824
B128F
W191f

824
B128F
W191f   Wallace
              Francis Bacon on the
          nature of man

D0895070

CHRISTIAN HERITAGE COLLEGE
2100 Greenfield Dr.
El Cajon, CA 92021

Francis Bacon on the Nature of Man

Francis Bacon on the Nature of Man

The Faculties of Man's Soul: Understanding, Reason, Imagination, Memory, Will, and Appetite

Karl R. Wallace

UNIVERSITY OF ILLINOIS PRESS   Urbana · Chicago · London, 1967

© 1967 by the Board of Trustees of the University of Illinois
Manufactured in the United States of America
Library of Congress Catalog Card No. 67–21858

Contents

24409

Introduction

Francis Bacon has always been a fascinating Renaissance figure. He is acknowledged today as the first great English essayist and historian. In his own times, Ben Jonson and Dudley Carleton considered him the greatest of Parliamentary speakers. His reputation for legal reasoning and justice, marred at the end of his lord chancellorship by his confession of wrongdoing, make him a rival of Edward Coke. His standing among English epistemologists and empiricists may be slight today, particularly when compared with that of John Locke and David Hume; yet among philosophically minded scholars in the seventeenth and early eighteenth centuries he was widely respected. In investigating the philosophy of those years, Fulton Anderson found him the most often quoted.[1] The men of scientific cast who started the Royal Society venerated him as their teacher and model. Most of all, his own nature is intriguing. Driven by love of great place like most Renaissance men of superior talents, Bacon achieved fame as statesman, philosopher, and author. He probably preferred the active and public life to the contemplative, yet he spent much time in reading and writing. He was a modern in spirit and outlook, yet he owed much to classical and medieval tradition, whose virtues and vices he clearly discerned. He accepted the religious faith and theology of the English Church, yet he was habitually skeptical of much of men's thought and work. As a person, he presents the elements of paradox.

My interest in Bacon has been primarily in his theory of rhetoric

---

[1] Fulton H. Anderson, *The Philosophy of Francis Bacon* (Chicago: University of Chicago Press, 1948), p. 1.

and communication and in his practice thereof.[2] The interest began in the early thirties and has been sustained as time and duties have allowed. Gradually it became evident that an exact understanding of any aspect of Bacon's thought can be approximated only when one understands the foundation of his system of knowledge and learning. The foundation was announced first in the *Advancement of Learning* (1605) and was augmented eighteen years later. Its central pillars are the psychological faculties. The chief ones — reason, imagination, and memory — give rise to philosophy, poetry, and history. As the full system of learning was developed, the complete number of faculties appeared. Bacon specified six: understanding, reason, imagination, memory, will, and appetite. These were well known, he said, and in view of his audience he does not explain their nature and remarks only occasionally upon their functions. So if the modern student wants to know what Bacon knew, he must discover what was well known about man's faculties during the period of Bacon's lifetime. In illuminating the bases of Bacon's thought, one illuminates the psychology of the period, and in dealing with the psychology of the times, one finds much of it illustrated in Bacon.

This book endeavors to explain what Bacon meant by his six psychological concepts. The explanation is set in a somewhat broader frame than my purpose suggests, because the six faculties are parts of a whole, the human being. The period, which for my ends includes the ideas of John Locke, did not use the term *psychology*. Instead, as a rough equivalent, men spoke of the nature of man or of man's soul. Although the study can be considered a small chapter in the history of psychology, I have avoided for

---

[2] Karl R. Wallace, *Francis Bacon on Communication and Rhetoric* (Chapel Hill, N.C.: University of North Carolina Press, 1943); "Bacon's Conception of Rhetoric," *Speech Monographs*, III (1936), 21–48 (reprinted in *Historical Studies of Rhetoric and Rhetoricians*, ed. R. F. Howes [Ithaca, N.Y.: Cornell University Press, 1961]); "Early English Rhetoricians on the Structure of Rhetorical Prose," *Papers in Rhetoric*, ed. D. C. Bryant (St. Louis: Washington University, 1940; "Rhetorical Exercises in Tudor Education," *Quarterly Journal of Speech*, XXII (February, 1936), 28–51; "Aspects of Modern Rhetoric in Francis Bacon," *Quarterly Journal of Speech*, XLII (December, 1956), 398–406; "Discussion in Parliament and Francis Bacon," *Quarterly Journal of Speech*, XLIII (February, 1957), 12–21; "Imagination and Francis Bacon's View of Rhetoric," *Dimensions of Rhetorical Scholarship*, ed. Roger E. Nebergall (Norman, Okla.: University of Oklahoma Department of Speech, 1963), 65–81; "Francis Bacon on Understanding, Reason, and Rhetoric" (in press).

the most part the terms and vocabulary that later became the special property of psychology, and have preferred the language of the period. The preference does not make exposition easy. Bacon himself recognized the difficulties. The ordinary language, whether Latin or English, sometimes was not equal to designate a "new," technical idea. Bacon knew, for example, that "induction," or the term he adopted, "new induction," did not quite signify what he meant. He chose not to coin new terms, partly because they would introduce a worse confusion than ambiguous familiar words, and partly because they would be unintelligible to his audience. Bacon was always the rhetorician as well as the specialist. Desirous of financial aid for his projects, he addressed men of power and influence; he had to be persuasive and meet the requirements of decorum, the demands of the fitting and appropriate. His habit was to talk about the nature of man in ordinary language. Occasionally he used the language that had crept into the educated man's parlance from classical and medieval metaphysics and theology, the categories of being and of physical movement, and the terms of logic, rhetoric, anatomy, physiology, and medicine. All of these studies had long had something to say about the nature of man. Their vocabulary, as Bacon aptly observed, presented "a certain rhapsody and incongruous mass of Theology, of Logic, and of some parts of Natural Philosophy (as those concerning First Principles and the Soul), all mixed up and confused. . . ."[3]

Two principal groups of source materials have been relied upon. First are Bacon's own works and the many interpretations of them. The Spedding, Ellis, and Heath edition with its learned notes and introductions, its Latin texts and many translations, its life and letters, is still standard. Fulton Anderson's interpretations have occasionally been most helpful; so have Farrington's recent translations of three works.[4] Bacon himself is usually clearer than his

---

[3] *De Augmentis Scientiarum*, or *Of the Dignity and Advancement of Learning*, in *The Works of Francis Bacon, Baron of Verulam, Viscount St. Alban, and Lord High Chancellor of England*, collected and edited by James Spedding, Robert Leslie Ellis, and Douglas Denton Heath (7 vols.; London: Longmans & Co. . . . Virtue & Co., 1879), IV, 337. Cf. *ibid.* IX.

[4] *Temporis Partus Masculus*; *Cogitata et Visa: de Interpretatione Naturae, Sine de Scientia Operativa*; *Redargutio Philosophiarum*, in Benjamin Farrington, *The Philosophy of Francis Bacon* (Liverpool, England: Liverpool University Press, 1964).

interpreters, especially if one knows the intellectual climate and context in which he was writing. It is worth repeating Anderson's wry remark, that persons who interpret Bacon ought to read him.

The second group of materials is probably less familiar to students of Bacon and his times. It is chiefly the literature of the period that deals with the psychology of man, with the nature and soul of man, and secondarily the literature dealing with the arts and principles of logic and rhetoric. These arts reflected man's attempt to think, act, and communicate as a man.

Fundamental to the writings about man is the long tradition of thought they mirror. The heart of the tradition is represented, naturally enough, by Plato (particularly by the *Meno*, *Timaeus*, *Phaedrus*, and *Republic*), by the neo-Platonists like Plotinus, by Aristotle (especially his books on logic, dialectic, rhetoric, physics, and ethics; and those treating directly of man's nature: *De Anima*, *De Sensu*, and *De Reminiscentia*), and by Galen and his works on medicine, or "physic." The lines of thought started by these men ran down to the English Renaissance through commentaries and translations (such as those of *De Anima* available through Melanchthon and Vives), through summaries and epitomes by university lecturers, and through major figures such as Pico della Mirandola, St. Augustine, and St. Thomas Aquinas. There is a host of minor figures, unknown today to the popular reader but familiar to large numbers of literate Elizabethans and Jacobeans. There were the divines who wrote special treatises aimed at helping educated persons master passion and live the life of reason. Such were Nicolas Coffeteau, John Woolton, Thomas Wright, Robert Burton, Edward Reynoldes, and Joseph Glanvill.[5] These men and others like them often include complete sketches of the soul of man, as well as base their extended expositions and arguments on their understanding of the soul's operations. There were the cyclopedists, most of them continental authors and known in England either in Latin or in translation; for example, Nicolas Mirabellus, Bartholomaeus, La Primaudaye, and Pierre Charron. Offering surveys and classifications of all knowledge, they include chapters on human nature. Some books were by physicians who either address their fellows or the general public on anatomy, physiology, and health. From them one learns much about the

---

[5] The works of these men, and of the authors mentioned below, appear in the bibliography in the editions I have used.

elements and humours which were thought to affect the soul's functions and determine character. In this group are such men as John Jones, John Banister, Helkiah Crooke, Timothy Bright, Lemnius, Valentinus, Vesalius, and Thomas Vicary. Possibly in their company should fall Thomas Rogers, a divine, whose general survey of the anatomy of the mind probably mirrored what he absorbed at Oxford. Then there were others who may be thought of as philosophers: Sir Kenelm Digby and Thomas Hobbes. The writers on moral philosophy (ethics and politics) sometimes pay their respects to psychology; among them are William Baldwin, Lewis Bryskett, Daniel Tuvil, and William Jewell. There was, finally, a small class of didactic poets who attempted compact accounts of the faculties. Chief among them are Phineas Fletcher, Sir John Davies, and John Davies of Hereford. I have made no direct use of poetic and dramatic literature, nor of the sermon and the literature of controversy. Such writing abounds in psychological allusions, but by nature and purpose it does not attempt systematic analysis of the powers of soul and mind.

Materials concerning logic and rhetoric are probably more familiar to students of the period and the vocabulary is more stable and less confused than the terminology used to describe the faculties of the soul. Rhetoric, dialectic, and syllogistic logic had been recognized for centuries as settled disciplines, and their categories and terms had acquired standard meanings. In recent years the scholarship of W. S. Howell and Father Walter J. Ong has directed attention again to the books and materials one must take account of in the seventeenth and eighteenth centuries in England. These men also have helped characterize the flow of logical and rhetorical thought from its classical, medieval, and Ramean sources. It is perhaps sufficient to remark here that although the logics and rhetorics make little mention of the faculties and their behavior, their authors assumed to know how the mind functioned and how it should act when it reasoned and communicated properly.

The background literature dealing with man's nature and soul is used only for purposes of comparison and contrast, to illuminate or give emphasis to Bacon. For the same purposes, there is an occasional reference to Descartes and Locke. There is no attempt, furthermore, to trace Bacon's ideas to specific sources. The task would be formidable indeed, and is sufficient for a separate book. This study, then, focuses simply on what Bacon thought made man a man.

The presentation begins with the physical basis of man and proceeds to the higher, mental processes; it ascends from bodily, sensory behavior to intellectual behavior. The portion dealing with imagination, reason, and understanding looms large because Bacon has more to say about those faculties than the others. He was a rationalist, and believed that man ought to use his head rather than his muscles if knowledge was to grow and behavior be rational. The account of the faculties is followed by observations on the significance of Bacon's psychology.

In anticipation of the final observations, expressed here in general rather than technical terms, we shall say that Bacon's view of the mind has a place in the history of faculty psychology. He was vexed with the vagueness and complexity of the classical-medieval account of man's soul and its powers, and favored a simpler, more dynamic explanation. His view of "scientific" discovery merits first place in the history of man's attempts to methodize creative thought and set the stage for "insight." His view of man's mental equipment told him that he who searched for nature's secrets must do more than direct his understanding and reason to what man had preserved in language, and do more than spin out new designs from the familiar fabric of a traditional mind. Rather, he who probes for new truth must teach his understanding to respect the reports of the senses, to dwell upon their data methodically, and to curb premature abstraction from the facts. Bacon tried to show the scientist how to bind the understanding to the senses, to dissect nature, not merely to dissect language. As a result, Bacon invented not a new kind of induction (as induction is understood by logicians), but a psychology of discovery. His unique view of the creative function of imagination made him the first person to formulate a psychological foundation for a rhetoric that by nature had to be reasonable, moral, and appealing. It can be said that Bacon taught men how to think originally and how to communicate well, but he did not achieve these without first having his own picture of how the mind worked.

I hope this book will prove informative to anyone interested in himself, his own education, and a belief in an orderly world. To read profitably he need not be a student of Francis Bacon, or a historian of psychology, or a teacher and critic who focuses on the literature of the period. He need only be interested in his own nature and in the characteristics that make him human, namely, the ability to make signs and symbols, as in speech, music, and mathematics, and the ability to reason. Historically, these abilities were attributed to the two highest faculties or powers of the human animal, understanding and reason. These enabled man to abstract from and organize his sensory experience and imagery, aided by memory, into forms and combinations of forms that could exist and be manipulated quite independent of the "real" world. The better a man could abstract and handle his abstractions, the more manlike he was. At the pinnacles of abstract thought, his spirit might be in tune with the divine spirit, or be in touch with other human spirits. In the sloughs of behavior, his sensations and biological processes reduced him to the level of animals. Hence, rationality, at least in western cultures, has always been regarded more highly than emotionality. The elaboration of the faculties of the soul and of the kinds and levels of bodily behavior at the hands of philosophers, physicians, theologians, and educators has been so extensive and has gone on for so many generations of man that its influence is evident even today. The vocabulary introduced by the new experimental psychology has not yet permeated everyday speech. Most of the words and many of the ideas we use in talking about ourselves are the direct legacy of the old faculty psychology.

Anyone concerned about methods and procedures in formal education today is aware of the renewed interest in literacy. Not only is skill in handling one's native language held to be valuable in itself, but also the ability to read and speak, listen, and write, with accuracy and readiness, is essential to learning and mastering one's specialty, whether specialization be in the humanities, technologies, or sciences. This article of faith, in the English speaking world at any rate, has never been so rigorously followed as it was in the England of the Tudors and the first Stuarts. Educational practice in the period reflected the belief that the powers of understanding and reason were manifested primarily in language behavior, and that training in speech and language, undertaken and sustained from age five to twenty, would certainly develop the powers of reason and memory and require the use of the imagination. This belief is seen in the trivium and its methods. The schoolboy worked with limited materials which he virtually memorized as he learned the vocabulary and syntax of Latin and English. He was engaged in exacting "double" translation as he worked from one language to the other and back. He was exercised in the *elements* of composition — the subunits of a larger whole. He wrote letters and constructed speeches after the models placed before him. In his university days, if not before, he mastered the art of disputation which, supported by lecture and reading, was the method of learning and examination in every subject, particularly in the studies of the higher school and the university. Essentially these endeavors did not require sensory and motor experiences of life directly; they were linguistic and symbolic. They immersed youth in the form and structure of ideas, in analysis and synthesis. Analysis was necessary to the grasp of the "sentence," the tropes and schemes of speech, the logical and dialectical attributes and uses of syllogistic reasoning, and the representative nature of character portrayal and dramatic action. Synthesis was illustrated in old and new combinations of ideas, in inventing tropes and schemes of language, in inventing arguments and imitations of action, and in managing the order and progress of ideas in speeches, poetry, and disputations. The finished composition became the object of criticism and was subjected to standards of truth and goodness. In a word, thoughtful men, aware of man's nature, regarded grammar, logic, and rhetoric both as tools of practical discourse and as intellectual instruments of learning. All such activity was held to be rational, distinctively human, and was better, "nobler," than emotional behavior merely.

Most persons believe that the world is orderly rather than chaotic. If it is not more organized than disorganized, why bother to learn? This article of man's faith and comfort is illustrated *par excellence* in the intellectual climate of Bacon's day, although its history is very old. Richard Hooker reflects the Elizabethan's belief in the order of things. First there is eternal law "laid up in the bosom of God." Then: "That part of which ordereth natural agents we call usually *Nature's* law; that which angels do clearly behold and without any swerving observe is a law *Celestial* and heavenly; the law of *Reason*, that which bindeth creatures reasonable in this world, and with which by reason they may most plainly perceive themselves bound; that which bindeth them, and is not known but by special revelation from God, *Divine* law; *Human* law, that which out of the law either of reason or of God men probably gathering to be expedient, they make it a law." [6] Man had his place in Nature's hierarchy, with degrees and levels thereof. Nature was arranged from low to high, from plant, insect, and animal to man. Man's levels of soul ranged from the vegetative through the sensory to the rational, and his faculties from the sensory up through memory, imagination, reason, and understanding. The scheme was labeled the chain of being, or the spiral of life. Each level, grade, or "degree" linked into the grade above and shared some of its qualities. Each level also developed branching links of its own. Individual man, for example, was analogous in structure and function to the family, the community, the nation. Hence in problems of morality and conduct, viewed both theoretically and practically, the understanding was sovereign in man in precisely the way that Queen Elizabeth was sovereign. The chain of being represented a great system, and among its complexities man set out to discover its causes and explain its order. As a result, he might be able to control nature and predict behavior.

For encouragement and help in this study I am indebted to a larger number of persons and institutions than can be specified here. Especially helpful have been four libraries rich in English printed and manuscript materials, 1500–1700. Their facilities are remarkable and their staffs have been cordial: The Folger Shakespeare Memorial Library, and Dorothy Mason and Giles Dawson; The Henry E. Huntington Library, and Mary Alice Fry and John M. Steadman; The Francis Bacon Foundation, Inc., and Elizabeth Wrigley; the University of Illinois Library, especially its Rare Book Room, presided over by Isabelle F. Grant and Marian Harman. Especially flattering were the attentions of the staff of the libraries at University College (London), the University of London, and Cambridge University. To Marvin T. Herrick and Harris Fletcher I owe much for initial criticism and steady example. From time to time I have benefited from the funds of the Research Board of the University of Illinois. I am grateful,

[6] Richard Hooker, *Of the Laws of Ecclesiastical Policy*, in *The Works of . . . Mr. Richard Hooker . . .* , arr. Rev. John Keble (3 vols.; 7th ed.; Oxford: The Clarendon Press, 1888), I, 205.

finally, to Katherine Mullen and Mary Furman for much typing at odd hours. The ultimate obligation is to Herbert Wichelns, wise teacher and exemplar intellect, and to the Cornell tradition in rhetoric and public address.[7]

[7] Appreciation should be expressed also to the University of Oklahoma and the University of California at Los Angeles for the stimulation they provided in asking me to lecture on the relationships Bacon saw between rhetoric, imagination, reason, and understanding. If a little of the language here and there is that of the lectures, they understand.

CHAPTER 1

General View of Man's Nature

Francis Bacon's general view of the nature of man is set within the frame of his proposals for the advancement of learning. Bacon believed he could make his proposals clear only by presenting a classification of knowledge, showing what things man had learned about himself and nature and what things he was ignorant of. The basic categories Bacon used in classifying knowledge are reflected in his view of human nature; hence in our attempt to sketch the human being as Bacon understood him it will be prudent to respect his frame of reference and his terms. If we can do so, we can avoid some of the subtleties, ambiguities, and exasperations of metaphysical language — which Bacon himself often inveighed against — and if we cannot, the reader can at once detect the trouble.

The classification of knowledge in *The Advancement of Learning* and the *De Augmentis Scientiarum* reflects the problem of acquiring knowledge and of using it. In effect Bacon says: From what do we learn? What are the sources of knowledge and behavior? He answers: From nature about us, from each other, and from God. How do we learn? He replies: Through the faculties of the mind we learn by rational methods about all natural phenomena. Through the divine spirit of the soul we learn by revelation of things divine. For what is our learning used? For speculative purposes, i.e., for the sake of theoretical knowledge, and of understanding ourselves in relation to God and nature. For practical or "operative" purposes, i.e., for the sake of controlling natural forces wherever we can and of living with one another in harmony and virtue. Although Bacon says frankly that he is more interested in knowledge for use than in knowledge for its own sake, he is above all concerned with man's ways and methods of knowing. In seeking to understand nature and to control her forces to his own advantage, man can do but two things: study nature directly, "in fact"; and study his own thoughts and interpretations that he has derived from direct observation. ". . . man is but the servant and interpreter of nature: what he does and what he knows is only what he has observed of nature's order in fact or in thought; beyond this he knows nothing and can do nothing."[1]

Man's Faculties and His Soul

Probably Bacon's interest in the ways and channels of acquiring knowledge led him to classify learning in terms of the faculties and powers by which and through which man came to grips with reality and his own behavior. In announcing his classification he simultaneously declares it to be the best: "The best division of human learning is that derived from the three faculties of the rational soul, which is the seat of learning. History has reference to the Memory, poesy to the Imagination, and philosophy to the Reason."[2] From the human soul and its "treasures," "all other doctrines are derived."[3] Among the subdivisions of philosophy Bacon placed moral and civil knowledge — ethics and politics, to the modern ear — and with them he linked the faculties of will and appetite. When speaking of "the use and objects" of man's faculties as they are manifest in "the logical and ethical sciences" — what today we would call the behavioral sciences — he produces his complete list of human powers: understanding, reason, imagination, memory, appetite, and will.[4] By these powers man knows and acts, and chiefly in their terms Bacon understood the human being. Our description of Bacon's man will adopt his names of the faculties and will focus on their nature and function. What does man do when he understands, reasons, and remembers? What is supposed to be going on when he imagines and feels and and when he is moved by his appetite and his will?

In descriptions of what man is, how he thinks and behaves, the

---

[1] *Works* IV, 32.   [2] *De Aug.* II, 1; *Works* IV, 292.
[3] *De Aug.* IV, 3; *Works* IV, 396.   [4] *Ibid.*, p. 398.

faculties have always been regarded in some way as subsidiary "parts" of a whole. The label for the whole was *soul*. The part-whole relationship entailed is hinted at in the stock phrase, the faculties *of* the soul. It would be helpful to our study if we could discover in Bacon a dominant concept of the soul. But he does not give us one. In no place does he care to offer a characterization or formulate a definition after the custom of others with whom he was unquestionably familiar.

In the English Renaissance, *soul* referred to that which marked the difference between the living and the nonliving. The conception is at least as old as Aristotle. Hammond expresses it as the actuality of a body having life potentiality within it; it is "the first grade of actuality of a natural organized body." [5] Hett interprets the notion of actuality thus: "If you have the capacity to acquire knowledge of a subject, you may be said to have potential knowledge of it, which may become actual by study. In another sense, if you possess knowledge which you are not using, it may be called potential, actual only when you are using it." [6] St. Thomas Aquinas defined the soul as "the first principle of life in those things in our world which live," and added that particular emphasis should be given to *first*, for "not every principle of vital action is a soul. . . ." [7] Concentrating on the human being as distinguished from the animal, Robert Burton reminded his readers that the soul "is defined by Philosophers to be *the first substantial act of a natural, human, organical body, by which a man lives, perceives, and understands, freely doing all things, and with election.*" [8] The soul, then, could be conceived of as a formal principle, an organizing principle, whereby inanimate matter became

[5] W. A. Hammond, *Aristotle's Psychology* (New York: The Macmillan Co., 1902), p. xxii; compare J. A. Smith's translation of Aristotle: The soul is "the first grade of actuality of a natural body having life potentially in it." *De Anima*, trans. by J. A. Smith, in *The Works of Aristotle Translated into English Under the Editorship of W. D. Ross* (Oxford: The Clarendon Press, 1931), 412 a 30.

[6] *Aristotle on the Soul, Parva Naturalia, On Breath*, with an English translation by W. S. Hett (London: William Heineman, Ltd., and Cambridge, Mass.: Harvard University Press, 1957), pp. 66–67.

[7] *Summa Theologica*, 75.1, in *Basic Writings of Saint Thomas Aquinas*, edited and annotated, with an introduction by Anton C. Pegis (2 vols.; New York: Random House, 1945).

[8] Robert Burton, *The Anatomy of Melancholy*, eds. Floyd Dell and Paul Jordan-Smith (New York: Farrar and Rinehart, 1938), p. 144.

animate. The lowest signs of the living could be detected in the processes of nutrition through which the body grew, sustained itself, and decayed. This kind of organic activity appeared to be so distinct from other life that it was often thought to be dominated by a separate soul, the vegetative or nutritive soul. Signs of a higher grade of life were to be seen in sensory activity and its accompanying feelings of pleasure and pain, these associated with something called the sensitive soul. Signs of the highest grade of life were thinking, reasoning, imagining, remembering, and self-consciousness. These were a group of related activities associated with, and sometimes assigned to, the rational soul.

How many souls were there? One? Many? Historically these questions had been foci of controversy. Probably the educated Elizabethan and Jacobean believed that different grades and types of behavior were manifestations of a single soul, ranging from the complex and abstract to the simple and concrete, as one observed them from the top down, in human life, animal life, and vegetable life. The influence of Plato and Cicero, weighted with the doctrine of separate souls and separate faculties, seems to have been running out in Bacon's England. The view of Aristotle and his commentators, that there was one soul having manifold powers, was dominant. Timothy Bright, for example, would not allow a plurality of souls nor a multiplicity of faculties. He asserted flatly: "I say the facultie, and not the faculties."[9] He insisted that the soul was simple, like an element, and that the notion of many faculties invited the notion of many souls, thus tending to destroy the unity of soul and man. The soul was to all human action what the "one right and straight motion, through the aptnesse of the first wheele" was to the variety of motion in the clock.[10]

Bacon entered this climate of belief not by speculating on the nature of the soul but by declaring in favor of two souls. One was the rational soul, present only in human beings. The other was the irrational soul, shared by man and brutes.[11] Bacon was convinced that intellectual behavior and animal behavior were so radically different as to constitute a difference in kind, not merely of de-

---

[9] Timothy Bright, A Treatise of Melancholy . . . (London, 1613), p. 51.
[10] Ibid., p. 82.   [11] De Aug. IV, 3; Works IV, 396.

gree: "there are many and great excellencies of the human soul
above the souls of brutes. . . . Now wherever the mark of so
many and great excellencies is found, there also a specific difference ought to be constituted; and therefore I do not much like
the confused and promiscuous manner in which philosophers
have handled the functions of the soul; as if the human soul dif-
fered from the spirit of brutes in degree rather than in kind; as
the sun differs from the stars, or gold from metals."[12] Bacon's
belief in separate souls was perhaps influenced by his religious belief, for he thought that the origins of the souls were different. The rational soul was "divine," and sprang from "the breath
of God. . . . For touching the first generation of the rational
soul, the Scripture says, 'He hath made man of the dust of the
earth, and breathed into his nostrils the breath of life. . . .'"[13]
On the other hand, "the generation of the irrational soul, or that
of brutes, was effected by the words, 'Let the water bring forth;
let the earth bring forth.'" The brute soul was the "Sensible or
Produced Soul." Man thus was of dual natures, of the dust of
the earth and of the breath of God.

In believing that the brute soul and the rational soul were
radically different Bacon was in good philosophical company.
Writing only some thirteen years later than Bacon, Descartes
thought that one of the great sources of human error was to
believe that "the soul of a brute is of the same nature as our
own. . . ."[14] But although the Frenchman felt he had to pro-
claim the immortality of the soul, Bacon left this matter, and
similar ones, to the theologians. He was content merely to restate
his conviction that "the substance of the soul in its creation was
not extracted or produced out of the mass of heaven and earth,
but was immediately inspired from God. . . ."[15]

---

[12] *Ibid.*, p. 397.
[13] *Ibid.*, p. 396. Bacon's belief in two souls, a rational soul and an irrational one, was respected by the deists as late as 1695. See M.S., *A Philosophical Discourse of the Nature of Rational and Irrational Souls* (London,
1695), pp. 7, 26.
[14] René Descartes, *Discourse on the Method of Rightly Conducting the
Reason and Seeking for Truth in the Sciences* (1637), in *The Philosophical
Works of Descartes*, trans. Elizabeth S. Haldane and G. R. T. Ross (2 vols.;
New York: Dover Publications, 1955), I, 118.
[15] *De Aug.* IV, 3; *Works* IV, 398.

Brute Soul and Its Substance

Speculations about the nature of the soul always included these questions: Was the soul substantial? Was it material? Bacon was deeply interested in physical reality. He believed that its matter and behavior could be convincingly explained if his method of scientific investigation were followed and if the inquiry were directed to the discovery of efficient and material causes.[16] So with respect to the brute soul, Bacon expressed confidence. It "must clearly be regarded as a corporeal substance" and was certainly material. Because it was breathlike and unobservable, it might be better termed "spirit." It was "attenuated and made invisible by heat; a breath (I say) compounded of the natures of flame and air, having the softness of air to receive impressions, and the vigour of fire to propagate its actions. . . ." It was within the body; indeed, it was "clothed with the body." And "in perfect animals" it resided "chiefly in the head, running along the nerves, and refreshed and repaired by the spirituous blood of the arteries; as Bernardinus Telesius and his pupil Augustinus Donius have in part . . . maintained."[17] (Bacon's view of *spirit* we shall discuss later.) The substance of the animal soul can be fruitfully investigated if it be treated as matter in motion. But Bacon would not have the study of the soul's substance mixed up with metaphysical guesswork and nomenclature, with assertions that the soul is the first actuality or first principle of a living body and that the soul is related to body as form is to matter. "For of what service are such terms as *ultimate act, form of the body*, and such toys of logic, to the doctrine concerning the substance of the soul?"

About the brute soul as a material substance, Bacon makes two other observations. Contrasted with man's body, the soul is "the simplest of substances. . . ." It is also among the most active of things; it enjoys no rest.[18] It seeks to escape from the body, to join its own kind, the spirits permeating the world. On the other

---

[16] In *De Augmentis* III, 4, Bacon assigns to Physic the inquiry into efficient and material causes, and to Metaphysic the inquiry into formal and final causes. In the *Novum organum sive indica de interpretatione naturae* (London, 1620), I, 2, he observes that final causes are also relevant to sciences having to do "with human action."

[17] *De Aug.* IV, 3; *Works* IV, 398.

[18] *De Aug.* IV, 2; *Works* IV, 380.

hand, the body is complex; "of all substances which nature has produced man's body is the most multifariously compounded."[19]

Rational Soul

What of the nature of the rational soul? Is it substantial? Bacon takes no stand. He hands over to theology for study not only the doctrine concerning "the breath of life," but also "the doctrine concerning the substance of the rational soul."[20] He would reserve for the theologians other traditional questions concerning the nature of soul. Is it native to the body from the beginning? Does it join the body from without at birth? Is it separable from the body, or inseparable? Is it mortal, or immortal? How far is it "tied to the laws of matter, how far exempted from them?"[21] Robert Ellis has suggested that Bacon had to admit the substantiality of the rational soul, because the Clementine constitutions made it heretical to deny that the rational soul is the substantial form of man. If Bacon believed in the substantiality of the rational soul, it can only be discovered by implication. He accepted the idea that the soul is the form of forms, *anima forma formarum*.[22] He censured Plato for pursuing perfectly abstract forms, for the idea of form was unintelligible without its correlative idea, matter.[23] He was probably well aware of the hoary philosophical position that when one inquired into the *nature* of anything both material and formal aspects of it were regarded as substance. Every corporeal substance, so the argument ran, consisted of two principles, a potential principle called *materia prima* and an actual principle called the *form*. "Thus in man the body is the potential or material principle, and the soul the actualizing, vivifying, formal principle. Hence man is a composite, neither principle alone making him a man as such, both being equally necessary. Nor is either less a substance because each is incomplete in itself. Substantial change must be a change in one of these con-

---

[19] *Ibid.*

[20] *De Aug.* IV, 3; *Works* IV, 397.

[21] *Ibid.* Pierre Charron catalogues the ten "topics" of the soul. *Of Wisdome Three Bookes*, trans. Samson Leonard (London, 1658), Chap. 7. Like any educated Elizabethan, Bacon doubtless knew them all.

[22] *De Aug.* V, 1; *Works* I, 616; IV, 407.

[23] *De Aug.* III, 4; *Works* IV, 360.

stituents. The substance of man as form, dynamically considered as the source or principle of his activities, is known as nature."[24] Holding such notions, Bacon could have asserted the substance of the rational soul. But he appears never to have done so. He might have said, as Alexander Pope wrote much later, that the soul is form and doth the body make. But he did not.

Faculties as Activities of the Soul

Bacon appears to be far more interested in the behavior and function of the rational soul than he is in its substance and its divinity. The rational soul makes use of the brute soul, or spirit, as an instrument.[25] This spirit is dynamic and is never at rest as long as there is life. If the soul requires an instrument or organ when it functions, manifestations of its activity must reflect a dynamic state of affairs although these are not available to sense perception. Rational life, then, does not reflect static entities. Rational life involves movement, and its faculties and powers involve movement. Consequently, *understanding, reason, imagination, memory,* and *will* are names that designate types or classes of the soul's activity. Bacon seems to be saying all this when he calls for "a true Physic of Abstracts" which entails the measurement of motion. In animate and inanimate things there are motions, simple and compound, which invite meticulous study. In the life of creatures and human beings, for example, there is "voluntary motion in animals; the motion which takes place in the actions of the senses; motion of imagination, appetite, and will; motion of the mind, determination, and intellectual faculties. . . ."[26] There is nothing static about man and his powers. He is a vibrant, dynamic mechanism. To Bacon man's faculties were distinctive types of movements.

Conceived of as movements, the faculties are looked at in two ways: their origin and their functions. Bacon thought that they were "innate and inherent" in the soul and that they could be profitably studied from the point of view of their beginnings in

---

[24] Charles A. Hart, *The Thomistic Concept of Mental Faculty* (Washington, D.C.: The Catholic University of America Press, 1930), p. 29.
[25] *De Aug.* IV, 3; *Works* IV, 397.
[26] *De Aug.* III, 4; *Works* IV, 357.

the spirit-substance of the human beings. They could, and should, be analyzed as physical phenomena.[27] He believed that our chief information about them was to be derived from observing them at work. They have their uses and objects, and these are best seen in the sciences of logic and ethics. The object of logical behavior is to produce true knowledge and information rather than false, the object of ethical behavior to secure good actions rather than evil. The one "produces determinations, the other actions," the one is judicial in character, the other is ministerial.[28] To accomplish such objects, logical behavior uses the understanding and reason, and the science of logic treats of these faculties. Ethical behavior utilizes the will, appetite, and affections, and the science of ethics handles these faculties. Both provinces, the judicial and the ministerial, use the imagination and memory. The faculties may be found at work also in the arts of production: rhetoric and poetry. Rhetoric uses all the faculties, though it employs reason and imagination in a distinctive way. Poesy illustrates primarily the work of the imagination. We shall in later chapters treat these faculties at length.

Man's Person and the League of Mind and Body

So much for what Bacon says directly about the rational soul of man. Bacon also speaks indirectly of man's form and essence when he treats briefly of what he terms "the Person" of man and "the League of Mind and Body." These are the heads or "divisions" or "parts" he announces in embarking upon his discussion of "the Nature or State of Man." It must be observed that Bacon is never rigid in dividing and subdividing his subject matter into parts and categories. He castigated Ramus for his strict dichotomizing. Although the structuring and ordering of reality and behavior were necessary to the understanding and explanation of men and things, the process of anatomizing in itself endangered the unity and continuity of life and learning. So when he treats of human nature, he warns the reader: "generally let this be a rule; that all divisions of knowledges be accepted and used rather for lines to mark or distinguish, than sections to divide and separate them;

---

[27] *De Aug.* IV, 3; *Works* IV, 399.   [28] *De Aug.* V, 1; *Works* IV, 405.

in order that the continuance and entireness of knowledge be preserved." [29] There is a general science that can consider the soul and the body as separate from each other. There are other studies that will consider "the nature of man undivided," that is, man viewed as a person; and that will consider "the bond and connexion between the mind and body," that is, the league of mind and body. The study of man, the person, will delineate the failures of the race, comprising a history of incidents in which man's conduct has brought him "miseries." It will also record the triumphs of men, when they have conducted themselves at the *"tops* or *summits"* of their humanity. The history would include both intellectual and moral successes as, for example, the feat of a great rhetorician, like Protagoras or Gorgias, and the patience of Job. Bacon is clearly thinking of man as a unit or whole engaged in conduct that demands his entire being, not a segment or single faculty thereof.

In treating of the league, Bacon does not try to label the relationship between mind and body. He simply asserts that there is a connection, a connection that is no clearer than that of mutual "influence." There *must* be a connection, first, because one can infer something about the state of the soul by observing the movements and gestures of the body. The "lineaments of the body" and the "motions and gestures of the countenance" disclose "the dispositions and inclinations of the mind in general." [30] Bacon believed that gestural signs are reliable indicators of mental states. If information about them were extended and organized, one could build an art of "prediction." Persons could know whether their listeners were ripe for a proposal, whether, in Bacon's picturesque phrase, they were in a "season of access." After all, "we laugh and weep and frown and blush nearly in the same fashion; and so it is (for the most part) in the more subtle motions." [31] Dreams, also, indicate inner states of being — moods, dispositions, affections, and perturbations. Bacon recognizes that the interpretation of dreams has been handled by many writers and that it is "full of follies"; nevertheless, dreams should

---

[29] *De Aug.* IV, 1; *Works* IV, 373; *The Twoo Bookes of Francis Bacon of the Proficience and Advancement of Learning Divine and Humane* (London, 1605), II (cited hereafter as *Advancement of Learning*); *Works* III, 366–367. My rendering.
[30] *De Aug.* IV, 1; *Works* IV, 376.   [31] *Ibid.*

be studied seriously. In brief, mental states influence bodily states as revealed by outward signs.

It is evident, second, that bodily states influence mental states. The relationship of body and mind entails an antistrophe. The "humours and temperament of the body alter and work upon the mind," and the "passions and apprehensions of the mind alter and work upon the body." As for the first: "physicians prescribe drugs to heal mental diseases, as in the treatment of phrensy and melancholy; and pretend also to exhibit medicines to exhilarate the mind, to fortify the heart and thereby confirm the courage, to clarify the wits, to corroborate the memory, and the like. . . . The root and life of all which prescripts consist in . . . the sympathy of the mind with the state and disposition of the body." [32] As for mental and emotional states directly working upon bodily states, Bacon simply points out that "there is no physician of any skill who does not attend to the accidents of the mind, as a thing most material towards recoveries, and of the greatest force to further or hinder other remedies." [33] Bacon is obviously alive to the phenomena of suggestion, and he suspects that among the faculties the imagination, as well as the affections, is implicated. As will be evident in the chapter on imagination, he felt that images had the power of working on the body of the imaginant and that they also had the power of affecting the body of another.

The apparent interplay of mental and physical conditions seems to have suggested to Bacon that mental events might be physiological in character and be localized within the body. Some medical men had for centuries held a similar opinion. In Bacon's day Helkiah Crooke, a respected teacher of medicine, swiftly reviewed the history of medical opinion on the subject and concluded that in the forepart or front ventricles of the brain, imagination was dominant; in the middle portion, reason ruled; and in the rear part, memory was chiefly localized. [34] Such beliefs may be true in part, says Bacon. [35] He invites further scrutiny of Plato's opinion that understanding had been placed in the brain as in a castle, animosity in the heart, and "concupiscence and sensuality in the liver. . . ." [36] He seems to believe that in some degree,

---

[32] *De Aug.*, IV, 1; *Works* IV, 377.   [33] *Ibid.*, p. 378.
[34] Helkiah Crooke, *Microcosmographia* (London, 1615), pp. 504–505.
[35] *De Aug.* IV, 2; *Works* IV, 378.
[36] *Ibid.*

perhaps to a considerable degree, both intellectual and emotional behavior depend upon bodily functions.

We can conclude, then, that the most general dimension of man is his vitality. He is something that lives and can maintain life. In these respects he is no different from other creatures who are lower in the scale of animate beings. Another general dimension is man's sentience. He senses and feels, and is thus a responding, dynamic creature. His vitality and sentience are evident in movement and in patterns of movement whose necessary and material basis is spirit. Such a complex of organized movement has the name of "soul," and because in these ways man is like animals he may be said to have a brute soul, or irrational soul. It is somehow produced from the elements of heaven and earth, and it is in man's body from the instant of living until he dies.

Man's more special dimensions are his understanding, reason, imagination, and will. These enable man to move and act in ways so complicated and refined as to mark off his behavior sharply from that of animals. The difference is so great it should be considered one of kind, not of degree. Such highly organized behavior has the name of "rational soul." God gave this ability, this soul, to man. Man uses his distinctive ability to produce knowledge and opinion and to communicate them. By it he makes his philosophy and science, his history, and his poetry. The types of movements by which the rational soul discharges its distinctive function are known as the faculties of the mind.

CHAPTER 2

The Instrument of the Rational Soul: Spirit

Bacon held that the irrational soul could properly be called spirit. He declared, too, that this spirit was the instrument and organ of the rational soul. If we are to understand Bacon's account of man's mental faculties, we must try to grasp what Bacon meant by "spirit" and, in its plural form, "spirits." The endeavor is important, because among the kinds of spirits Bacon recognized, the living spirit had as its organ or instrument "the fabric of the parts" of the body. The parts, of course, were those that any standard anatomist would refer to in teaching his subject — the principal regions of the body (head, chest, and abdomen) and the more specific parts, such as brain and nerves, bones and muscles, heart and lungs, arteries and veins, liver and stomach and the intestines (the guts), kidneys and spleen, and the genitals. These parts, structured and fleshed as they appear in the human frame, were the body's fabric.[1] There were but two things in the body, namely, "spirits and parts,"[2] and "the nature of spirits is as it were the master-wheel which turns the other wheels in the body of man. . . ."[3]

Bacon seems to have regarded things material in two ways. First, there is an ultimate particle of matter. This notion may be taken in two senses: either as "the last term or smallest portion" when one is dividing and fractionating bodies, or as "a body without vacuity."[4] The particle might be thought of as atom-like, al-

---

[1] *History of Life and Death, Works* V, 335.
[2] *Ibid.,* p. 332. Compare Bacon's statement that he treats of human philosophy or "man segregate . . . as he consisteth of body and spirit."*Advancement of Learning,* II; *Works* III, 444.
[3] *Ibid.,* p. 330.
[4] *Thoughts on the Nature of Things, Works* V, 419.

though Bacon did not accept Democritus' view of the atom. Second, quite different from particles of matter, there is something called *spirit* in all things. So the material world consisted of body stuff and spirit stuff, made up of bits so small that they were inaccessible to man's senses. Spirits in particular were essential to all kinds of change and movement in both inanimate and animate things. They were never at rest.

Kinds of Spirits

Bacon conceived of two chief kinds of spirits. There are "lifeless spirits, such as are in bodies inanimate, and in addition to them a living spirit."[5] Both kinds are found in living bodies, though the vital spirit is unique to animate life. The two kinds reveal different characteristics.

In lifeless spirits, the dominant element is air; they are confined "pneumaticals." They are "diffused in the substance of every part of the human body . . ." in "the flesh, bones, membranes, organs and the like. . . ."[6] They are in the substance of the body not only during its lifetime, but also after death; they "remain in the corpse."[7] In the vital spirit, the principal element is flamelike, though the breathlike element is present also. Indeed, it appears to be "a mysterious combination of a flammeous and aerial nature."[8] Bacon does not say what happens to the vital spirit after death. It is clear that the elemental difference between the two kinds of spirits is one of degree. Indeed, we are not to miss the point that lifeless spirits, as well as vital spirits, possess a flammeous component; "inanimate bodies have their spirits no whit inflamed or kindled."[9] We are told, too, that "the inflammation of the vital spirits is gentler by many degrees than the softest flame," softer than the warmth detectable in the "spirit of wine."[10]

---

[5] *History of Life and Death, Works* V, 322. Bacon's Latin for "lifeless spirits" is *spiritus mortuales.* The word *lifeless* perhaps implies unfortunately that spirits are without motion, or are typically at rest. What Bacon means is that there is a kind of spirit in lifeless bodies that is different from another kind of spirit found only in living bodies.

[6] *Ibid.*   [7] *Ibid.*   [8] *Ibid.,* pp. 323–324.

[9] *Sylva Sylvarum*; or *A Natural Historie* (London, 1627), 601; *Works* II, 528.

[10] *History of Life and Death, Works* V, 323.

The flamelike material of the spirits accounts in part for motion that is imperceptible to us. Bacon believed that heat was invariably associated with motion, and this idea applied to the activity of spirits in both living and nonliving bodies helped him to account, among other things, for the outline or shape of objects. The spirits literally swelled and pushed out the particles of natural things into the shapes and figures we see, to form a particular person, a tree, a flower, a stone. In the shaping of things, however, there is a radical difference between the work of spirits in living and nonliving beings. In animate things, spirits are constrained to relatively few contours; in inanimate things, they are relatively free to make a great variety of shapes: "plants are all figurate and determinate; which inanimate bodies are not . . . look how far the spirit is able to spread and continue itself, [only] so far goeth the shape of figure, and then is determined."[11]

The two kinds of spirits differ in another way. Lifeless spirits considered as bits of substance are separable from one another. They need not be in direct contact; they need not rub shoulders. ". . . they are not continued in themselves, but are as it were cut off and surrounded by the grosser body which intercepts them . . . [and] are shut in . . . by the tangible parts. . . ."[12] But vital spirits are "integral" and are continued in themselves. They are systems, one type being a branching network and permeating the body "through small thread-like channels" and "in veins and secret canals" much as blood is dispersed throughout the body. The other type has in the head "certain cells or seats, where the principal spirits do reside, and whereunto the rest do resort," the cells being "the fountain of the streamlets which diverge from thence."[13] The image Bacon thus creates is reminiscent of the "animal" spirit, described for centuries by anatomists as being concocted in the brain and sent throughout the body over nerves and invisible threads to control bodily movement. Bacon is certainly aware of such a spirit, but his conception of vital spirits, or living spirits, is not to be confused with it. This he makes clear when he says that "the principal seat of the spirits

[11] *Sylva Sylvarum*, 602; *Works* II, 529.

[12] *History of Lfe and Death*, *Works* V, 322; *Sylva Sylvarum*, 601; *Works* II, 528.

[13] *Sylva Sylvarum*, 601; *Works* II, 528; *History of Life and Death*, *Works* V, 323.

is doubtless in the head; and though this is commonly referred only to the animal spirits [*ad animales spiritus*], yet it applies to all."[14]

Another characteristic is said to distinguish lifeless spirits from living spirits. The former feed directly on the body materials adjacent to them. Bacon was much interested in the causes of bodily corruption and of prolongation of life. He believed that decay was due chiefly to the parasitic action of the lifeless spirits and that if this action could be controlled life could be extended. In *The History of Life and Death*, he thought he was on the way to solving the problem and was pointing the direction to others. Living spirits, on the other hand, seem to be "self-subsisting." They need a friendly body if they are to exist; yet they are essential to life itself and thus seem more to give to living processes than to take away. It is obvious that on this point Bacon is very close to the theological question: Does the soul — or does *a* soul —live after death? If the living spirit is not immortal, how does it maintain itself?

In a section of the *History*, intriguingly subtitled "The Porches of Death," Bacon states that "the living spirit seems to require three things for its subsistence. . . ."[15] First, the spirit must have room to move according to its nature, particulary requiring space "for its motion in the ventricles of the brain and the nerves perpetually. . . ." Blows to the head and some parts of the body constrict its movement and sometimes kill it. Its own motion is constantly reinforced by the pulsations of the heart and the rhythms of breathing. Second, though its own nature is flammeous, its condition must be more cold than hot, and respiration provides the proper "refrigeration." Third, the body, as the home of the spirit, must be properly fed and maintain a state of good health. Feeding, or alimentation, involves the organs and parts of the body directly, and concerns the spirit, if at all, only indirectly. As for the requirement "of aliment, it seems to belong more to the parts than to the living spirit. . . ." Consequently, "a man may easily believe that the living spirit subsists in identity, and not by succession or renovation."[16] What Bacon had in mind here is that the vital spirit has a long, continuous period of exist-

---

[14] *History of Life and Death, Works* V, 240.
[15] *Ibid.*, p. 311.   [16] *Ibid.*, pp. 313–314.

ence, probably from the birth of the body to its death. Its vital force does not flare up and down, like a flame, being "perpetually generated and extinguished, and . . . of no sensible duration."[17] This spirit must not, Bacon is prompt to say, be confused with the rational soul in man, which is certainly "not propagated, nor subject either to repair or death." He seems to say, also, that it should not be confused with "the natural spirit of animals and even of vegetables," which differs from the rational soul "in essence and in form."[18] Well aware of the belief that the vital spirit, as commonly regarded, was engendered from the blood in the heart and coursed through the arteries, Bacon perhaps thought that his kind of spirit received some sustenance by being merely in contact with the blood. If the spirit needs food, it is at the end of one's life. At that time the food "should be of such a kind and so prepared and applied that the spirit can act upon it." What occasions atrophy in old age is that "although there be flesh and blood . . . the spirit has become so scanty and thin, and the juices and the blood are so exhausted and obstinate, that they are not equal to alimentation."[19] Bacon concludes, apparently, that "the blood of the veins supplies the blood of the arteries, which again supplies the spirit."[20]

The two kinds of spirits, finally, differ in their desires or appetites. The vital spirit has a special affinity for the body; indeed, it abhors leaving the flesh, because it has "no connaturals near at hand." It may, perhaps, rush to the extremities of the body, to meet something that it loves, but . . . it is loth to go forth."[21] Nonvital spirits have two appetites. They desire to multiply. Unhappily finding nothing like themselves within their prison, they are impelled to create their own kind. They desire, furthermore, to escape from the body and join their fellow pneumaticals in the ambient air. Bacon's explanation of this action makes full use of the principle of natural sympathy, that like attracts like: "One drop of water moves towards another, and flame to flame; but much more does this appear in the escape of the spirit into the external air, because it is not carried to a particle like itself, but to a very world of connaturals . . . the going forth and escape of the spirit into the air is a double action, arising partly

---

[17] *Ibid.*, p. 315.   [18] *Ibid.*, p. 314.   [19] *Ibid.*, p. 315.
[20] *Ibid.*, p. 314.   [21] *Ibid.*, p. 325.

from the appetite of the spirit, and partly from the appetite of the air; for the common air is a needy thing, and seizes everything with avidity, as spirits, odours, rays, sounds, and the like."[22]

The vital spirit is held to exercise two functions that nonvital spirits do not reveal. First, it seems to play a controlling role in governing the growth and decay of body parts and tissues. The lifeless spirit maintains itself by feeding on adjacent parts. The amount and rate of its feeding determine the time span of its host's existence. Since inanimate things exist far longer than animate beings, Bacon reasoned that the vital spirit, present only in things living, was in part responsible for the body's growth, sustenance, and corruption. It "disturbs and restrains" and "intensifies and increases" the processes involved in the "consumption or depredation of the human body" and "the repair or refreshment thereof. . . ." In the most direct of ways, then, the vital spirit is vital.

The vital spirit, in the second place, seems to be the efficient cause of all actions and functions undertaken by the body's principal organs and members. Digestion is the function of the stomach, seeing that of the eye, and so on. The action in each case is "properly" that of the organ and member involved. They can be regarded as the material cause of the action. But no action, no matter how specific to a member, would come about if the vital spirit were not present: "The actions or functions of the individual members follow the nature of the members themselves; as attraction, retention, digestion, assimilation, separation, excretion, perspiration, and even the sense itself, depend upon the properties of the several organs, as the stomach, liver, heart, spleen, gall, brain, eye, ear, and the rest. But yet none of these actions would ever be set in motion without the vigour, presence, and heat of the vital spirit. . . ."[23] Thus Bacon seems to think that the vital spirit is some sort of force-carrying, or force-bearing, substance without which no animal or human activity is possible. Perhaps the notion of "vehicle" fits here. If so, we are reminded of one of Bacon's more general philosophical tenets, "the efficient cause . . . is nothing else than the vehicle of the form."[24]

---

[22] Ibid.
[23] Ibid., p. 324.
[24] De Aug. III, 4; Works IV, 361.

Of Spirits in General

Of each kind of spirit, lifeless and vital, we now know the chief characteristics. Of spirits in general, unqualified by the adjectives "lifeless" and "vital," something more can be said. One must, however, interpret the evidence with caution because of Bacon's habit of using "spirit" and "spirits" interchangeably, the singular form often doing service for the plural. Often, also, the terms are unqualified and their contexts do not always make clear how they are to be understood. Despite ambiguities, there emerge two important bits of information. The first involves spirit in its role of vehicle. Bacon discusses the problems entailed in learning about unseen forces by studying phenomena that can be observed. During the discussion, he expresses the conviction that from the spirits "and their motions principally proceed arefaction, colliquation, concoction, maturation, putrefaction, vivification, and most of the effects of nature. . . ."[25] The bodily processes here — drying out of tissues, melting and dissolving of flesh, and putrefaction — are additions to those mentioned or implied above, and the additional processes have elsewhere been attributed chiefly to the parasitic action of the lifeless spirit. Thus spirit of any kind is the vehicle of physiological action. Our interpretation is reinforced by Bacon's unqualified assertion that "the spirits are the agents and workmen that produce all the effects in the body. This appears manifest both by general consent and by innumerable instances."[26] It is obvious that the idea of agent and the image of workman are not inconsistent with the notion of vehicle. We cannot do some things except by means of and through somebody else.

Concerning spirit and spirits, the second piece of information links spirit with the brain and with what Bacon calls the "Thinking Faculty." In making the point that the power of acquiring knowledge demands labor and that "as well in inventing as in executing," he asserts that the kind of effort required is "chiefly that labour and travel which is described [descried?] by the sweat of the brows more than of the body; that is such travel as is joined with the working and discursion of the spirits in the

---

[25] *Sylva Sylvarum*, 98; *Works* II, 381.
[26] *History of Life and Death*, *Works* V, 268.

brain. . . ."[27] Bacon's illustration of intellectual effort and "discursion" is that required in "the election of the mean." It is the movement of reason when one finds the common idea that links a major premise with a minor premise and leads to the conclusion. It is the process of illuminating a lesser known, particular case by bringing it within better known, general knowledge. Movement there is, both literally and metaphorically, and Bacon hints strongly that the actual movement is that of the spirit. In one other passage, Bacon asserts that all the powers of the soul involve motion; when one thinks, the spirits "dance" as it were. He commends Donius[28] for criticizing those ancients who "too eagerly fixing their eyes and thoughts on the memory, imagination, and reason, have neglected the Thinking Faculty. . . ." This power holds "the first place." "For he who remembers or recollects, thinks; he who imagines, thinks; he who reasons, thinks; and in a word the spirit of man, whether prompted by sense or left to itself, whether in the functions of the intellect, or of the will and affections, dances to the tune of the thoughts. . . ."[29] Possibly it is animal spirits that dance. A late seventeenth-century source, purporting to be aware of Bacon's views of the soul, asserts that animal spirits are "the efficient cause of all Sensation. . . ." They are responsible, moreover, for "ideas" derived from the object world: "Outward Objects . . . affect the Animal Spirits, and the Animal Spirits must make traces in the Brain, and [there] lodge those Ideas [of outward objects]."[30] The ideas turn out to be appearances, for "The Animal Spirits make no other impression upon the Brain than as things appear. . . ."[31]

Bacon's description of the spirits leaves no basis for doubting that spirit is substantial and material. If there be spirit that is

---

[27] *Of the Interpretation of Nature, Works* III, 223.

[28] Antonio F. Doni, *De natura hominis* (Lyon, 1581).

[29] *De Aug.* II, 13; *Works* IV, 325. In the passage Spedding has translated *Anima* as "the spirit of man." Wats and Shaw prefer "soul," and so do I. Nevertheless, the basic point remains: there is a material vehicle in motion whenever thinking goes on. *Of the Advancement and Proficience of Learning, or the Partitions of Sciences, IX Bookes* . . . Interpreted by Gilbert Wats (Oxford, 1640); *The Philosophical Works of Francis Bacon* . . . Methodized, and Made English, from the Originals . . . by Peter Shaw (3 vols.; 2nd ed.; London, 1737).

[30] M.S., *A Philosophical Discourse of the Nature of Rational and Irrational Souls,* p. 12.

[31] *Ibid.,* p. 24.

conceivable as sheer form and that requires no correlative idea of material to render it intelligible or real, Bacon is leaving such a conception to religion and theology. The term "spirits" falls into the category of substance, and the term refers to things that are real. In fact, says Bacon, spirits are "things by themselves." No abstract entity is entailed here, but "a natural body. . . ." And natural bodies are "no less differing one from the other than the dense or tangible parts" which embrace them.[32] In the *Sylva*, Bacon deliberately reinforces his statement by the device of contrast. Sometimes spirits are taken for "*vacuum*," but they are really "the most active of bodies." Sometimes they are taken for air, but from this "they differ exceedingly." Sometimes they are regarded as virtues and qualities of tangible parts, but they are actually things by themselves. Sometimes they have been called souls of plants and living creatures, but they are not such.[33] Later in the same section of the *Sylva*, he refers to spirits as "minute parts" and calls for special study of their effects and manifestations in order that we may learn about their "motions." When speaking of the errors and idols to which man is prey, Bacon calls attention to the homogeneous state of a substance, as indicated by the uniform nature of its particles and the evenness of their distribution. This state is a condition of man's spirit and gives rise to error. In Bacon's language: "The spirit of man (being of an equal and uniform substance) pre-supposes and feigns in nature a greater equality and uniformity than really is."[34]

In completing our description of spirit substance as Bacon understood it, it is well to recognize what he did not have in mind. He did not think of spirit as an immaterial substance as Joseph Glanvill did.[35] His *spiritus* is less complicated and complex than

---

[32] The quotations are from *Sylva Sylvarum*, 98; *Works* II, 381. *The History of Life and Death*, probably a slightly earlier work than the *Sylva*, makes the same point, although I am not certain that Bacon is speaking of spirit in general rather than of the lifeless kind only. ". . . this spirit, whereof I am speaking, is . . . a body thin and invisible, and yet having place and dimension, and real." *Works* V, 321.

[33] *Sylva Sylvarum*, 98; *Works* II, 380–381.

[34] *De Aug.* V, 4; *Works* IV, 432.

[35] Glanvill's formal definition of spirit: it is "an Immaterial Substance intrinsically endued with Life and the faculty of Motion." [*An Appendage . . . Concerning the Possibility of Apparitions and Witchcraft. Containing the Explication of the Nature of a Spirit . . .* (London, 1681). Bound as part of *Saducismus Triumphans* (London, 1681), p. 141.]

the doctrine of spirits he inherited or the views in vogue among his contemporaries. He did not build up a conception of spirit beyond what he thought would be useful in accounting for the changes and movements he saw throughout the natural world. His two kinds of spirits, lifeless and living, possibly embrace all that was customarily thought of as three kinds of spirits, natural, vital, and animal. As we have already noticed, he referred to the vital spirit by name. At times he spoke of an animal spirit. For example, in commenting on Fracastorius' heated head pan that alleviated the symptoms of apoplexy, he explained that the device "manifestly expands the animal spirits. . . ."[36] This sort of spirit was employed to account for certain vague and very faint sensations beyond the range of responses assignable to the external senses. Animal spirits, for instance, may possess "a sense of heat and cold" more exquisite than the sense of touch.[37] Only rarely did Bacon speak of the natural spirit, and when he did he seemed skeptical of its existence: "Men talk . . . of the natural spirit of animals and even of vegetables, which differs from the other soul [i.e., the rational soul] both in essence and in form."[38]

Bacon did not see his spirits as the manifestation of some higher, rarer spirit, something that was divine. Nor did he see spirit as something intermediary between the rational soul and the body. Rather, the irrational or brute soul was the instrument of the rational soul and thus was considered a necessary and integral aspect of all mental activity. As far as he could he avoided meta-physical speculation. What he did not do may be suggested if

---

[36] *Novum Organum* II, 25; *Works* IV, 177.

[37] *Ibid.*, 13, p. 144.

[38] *History of Life and Death, Works* V, 314. In the sixteenth century the physiology of the three spirits is neatly represented by the revered Galen. The liver was the center of nutrition, the heart of blood circulation and heat regulation, and the brain of sensation and movement. The liver engendered the natural spirit (*pneuma physicon*) and mixed it in the blood. The heart added the vital spirit (*pneuma zoticon*) to the blood stream. The brain provided the animal spirit (*pneuma psychion*) which permeated the nerves. See Arturo Castiglioni, *A History of Medicine*, trans. E. B. Krumbhaar (New York: Alfred A. Knopf, Inc., 1941), p. 221. Renaissance anatomists offered variations upon Galen. Valentinus saw but two kinds of spirits, vital and animal. He had the vital spirit manufactured from blood by the heart. He regarded it as the *matter* of the animal spirit. For Valentinus' full account see his *Enchiridion medicum* . . . (London, 1608), pp. 10–11. Crooke saw the lungs as "the shoppe of the spirites" where inhaled air was prepared for the heart and the "in-bred spirite. . . ." *Microcosmographia*, p. 387.

we but briefly refer to the speculative thought of some of his contemporaries.

Helkiah Crooke seems to have been a respected writer on anatomy in the days of Bacon. Holder of three medical degrees and personal physician to James I, he published his *Microcosmographia: A Description of the Body of Man*, 1111 folio pages, in 1615. He is certainly more thorough and accurate than the authors of general compendia and of popular health books. Crooke accepts the traditional three spirits, natural, vital, and animal. At times, like Bacon, he is skeptical of a natural spirit and reports that some writers deny its being. But he thinks that Columbus had established it "by argument," and goes on to say that it is produced in the liver and feeds the "Nourishing Soule as they call it, which is seated in euery part of the body."[39] Crooke is confident that there is a vital spirit, and in discussing it he speculates about the body-soul relationship in a manner that Bacon, in his best critical moments, would reject. It is "primarily seated in the Left caue or denne of the heart. . . ." There it has been extracted from the blood, "creamed as it were off the bloud, and by the heat of the heart rarified into an aetherial consistence." Its substance must be as close to the soul like as its mortality will permit: "For the Soule it selfe being a denison of heauen . . . how could it bee tyed to this house of clay vnlesse it were by the mediation of some middle Nature, participating (as neere as mortality will suffer) of the purity of the Soule and yet hauing his originall from the body, that the Soule might haue a nimble and agile instrument to follow her sudden designes." A man's position on the manner in which the vital spirit is nourished can well indicate his position on the immortality of the soul. As we have seen, Bacon felt that the spirit was "supplied" by the blood. Crooke asserts that the spirit is nourished by the blood, but not "like the nourishment of the partes, but rather is an illumination, vnition and establishment of them. . . ." In describing the function of the spirit, Crooke is lyrical: "This spirit whilest it shineth in his brightnes and spredeth it selfe through all the Theatre of the body, as the Sunne ouer the earth, it blesseth all partes with ioy and iolitie and dies them with a Rosie colour; but on the contrary when it is retracted, intercepted or extinguished, all things

---

[39] *Ibid.*, p. 134.

become horrid wanne and pale and finally do vtterly perish." So wonderful are its powers that Hippocrates and Galen called the vital spirit soul. Crooke's best judgment is that the vital spirit is really "the chief instrument of the Soule."[40]

In view of Bacon's acceptance of the animal spirit, Crooke's handling of it is especially interesting. He repeats the belief that it is made in the brain and its matter is air and the vital spirit. He also allows that it is responsible for bodily motion and sense, the animal spirits being the stuff of the sense organs and most readily moved. He becomes interesting — and metaphysical — when he describes the character of movement, first, outside the brain, and then within it. The spirits "transferre the *species* or formes of all outward things perceiued by the outward Sences vnto the brain. . . ." Within the brain, they "conceiue" the "images of those outward thinges, so that the Animall spirit may bee called the place and promptuarie of the *species* or formes."[41] So the "principall" faculties of the brain use "the ministry and helpe of this spirit"; it is their "vehicle."[42]

Among the nonanatomists in Bacon's time, there is considerable agreement on the number and kinds of spirits. Burton, for example, accepts the traditional three, though he follows Melanchthon in thinking that the fountain of all the spirits is in the heart. Timothy Bright recognizes the three, but he sees them as manifestations of a single spirit. Unlike Bacon, these men are somewhat more explicit about the relationship of spirit to the rational soul. For Bright, the spirit is "the most universal instrument of the soule," the three spirits being but "diverse offices of one Spirit." Spirit is not only the soul's instrument; it is the "mean," a "Sacred band of unitie," between soul and body.[43] For Burton, "spirit is a most subtle vapour, which is expressed from the *blood,*

---

[40] *Ibid.* All quotations above are from p. 410.

[41] *Ibid.,* p. 517. The page should be numbered 515. Cf. the edition of 1631.

[42] *Ibid.,* p. 519. See John Banister, *The Historie of Man* . . . (London, 1578), fols. 98–100; John Woolton, *A Newe Anatomie of the Whole Man as Well of His Body as of His Soul* (London, 1576), fol. 75, and *A Treatise on the Immortalitie of the Soule* (London, 1576), fols. 74–75; Valentinus, *Enchiridion medicum,* pp. 10–11. Banister (or Banester) was a surgeon during Elizabeth's reign, and Valentinus an anatomist in the classical vein. Woolton, a divine, writes better psychology than anatomy. Among the popular health books see that of Thomas Elyot, *The Castele of Health* (London, 1610), pp. 16–17.

[43] Bright, *A Treatise of Melancholy,* pp. 47 ff.

and the instrument of the soul, to perform all his actions; a common tie or *medium* betwixt the body and soul, as some will have it. . . ."[44] Sir Thomas Browne is somewhat more mystical. "'I am sure there is a common Spirit that plays within us, yet makes no part of us: and that is the Spirit of God, the fire and scintillation of that noble and mighty Essence, which is the life and radical heat of Spirits, and those essences that know not the virtue of the Sun.'" "'Conceive light invisible,'" said Browne, "'and that is spirit.'"[45] Descartes provided a more detailed account of animal spirits than Bacon. To the Frenchman, they were minute, fast-moving, material bodies essential to both voluntary and involuntary movement.[46]

If Bacon was not as complex and metaphysical as his fellows, what do his spirits amount to? They are minute, imperceptible substances, breathlike and flamelike, quite separate from inert particles of matter. They move so much as to seem never at rest. They help to account for natural movement and change, for they come into being and pass away. To maintain itself, nonvital spirit feeds on adjacent particles of matter, the evidence of its activity being illustrated by rust in metals, and the shrinkage of flesh and the slowing down of bodily organs in human beings. In all animate life, the living spirit is the efficient cause and vehicle of motion. Although movements of the body that were observable and local could be explained in part by sensory action, the initiation and persistence of them could better be accounted for by assuming a pervasive, dynamic, spirit-substance than some mysterious force or soul. One does not go far, says Bacon in effect, in either explaining nature or in examining her if at every point of difficulty one calls upon a vague force, invents an entity, or devises a special principle to fit the case. Rather, one looks for the simplest thing, the single principle, that will account systematically for the largest number of phenomena. Among those persons who had attempted various kinds of explanations, Bacon preferred those "who make the principle of things one in substance, and that fixed and invariable; but deduce the diversity

[44] Burton, *The Anatomy of Melancholy*, p. 129.
[45] From Egan S. Merton, *Science and Imagination in Sir Thomas Browne* (New York: Columbia University Press, 1949), p. 68.
[46] Descartes, *The Passions of the Soul* (1649), articles 13–16, in *Philosophical Works*, I, 337–340. Cf. *Discourse on Method, ibid.*, p. 115.

of beings from the different magnitudes, configurations, and positions of that same principle." So Bacon adopted the two spirits as principles, principles that postulated a substance of the kind we have tried to describe in his own terms. Not much progress was made in understanding the sensible soul until it was regarded as a substance rather than a function. Now, says Bacon, we will assume a spirit and inquire "by what efforts a spirit so small and tender can put in motion bodies so gross and hard."[47]

Spirit in the human being is a substance so responsive to the two sources of knowledge that it reverberates to each — to God's revelations and to man's observations of nature. ". . . the informations of revelation and of sense differ no doubt in matter and manner of entrance and conveyance" to us; "yet the human spirit is one and the same; and it is but as if different liquors were poured through different funnels into one and the same vessel."[48] The human spirit responds both to divine sources of stimulation and to natural things. This is the kind of spirit man uses when he exercises the faculties of his soul — his understanding, reason, imagination, memory, appetite, and will. As the instrument of man's faculties it is both efficient cause and vehicle without which there is no human behavior.

Bacon's conception of the living spirit may not be significantly different from that of Bernard Telesius, from whom Bacon may have derived it.[49] If we may accept N. C. Van Deusen's description of the Italian's *spiritus*, it was an extremely tenuous substance continuous with itself throughout the body. It was capable of being dilated by heat and cold — these being two qualities of matter — and responded instantly to movement and caused movement. Telesius endowed this spirit with powers, not merely of motion, but of reason, imagination, sense, memory, and desire.[50]

---

[47] *De Aug.* IV, 3; *Works* IV, 401.

[48] *A Description of the Intellectual Globe, Works* V, 504.

[49] Bacon doubtless knew Telesius' *Bernardini Telesii consentini de rerum natura* . . . (Naples, 1597), for his *Principles and Origins* contains a long report of Telesian philosophy, with critical comment. Robert Ellis is confident that Bacon's spirit is Telesius' spirit. (*Works* I, 55.)

[50] Neil C. Van Deusen, "Telesio, the First of the Moderns," unpublished Ph.D. dissertation, Columbia University, New York, p. 53. Walker's interpretation of Telesius agrees with that of Van Deusen. Walker adds that Campanella's conception of spirit was much like Telesius', but that for Ficino spirit was a substance which functioned as "a medium of transmission by sentient and cognitive souls. . . ." D. P. Walker, *Spiritual and*

Bacon's *spiritus* is probably not much different in nature, but Bacon is somewhat more detailed in indicating what his spirit — and spirits — can do. This we shall see when we come to describe the faculties of man, for they will emerge as patterns of spirit behavior that may be discriminated both logically and functionally.

In taking the position that the ultimate basis of organic and inorganic existence consisted of particles of matter, some of them called spirit, Bacon was aware of the ideas and terms of the ontology he inherited. From the point of view of the physical world, the traditional elements were four, in the order of increasing density: fire, air, water, and earth.[51] Combinations of these gave four elemental compounds or matrices: mercury, sulphur, arsenic, and salt. From the point of view of physiological existence, the four elements gave rise to four "qualities": earth was responsible for coldness, water for moistness, air for dryness, and fire for heat. Each element, furthermore, could take on qualities other than the quality it originated; air, for example, could be hot and moist, or dry and cold. The possibility of a great variety of combinations, or "forms," is evident. Each element, also, was associated with degrees of density and rarity. Combinations and compounds of elements and qualities were called "tempers" when applied to things inorganic, and "temperatures" and "temperaments" when applied to animals and men. In nonliteral usage, one could of course speak of a person's temper. Some persons believed that the temperature of the brain determined "all the estate and action of the reasonable Soule."[52] Finally, when the notion of mixture and proportion of elements and compounds was applied specifically to the materials of the blood stream and the fluids of the body, there were four humours: Blood, Black Choler, Yellow Choler, and Flegm.[53] In this scheme of things, the element indispensable to life was heat, an essential element in Bacon's vital spirits, as it was also in the classical animal spirit.

Demonic Magic from Ficino to Campanella (London: Warburg Institute, University of London, 1958). See especially pp. 189–190, 216, 230.

[51] Corresponding with the four elements, so Farrington declares, were four fundamental processes: combustion, evaporation, solution, and condensation. Farrington, *The Philosophy of Francis Bacon*, p. 122.

[52] Charron, *Of Wisdome*, p. 49.

[53] For the physician's standard view of the humours and temperatures about 1600, see Valentinus, *Enchiridion medicum*, pp. 4–11. Galen called the humours "elements" of the blood, so his disciple, John Jones, understood. John Jones, *Galens Booke of Elements* (London, 1574), fol. 6.

Bacon doubted whether such a terminology reflected the true states of things. The originator of the four elements, said he, was Empedocles. Later it was "snapped up by the doctors and served as a pattern for further groups of four — four temperaments, four humours, four primary qualities." [54] At one time he wondered whether the element of fire existed; at another he was inclined to accept fire or flame, water, and air, and omit earth. [55] He accepted the vocabulary of the chemists, then offered his own opinion:

. . . two of these, namely, sulphur and mercury (in the sense in which I take them), I judge to be the most primeval natures, the most original configurations of matter. . . . But these terms . . . may be varied, and receive different denominations; as, the oily, the watery, the fat, the crude, the inflammable, the non-inflammable, and the like. For they appear to be those two enormous tribes of things which occupy and penetrate the universe. In the subterranean world we find sulphur and mercury . . . ; in the animal and vegetable world we find oil and water; in pneumatical bodies of the lower order we find air and flame; in the celestial regions we find starry body and pure ether. But of this last pair I do not as yet pronounce decisively. . . . [56]

Of these terms he made full use in describing conditions that influenced spirit activity. The ideas of the dense and rare he regarded as fundamental states of matter, perhaps properties; they pervaded "all other natures without being subject to their laws." [57] The jargon of temper, temperature, and the humours, he never submitted to sustained analysis. When he employs the vocabulary at all, he usually speaks seriously. The spirits, for

---

[54] *The Refutation of Philosophies*, in Farrington, *The Philosophy of Francis Bacon*, p. 125.

[55] *Novum Organum* I, 60; *Works* IV, 61; *History of Dense and Rare*, *Works* V, 344. The chemists of his time, he says, preferred earth, water, air, and ether — elements regarded not as matter but as elements out of which things are generated. Instead of "First Matter, they substitute three things, sulphur, mercury, and salt. . . ." *History of Sulphur, Mercury, and Salt*, *Works* V, 205.

[56] *Ibid.*

[57] *History of Dense and Rare*, *Works* V, 346. An interesting possibility is that Bacon regarded the elements not as particles of matter but as forms. In writing on the principles and origins of things, he referred to the scriptural mention of earth and water, and added, "which are the names of forms. . . ." (*Works* V, 468.) The meaning here conforms with that in the *Novum Organum*, in which the investigation of natures is equivalent to the investigation of forms.

example, temper the movements of bodily parts.[58] Some infectious diseases are "chiefly in the spirits, and not so much in the humours. . . ."[59] He is "certain that there be humours, which somewhere placed in the body, are quiet and do little hurt; in other places (especially passages) do much mischief."[60] The "individual and personal" features in the manners of men might indeed reflect their "temperatures."[61]

Hence, revisionist as Bacon may have been about some fundamentals of physical and physiological dogma, he had confidence in spirits. The living spirit partakes of the elements of fire and air, and partaking of both is "of a middle nature. . . ."[62] In man, as in all creatures, there are two kinds of materials, that of his "parts" and that of the spirit. The "fabric of the parts is the organ of the spirit," and the spirit in turn is "the organ of the reasonable soul. . . ."[63]

---

[58] *Novum Organum* II, 8; *Works* V, 228.
[59] *Sylva Sylvarum*, 297; *Works* II, 439.
[60] *Sylva Sylvarum* 65; *Works* II, 368. Cf. *De Aug.* IV, 2; *Works* IV, 385–386, 395, 396.
[61] *Advancement of Learning*, I; *Works* III, 277.
[62] *History of Life and Death*, *Works* V, 335.
[63] *Ibid.*

CHAPTER 3

Sense, Movement, and Appetite

A central problem in metaphysics has always been that of being and coming into being, and in turn this problem entailed attempts to describe and analyze movement and change. Of immediate interest to us in this chapter is Bacon's endeavor to describe human action and movement to the extent that these are influenced by man's sensory equipment.

If we may speak in the most general terms, it had been traditional to regard movement from two points of view, that involving change from place to place, and that involving change from state to state, or condition to condition. A man flexes a finger, picks up a hammer, or builds a house. An observer can see what is going on. The simple action appears to have a beginning and an end. So does the complex action, although the understanding of it may require its reduction into a sequence of component parts, continuous and contiguous but nevertheless separable in analysis. The other type of movement, that of change from one state to another state, proceeds so slowly or is so microscopic that it escapes observation. The hair is black in one year, gray in another. A man is five feet tall one year, six feet tall ten years later. He is in good health one day, ill the next. In this type of change, the terminal states can be located, the intervening stages are inaccessible to our senses. So we call upon the "intellect" and "reason" to infer and deduce what has gone on.

To understand a particular movement was to treat it as the outcome of one or more of four causes, the causes probably having their prime source in Aristotle's *Physics*. A movement was thought to have some end or purpose (the final cause), to be impossible without a material basis (the material cause), to require an agent or force to start it (the efficient cause), and to have a form or structure that was the product of one or a combination of the three causes. This last was of course the formal cause. A poem could be regarded as the result of such causes. As a completed thing, it was the final cause. Its material was language and its efficient cause was its author. The author, under the influence of his ideas for the poem, shaped them according to the skill and standards of his art, and made his product. Natural movements were explained similarly, whenever possible; and if it were not possible to name all the causes, it was assumed that man did not yet possess the ability or the tools to locate them. The efficient cause of many puzzling natural phenomena might be simply Nature, some mysterious or occult force, or a deity. To Aristotle and his disciples the efficient cause of *natural* events was linked with the final cause or "end." Bacon believed that Physics should be restricted to the search for material, formal, and efficient causes, these being sufficient to account for the appearance, structure, and function of a particular motion or action. He assigned to Metaphysics the consideration of final causes and the more abstract formal causes. He undoubtedly hoped that man's bodily movements, both external and internal, might eventually be understood in terms of their functions, material bases, and sources of stimulation.

Man's sensory equipment furnishes data for the directing of movement. In this respect man is like an animal; yet unlike animals he can learn to discipline his senses that they may supply better information and be better guides to conduct. The force of these statements may be appreciated by looking first to Bacon's two main modes of sensory stimulation and their chief effects.

The External Senses

Although he does not formally announce the fact, Bacon recognizes two classes of the sensory. First are the familiar, widely known, external senses, to which Bacon adds a sixth. Second is the living spirit, which in its "animal" aspect may behave like a sense.

So thoroughly does Bacon accept the traditional account of the external senses that he never feels the need to bring them together in a single place and discuss them formally. He of course often alludes to the usual five: sight, sound, touch, taste, and smell. To these he adds the "Venus sense," the recognition of which he attributes to Scaliger who did "well to make the pleasure of generation a sixth sense. . . ." Indeed, "the pleasure in the act of Venus is the greatest of the pleasures of the senses. . . ."[1] This pleasure is not merely a species of the sense of touch; rather, it is a separate sense. Other senses are characterized by the organs and spirits involved in discharging specific functions: "all the organs of the senses qualify the motions of the spirits; and make so many several species of motions, and pleasures or displeasures thereupon, as there be diversities of organs. The instruments of sight, hearing, taste, and smell, are of several frame, and so are the parts for generation."[2] Among the senses those of the eye and ear are *the purest.* As a consequence, so Bacon observed, the sciences thereof are the most learned, for they have "mathematics like a handmaid in their train."[3]

The functioning of the senses entails definite movement of the sense organs. Bacon makes no attempt to describe the motion, but in keeping with his desire that all types of body movements be investigated carefully, particularly as to the *measurements* thereof, he calls for an analysis of "the motion which takes place in the actions of the senses. . . ."[4]

The activity of the senses discloses their chief function: they are "reporters." As is true of all motion, sensory action is in response to "the stimulus of surrounding things," and presumably Bacon would include among "things" the structures adjacent to an organ and within it. The reports consist of information from sources external to the organ and they are made available to "the mind of man."[5] Indeed, it is from the senses that "all knowledge in nature must be sought, unless men mean to go mad. . . ."[6] Thus the senses provide for man's guidance the materials of knowledge and counsel with which the understanding, reason, and imagination must work. Among the reporters, the sense of sight has "the chief office in giving information."[7]

[1] *Sylva Sylvarum,* 693; *Works* II, 556.
[2] *Ibid.*
[3] *De Aug.* IV, 2; *Works* IV, 395.
[4] *De Aug.* III, 4; *Works* IV, 357.
[5] *Advancement of Learning, Works* III, 265.
[6] *Plan of the Work, Works* IV, 26.
[7] *Novum Organum* II, 39; *Works* IV, 192.

Bacon is most interested in the "audibles and visibles." In the *Sylva Sylvarum*, his Natural History, he gives over all of Century II and most of Century III to miscellaneous opinions, observations, and suggestions concerning them. Much of this material does not directly concern us, but it points toward the sciences of optics and acoustics. Bacon seems to be fully aware, for example, of contemporaneous opinion and fact on optical perspective and musical sounds. He suggests a complete classification of sound[8] that emerges from the basic distinction between tone and noise. "All sounds are either musical sounds, which we call tones; whereunto there may be an harmony; which sounds are ever equal; as singing, the sounds of stringed and wind instruments, the ringing of bells, etc.; or immusical sounds; which are ever unequal; such as the voice in speaking, all whisperings . . . all percussions of stones, wood . . ." and the like.[9] He is interested in the transmission of sight and sound, remarking among many other things "that visibles (except lights) are carried in right lines, and audibles in arcuate lines," "visibles are carried swiftlier to the sense than audibles," and dutifully recording much of what he had read or observed about the phenomena of reverberation, resonance, and echo, on the production and characteristics of speech sounds, and on the phenomena of color, reflection, and diffraction. Bacon appears to have believed that light is propagated by beams and "rays" emanating from both the object and the eye. Sound is propagated somewhat like "local motion," like "percussions or impressions made upon the air."[10] Bacon explains this only as a special type of motion, that of "*Signature* or *Impression*," which is an "operation without communication of substance."[11]

Of greater concern to us are the sense organs in their role as reporters. Specifically, what do they report? First, they respond to whatever is in their capacities, and they will do so with considerable accuracy if the source of stimulation is not too distant and if the intensity of stimulation is sufficient to activate the organ, is not painful, and the like. As will be seen later, the senses are not to be rejected as reporters that are intrinsically untrustworthy. They can be trained to provide accurate and reliable

[8] *Sylva Sylvarum*, 290; *Works* II, 436.
[9] *Sylva Sylvarum*, 101; *Works* II, 385.
[10] *Sylva Sylvarum*, 268; *Works* II, 430.
[11] *De Aug.* III, 4; *Works* IV, 356. Cf. *Sylva Sylvarum*, 288; *Works* II, 435.

data. Second, they report the "species" of things. With this idea we confront the nature of sense perception, particularly that point or moment at which sensation is thought to become meaningful, at which experience first takes on form and shape, at which experience is organized and becomes a "this" and not a "that." In metaphysical terms: how do physical and material things, such as objects and movements, sound and light, become "immaterial," mental events? One answer was that the sense organ itself makes an image of the object, the image being regarded as the sensory counterpart of the real thing and as the first step up the ladder of abstraction. The real tree, let us say, became the image of the tree. This was the level of response at which experience became discriminable, at which chaos became order, at which the organism dealt with a "this." In the diction of metaphysics, the experience was at the level of "sensible species." In the early seventeenth century, most of Aristotle's followers held that a sense organ not only sensed; it made an image. But the Arabian interpreters of Aristotle, particularly Avicenna, held that the species or "image" literally emanated from the object itself, and that the sense organs as reporters duly recorded them. Bacon seems to have held the same view. He does not say so flatly, but his language in talking of visibles and audibles permits of no other conclusion. "The species of visibles," he says, "seem to be emissions of beams from the objects seen; almost like odours; save that they are more incorporeal: but the species of audibles seem to participate more with local motion, like percussions or impressions made upon the air." [12] "All bodies," he continues, "seem to work in two manners." They communicate "their natures," and "the diffusion of species visible" seems to be of this sort. Or they communicate "by the impressions and signatures of their motions," and "the species audible" seem to be of this kind. [13] Often when Bacon speaks of "spiritual species" he is referring literally to external reality, not to man's power of interpretation. So far as I have observed, he does not use the term, "intelligible species," anywhere in his works. This was the level of abstraction, next above that of sensible species, that was said to be present in the conception and the idea. He is of course well aware of the problems and dangers

---

[12] *Sylva Sylvarum*, 268; *Works* II, 430.
[13] *Ibid.*

of abstraction; yet he avoided one of the technical terms associated traditionally with the process.

Perhaps Bacon wanted to avoid argument over the two kinds of species, intellectual and sensible. But one of his contemporaries, Thomas Hobbes, was not loath to argue. He thought he was rebelling against the current "philosophy-schools" which taught, he said, that an object sent forth a sensible species to the common sense, and the common sense in its turn sent an intelligible species to the understanding.[14] "*Sense*," he said, "*is a phantasm, made by the reaction and endeavour* [i.e., motion] *outwards in the organ of sense, caused by an endeavour inwards from the object, remaining for some time, more or less.*"[15] A sense organ responds to what are called "qualities" of objects, but the real source of the qualities is in the sentient being. As an act producing phantasms, sensing consists of two kinds of doing. It is an "appearance," an "apparition"; that is, in our vocabulary it is a sense image. Simultaneous with the appearance is "perception," a label that to Hobbes seems to mean the respondent's interpretation of the sense act. Or it is a conception. An appearance is an immediate act of sensing in response to an external object; a conception is a revival of sense activity in the absence of objects and in response to inner stimulation.[16] For Hobbes, then, the first level of organized experience occurred in sensing. For Bacon, the first level of organization was found in the object world and the senses duly reported what they encountered.

A third feature of seeing and hearing should be noted. Two aspects of sight are intrinsically pleasing. Color in itself is pleasing to the eye. So is order, which is the basis of proportion and harmony. And by analogy, so Bacon remarks, the same two kinds of experience are intrinsically pleasing to the ear. A single tone is as pleasing to the ear as a single color is to the eye. Order is as appealing to hearing as to sight, and involves the implicit measurement of intervals. "And therefore we see in garden knots, and the

---

[14] Thomas Hobbes, *Elements of Philosophy*, in *The English Works of Thomas Hobbes*, ed. Sir William Molesworth (11 vols., London: J. Bohn, 1839–45), III, 10. Cf. Hobbes, *Leviathan*, ed. M. Oakeshott (Oxford: B. Blackwell, [1946]), p. 13.

[15] Hobbes, *Works* I, 391.

[16] See *Ibid.*, pp. 389, 392. Hobbes may be the first Englishman to use the word perception as a modern psychologist would.

frets of houses, and all equal and well answering figures, (as globes, pyramids, cones, cylinders, etc.), how they please; whereas unequal figures are but deformities." On the basis of such observations, Bacon hints at a psychology of aesthetics: "both these pleasures, that of the eye, and that of the ear, are but the effects of equality, good proportion, or correspondence: so that (out of the question) equality and correspondence are the causes of harmony."[17] We should point out here that Bacon is particularly acute in making these observations, for he is referring only to the pleasing effect that directly attends the movement of the sense organs. In fact, he is self-consciously aware of his point, for he places in a quite different category such experience as "pictures and shapes . . . which are but secondary objects, and please or displease but in memory. . . ."[18] So some sense activity is directly pleasing and displeasing quite apart from effects that are stored in experience and learned through behavior.

Spirit and Sensation

The external senses, then, are the ordinary sources of experience. We turn now to another source of sensory experience, the spirits. We have already seen that the spirit in man's body is the efficient cause and necessary vehicle for the functioning of internal organs and processes. Bacon was much interested in vegetative and life-renewing mechanisms. They were dynamic mechanisms, and he wished that these, as well as motion in inanimate things, could be brought under the closest study. To do so would demand a classification of all motion into its smallest units — and Bacon offers a tentative classification under the head of the physics of "*Appetites* and *Motions*."[19] Yet, even if such a study should be completed and the mechanics of all movement be understood, there would doubtless remain the question in each case, What controls the process? Bacon's answer appears to be that the spirits possess something analogous to a sensing power and that this power initiates some kinds of movement and governs them. He gives to the animal spirit the sensation of pain. Perhaps it also responds

---

[17] *Sylva Sylvarum*, 111; *Works* II, 388.
[18] *Ibid.*
[19] See *De Aug.* III, 4; *Works* IV, 356–357.

to heat and cold; at least, "Sensible heat . . . is correctly defined
as merely the effect of heat on the animal spirits."[20] Because air
expands and contracts with changes of temperature, Bacon thinks
that air may have a "sense" of heat and cold, a sense "so subtle
and exquisite as far to exceed the perception of the human
touch. . . ." So by analogy of air with spirit, he remarks, "I
think that animal spirits have a sense of heat and cold more exquisite still, were it not that it is impeded and deadened by the
grossness of the body."[21] Possibly Bacon believed that in all
animate things internal motion not attributable to the influence
of the external senses was controlled by the sensory power of
spirit. I am inclined to think that he did. The living spirit seemed
to have a sense of its own.

But whether he believed that the "lifeless" spirit present in
all inanimate bodies exercised a sensory power is doubtful. Ellis
speculates on whether Bacon really followed Campanella's lead
and endowed all natural things with powers of sensation.[22] If
Bacon believed that a sense is required to initiate any and all
kinds of motion, he would have had nature alive with senses. But
this he did not believe. Sensation is a property of the animal
spirit—a property perhaps also shared by the vital spirit. Nevertheless, some things did not exhibit animal spirit. ". . . there is
no difference between the consents or sympathies of bodies endowed with sensation and those of inanimate bodies without
sensation, except that in the former an animal spirit is added to
the body so disposed, but is wanting in the latter."[23] Sense and
motion seem always to go together in the animate world, and this
circumstance leads Bacon to infer not that there are senses in
sticks and stones, but there are *motions* in inanimate things.
"Necessarily," he holds, "there are many more motions in inanimate bodies than there are senses in animate, on account of the

[20] *Novum Organum* II, 20; *Works* IV, 151.

[21] *Novum Organum* II, 15; *Works* IV, 144.

[22] "His whole doctrine of simple motions is full of expressions which it is
very difficult to understand without supposing that Bacon had for the time
adopted the notion of universally diffused sensation." Yet how far the
analogy "between animate and inanimate bodies ought to be carried, was
a doubtful question; and we need not be surprised to find that Bacon sometimes denies and sometimes appears to admit that the latter as well as the
former are, to a certain extent at least, consciously sentient." General
Preface, *Works* I, 54, 55.

[23] *Novum Organum* II, 27; *Works* IV, 165.

paucity of organs of sense."[24] Animals experience many kinds and varieties of pain and each involves motion. It is almost certain that there are as many motions in inanimate substances, "though they do not enter the senses for want of animal spirit."[25]

Appetite

What, then, accounts for motion under all conditions in which no sense organ is manifest? Among the classical explanations, Bacon preferred that of the Democritean atom, in which centripetal motion is the primary force and a secondary force is a sort of centrifugal motion that comes about when dense matter pushes away, or triumphs over, light or rare matter. But this theory was not entirely satisfactory to Bacon, for it was too general to encourage the study of nature in ways that would control her. To improve upon Democritus, Bacon from time to time considered certain "natural" mechanisms: "perception," consents and aversions, sympathies and antipathies, and appetites. He seems to have decided upon *appetite* as the single efficient and effective cause of motion. He applied it to both physical movement and to sense-controlled behavior. In this chapter we shall emphasize appetite as a feature of physical and biological motion and in another chapter deal with it, together with the Will, as the trigger of voluntary movement in human behavior.

Appetite is the power of receiving and giving. To Bacon this is the generic meaning of appetite and he employs it consistently. If moral philosophers and others would only cast their eyes "abroad upon nature" they would behold "the appetite that is in all things to receive and to give. . . ."[26] Things receive what is attractive and reject what is repugnant, and the "preference" of the receiver determines the action of the giver. Giving and receiving, furthermore, are motions, "the one motion affecting preservation and the other multiplication. . . ."[27]

With this concept as the controlling idea, two categories of appetite may be distinguished. First, there is motion whose effec-

---

[24] *Ibid.*
[25] *Ibid.*
[26] *Of the Interpretation of Nature, Works* III, 229.
[27] *Ibid.*

tive cause is "natural"; its own nature is its cause of movement. Giving and receiving are sufficient forces unto themselves. They must be, for many motions show no sign of sense or feeling. The class of motions having natural appetites is a large one. When Bacon undertakes his most precise analysis of the physics of motion, he captions the section, "*Appetites* and *Motions.*" He lists fifteen "simple motions, in which lies the root of all natural actions, subject to the conditions of the configurations of matter."[28] The name of each motion stands first as the name of the appetite, followed by a phrase describing its general function. There is, for example, the "motion of the *Second Connexion,*" or that to prevent the breakdown of the movement into disconnected parts. This movement is sometimes called the "appetite of union," illustrated by pitch and honey cleaving to a surface, and water forming drops to avoid dispersion.[29] In addition to the appetites of simple motions, there is the kind of appetite evident in the "figures" in "the universal frame of the world. . . ." The figures are given off "in the beams of heaven," and the earth receives them.[30] Called a kind of good, this appetitive motion is tersely referred to by Bacon as an "effecting or operation. . . ."[31] There is the appetite that binds the whole and its parts, or in Bacon's language, "the motion of congruity or situation of the parts in respect of the whole, evident in so many particulars. . . ." This entails a "consenting or proportion. . . ."[32] There is the appetite in which the inferior kind moves toward its superior kind. Like agrees with like "in small moments," as is seen when the magnet receives tiny iron particles; but iron in larger quantities will go to the earth, the kind superior to the magnet.[33] There is an appetite in every man to propagate the more general form of himself, i.e., to multiply his *species.*[34]

Within this scheme of natural appetites Bacon would doubtless

---

[28] *De Aug.* III, 4; *Works* IV, 356. Wats's translation: "according to the schemes and habitudes of matter."

[29] Note the three classes of appetite in *Sylva Sylvarum,* 293; *Works* II, 437.

[30] *Interpretation of Nature, Works* III, 229.

[31] *Ibid.,* p. 230.

[32] *Ibid.,* p. 229.

[33] *De Aug.* VII, 1; *Works* V, 7. In advising James on the union of England and Scotland, Bacon weaves this principle into an argument. *A Briefe Discovrse, Touching the Happie Vnion of the Kingdomes of England, and Scotland* (London, 1603), A 4.

[34] *Advancement of Learning,* II; *Works* III, 420, 425–426.

include what he calls "consents or aversions."[35] We are told concisely that "Consent is nothing else than the adaptation of Forms and Configurations to each other." From the point of view of Bacon's physics, configuration or scheme refers to the arrangement, perhaps the shape or figure, of particles of matter. Form refers to the principle or law that informs or illuminates the configuration, or the statement of the law or principle. Consent, then, seems to be a sort of structural appetite, and is perhaps not unlike the notion of valence in modern chemistry. Sometimes the giving and receiving will be dominated by the character of the material itself, sometimes by its scheme or figure. ". . . metals agree well together in quantity and density, especially as compared with vegetables, &c, but differ very widely in configuration; while . . . vegetables and animals vary almost infinitely in their configurations, but in quantity of matter or density their variation is confined to narrow limits."[36] The operations of the senses are illustrations of consents, for each sense does only what it can do and functions in its unique way. The eye is adapted to seeing, the ear to hearing, and neither can do the work of the other. A very few consents "have been approved by sure experiment; such as those of the magnet and iron, of gold and quicksilver, and the like."[37] There are the consents of medicines for certain parts, members, and operations of the body. "Nor should we omit," asserts Bacon, "the consents between the motions and changes of the moon and the affections of bodies below; such as may be gathered and admitted, after strict and honest scrutiny, from experiments in agriculture, navigation, medicine, and other sciences."[38] In every case of consent, appetite appears when the relationship of structure and material of one thing is similar to the relationship of structure and material of another thing. Giving and receiving is determined by a complex isomorphic relationship among things. Perhaps Bacon meant that they *are* such a relationship.

If appetite among physical things is of this nature, it clearly includes the mechanism of sympathy and antipathy. Bacon's most concrete use of sympathy may be seen in his discussion of musical sounds. "All concords and discords of music are (no doubt) sym-

---

[35] For Bacon's fullest discussion of these, see *Novum Organum* II; *Works* IV, 242–245.

[36] *Ibid.*, p. 243.　　[37] *Ibid.*, p. 244.　　[38] *Ibid.*

pathies and antipathies of sounds. And so likewise in that music which we call broken music, or consort music, some consorts of instruments are sweeter than others . . . as the Irish harp and base viol agree well . . . organs and the voice agree well. . . ."[39] But the Welsh harp and Irish harp "agree not so well." Bacon thus has observed similarities among kinds of sounds and among their patterns and qualities. He was keenly aware of the phenomenon of sympathetic vibration, in which one vibrating body will set a similar body into vibration. Indeed, in one passage he equates sympathy with similitude: "It seemeth, both in ear and eye, the instrument of sense hath a sympathy or similitude with that which giveth the reflexion . . . for as the sight of the eye is like a crystal, or glass, or water; so is the ear a sinuous cave, with a hard bone to stop and reverberate the sound; which is like to the places that report echoes."[40] Such useful and sound inferences as may be drawn from observing the resemblances of objects in motion might well be handled as consents and aversions. Operations that are deeply hid, as sympathies often are, invite superstition and abuse by magicians and alchemists. "I am," writes Bacon, "almost weary of the words sympathy and antipathy on account of the superstitions and vanities associated with them. . . ."[41] Furthermore, "what are called occult and specific properties, or sympathies and antipathies, are in great part corruptions of philosophy."[42] Nevertheless, Bacon intended to produce a treatise entitled "A History of the Sympathy and Antipathy of Things." He composed only a brief introduction which begins with this declaration: "Strife and friendship in nature are the spurs of motions and the keys of works."[43] From them are derived "the union and repulsion of bodies, the mixture and separation of parts, the deep and intimate impressions of virtues [i.e., innate forces and strengths], and that which is termed the junction of actives with passives; in a word, the *magnalia naturae*."[44] The power of correlative forces — what is active is potentially passive and what is passive is potentially active — was widely accepted, and is to be seen among the presuppositions of grammar, logic, and the nature of the intellect. There cannot be, however, "much hope of disco /-

[39] *Sylva Sylvarum*, 278; *Works* II, 433.
[40] *Sylva Sylvarum*, 282; *Works* II, 434.
[41] *Novum Organum* II, 50; *Works* IV, 244.
[42] *Ibid.*, p. 242.   [43] *Works* V, 203.   [44] *Ibid.*

ering the consents of things before the discovery of Forms and Simple Configurations."[45]

Another mechanism of motion mentioned by Bacon is what he chose to call "perception." Of all the deeply hidden mechanisms of movement Bacon is least clear about this one. It appears only in *Sylva Sylvarum* and *De Augmentis*, and in introducing it Bacon insists that students of the senses have neglected this "most noble subject. . . ." It ought to be scrutinized searchingly and be distinguished from the senses.[46] Bacon believes that all natural bodies exercise a sort of choice "in receiving what is agreeable, and avoiding what is hostile and foreign." The magnet attracts iron, the body assimilates food and rejects wastes, humours and juices course up and down the body, the heart and pulse beat — "all these and many other things are done without sense." Some bodies and substances near each other seem to feel or *perceive* each other's presence. They move in relation to each other only if "a reciprocal *perception* precede the operation. A body perceives the passages by which it enters; it perceives the force of another body to which it yields; it perceives the removal of another body which held it fast, when it recovers itself; it perceives the disruption of its continuity, which for a time it resists; in short there is Perception everywhere." Some of Bacon's illustrations of perception are also illustrations of consent, and he focuses on an aspect of experience that is at least close to touch and feeling. It is difficult to see that perception calls attention to anything that has not already been described under sense activity, consent, and appetite. Certainly he does not mean to endow all nature with universal sensation, for he censures persons who, with perception in mind, "have gone too far, and attributed *sense* to all bodies."

The second category of appetite is that of *desire*, a label simply meaning that the efficient causes of body actions are feelings of pleasure or of power often associated with successful sensory behavior. Sensory activity is taken to include that of the external senses and that of the spirits. The kinds of movement under sensory control are both external and internal — locomotion, instrumental use of hands and arms, gestures of body and face, and

---

[45] *Novum Organum* II, 50; *Works* IV, 242.
[46] The entire subject is discussed in *De Aug.* IV, 3; *Works* IV, 402–403. Cf. *Works* II, 602–603.

speech; and certain inner movements, such as those involved in digestion, nourishment, and respiration. Speaking in the broadest of terms, we may say that the activity involved is involuntary and habitual. It is set off by desire, for which another name in the classical literature of the senses is the sensitive appetite. Its presence as a guide to motion is felt as pleasure, and in creatures who are moved to preserve and multiply themselves the pleasure is that "of nourishment and generation. . . ."[47] In man its presence is felt either as pleasure or as a sense of power. The latter "sense" is one of achievement, as when one is aware of arriving at a goal or of accomplishing some object. The two feelings, says Bacon, are "the aptest and most natural division" of man's desires.[48]

Bacon's conception of appetite, as will become evident in Chapter 7, is not to be confused with his idea of Will. The latter faculty was often referred to by Bacon's predecessors and contemporaries as the intellectual appetite. When speaking of the will we are at the level of rational action and conduct, the level of voluntary movement. Will is the power, the efficient cause, of deliberative action. Indeed, will is related to voluntary movement precisely as desire is related to involuntary movement. In Chapter 7 we deal with will at some length.

In considering the physiological basis of man's nature Bacon recognized the primacy of movement and the need for understanding its most elementary mechanisms. He postulated something he was willing to call spirit or spirits. Spirit was a highly rarified substance, quite distinct from the divine spirit, the nature of which Bacon in his role as scientist left to the theologians. His concern was with the sensible or produced soul. The spirit was never at rest. Bodily changes and movements not manifestly influenced by the external senses — growth, maintenance of body functions, and decay — were to be explained by the natural powers of the spirit. The material nature of spirit was something like that of a particle, and particles possessed powers of giving and receiving, the chief forms of attraction being appetite and consent. Especially intriguing to Bacon was the mechanism of attraction whose power might lie in form and structure, in the

---

[47] *Interpretation of Nature, Works* III, 229.
[48] *Ibid.*

configurations of matter, in the conformities of shapes and figures for one another.

Bacon appears to have felt that all kinds of change, movement, and behavior must ultimately rely on sense activity or on something analogous to it. He seems to have assigned to spirit a sensory function in organic processes. In inorganic processes, the "lifeless" spirit acted *as if* it had sensory power. In all human behavior of which man could become conscious, the basic data of experience was undoubtedly supplied by the senses.

Bacon believed, as we have seen, that the basis of the rational soul was spirit activity; furthermore, rational life was related to spirit life as power is related to instrument and the vehicle thereof. As we turn to examine the faculties of the soul we are to focus upon the distinctive ways or modes in which man's six faculties or powers employ an instrument common to them all. The six are understanding, reason, imagination, memory, appetite, and will. Our explanation will follow that "natural" order that to Bacon and his contemporaries marked the grades of behavior from the sensory level to the intellectual. The final goal of individual life was to live rationally and this was achieved to the degree that a man could make his rational powers command his other powers. Respect for the understanding and for knowledge gained through the operations of reason, imagination, and memory and directed to informing the will and controlling the appetite led to exemplary conduct. The emphasis was on knowledge and its application. One can discern a logic and rhetoric in the process. Within man single — to use a Baconian locution — his faculties were in communication with each other; among men congregate, man single was in communication with his fellows.

The Faculties and Their Common Base

To understand each faculty is to grasp first the nature of the faculties in general, and their relationship to each other and to Bacon's divisions of knowledge.

The fundamental relationship among the faculties was that of knowledge to action. Understanding, reason, and imagination yielded contemplative knowledge and memory recorded and recalled it. Knowledge was a state or condition of the human being that constituted a potential for action. In any instance of rational behavior, action came about when an individual, confronted with the need to choose among alternatives, brought his knowledge to bear in ways that controlled appetite and directed his will. Rational conduct was thus knowledge actualized. Practical knowledge, on the other hand, was a state or condition built up chiefly through experience. It became rational to the extent that knowledge affected experience.

To Bacon the relationship among the principal classes of knowledge and the intellectual faculties was a definite one:

The best division of human learning is that derived from the three faculties of the rational soul, which is the seat of learning. . . . History is properly concerned with individuals, which are circumscribed by place and time. For though Natural History may seem to deal with species, yet this is only because of the general resemblance which in most cases natural objects of the same species bear to one another; so that when you know one, you know all. . . . All this relates to the Memory.

Poesy . . . is also concerned with individuals; that is, with individuals invented in imitation of those which are the subject of true history. . . . This is the work of Imagination.

Philosophy discards individuals; neither does it deal with the impressions immediately received from them, but with abstract notions derived from those impressions; in the composition and division whereof according to the law of nature and fact its business lies. And this is the office and work of Reason.[1]

In justifying this classification of knowledge, Bacon speaks of the chief operations of the senses and of the intellectual powers:

The sense, which is the door of the intellect, is affected by individuals only. The images of those individuals — that is, the impressions they make on the sense — fix themselves in the memory. . . . These the human mind proceeds to review and ruminate; and thereupon either simply rehearses them, or makes fanciful imitations of them, or analyses and classifies them. Wherefore from these three fountains, Memory, Imagination, and Reason, flow these three emanations, History, Poesy, and Philosophy. . . . I consider history and experience to be the same things, as also philosophy and the sciences.[2]

---

[1] De Aug. II, 1; Works IV, 292.   [2] Ibid., pp. 292–293.

These faculties or powers had as their vehicle the motions of spirits. Each faculty modulated, shaped, and figured spirit movement in ways peculiar to it:

some of the ancients, who in too eagerly fixing their eyes and thoughts on the memory, imagination, and reason, have neglected the faculty of thinking [or cogitation], which holds first place in the work of contemplating and considering [i.e., in the work of conception]. For he who remembers and also he who recollects, is thinking; he who imagines, is thinking; he who reasons, is thinking; and in a word the spirit of man, whether prompted by sense or left to itself, whether in the functions of the understanding, or of the will and affections, dances to the measure of thoughts.[3]

The context of the passage makes clear that by nature the souls of all living creatures are in infinite and endless motion, the human soul having its own mode of motion. That which is in motion is spirit. It seems evident, then, that thinking is a general mode of spirit activity in the rational soul and that the faculties designate distinctive types of motion. Thinking is like a radio carrier wave which is modulated according to the tasks it does. The faculties are types of modulation.

Although Bacon speculated much about spirit, the physical basis of mental life, he says very little about the anatomical location of mental activity. He was aware of the medical lore which located the faculties in the ventricles of the brain. "That arrangement," he said, "of the intellectual faculties (imagination, reason, and memory) according to the respective ventricles of the brain" was not entirely "destitute of error."[4] Yet he did observe, though almost as an aside, that "the cogitations of man . . . live in his head. . . ."[5] We are now ready to look at the faculties one by one.

Memory the Recorder and Storehouse

Memory is, first of all, the power of recording and storing whatever it receives. It receives the products of the senses, the understanding and reason, and the imagination.

---

[3] The rendering is in part mine. The Latin version is found in *De Aug.* II, 13; *Works* I, 528.
[4] *De Aug.* IV, 1; *Works* IV, 378.
[5] *Of the Wisdom of the Ancients, Works* VI, 763.

Bacon is explicit about the relationship of memory to the senses. The external senses respond to objects external to their organs; thus a sensory impression is made. Each response is to an individual object and each impression is an individual one. "The sense, which is the door of the intellect, is affected by individuals only." [6] Such impressions are images of objects. We shall call them sense images, to distinguish them from the work of the imagination. As "pictures and shapes," they are "secondary objects." Bacon offers this observation obliquely. In remarking on things pleasing to the sight, he points out that "pictures and shapes" are "but secondary objects, and please or displease but in memory. . . ." [7] Sense images are stored in the memory, for "the images of those individuals — that is, the impressions they make on the sense — fix themselves in the memory, and pass into it in the first instance entire as it were, just as they come." Memory also collects the affective aspects of experience; indeed, if we follow Bacon's hint, memory may contribute from its large and deep storehouse a scale of qualities marked by the "pleasant" at one end and "unpleasant" at the other. [8]

Memory received and preserved the work of the intellect and the imagination, as well as the work of the senses. Bacon almost ignores this function of memory, for he assumed what his contemporaries did, namely, that unless the human mechanism could retain intellectual experience it could not function in ways that were distinctively human. He recognized memory among four "intellectual" arts. The other three were invention, disposition, and transmission or communication. Memory preserved their work. With the principles and rules of an art as his anchoring point, Bacon writes more about improving the memory than he does about its operations. His helps for retention and recall recognize the difficulty of remembering abstract conceptions. The visual device of "Emblem," for example, helps memory to cope with "intellectual conceptions." [9]

Undoubtedly memory appeared to be a kind of experience; indeed to Bacon it was the record of experience. The relationship

---

[6] *De Aug.* II, 1; *Works* IV, 292–293.
[7] *Sylva Sylvarum*, 111, *Works* II, 388; cf. *Novum Organum* II, 26; *Works* IV, 163.
[8] *De Aug.* II, 1; *Works* IV, 293.
[9] *De Aug.* V, 5; *Works* IV, 437.

between man's experience and his recording of it seems to be Bacon's justification for tying together memory and history. The subject matter of history is "properly concerned with individuals, which are circumscribed by place and time." Such material "relates to the Memory."[10] When the mind "rehearses" what is retained in memory, it is thinking historically because it is dealing with experience. Hence Bacon can confidently assert, "I consider history and experience to be the same thing. . . ."[11] History is concerned, also, with things that have happened rather than with things that are happening or may happen. This fact helps to set off history from "Prophecy." Accordingly, if experience *per se* always implies a time reference to the past, memory includes all experience with the record of the past stamped upon it.

Helps to the Memory

Bacon's suggestions for the improvement of memory provide additional insights into the nature of the faculty. Indeed, the idea of improvement implies the chief functions that were traditionally imputed to memory, those of retention, recall, and recollection. If by recall is meant the recurrence of an experience and by recollection is meant recurrence of an experience attended by images of time and place, it must be recognized that Bacon did not name such functions. That he was fully aware of them, however, seems to be beyond doubt.

One group of aids to the memory suggests that we are dealing with a power that finds sense materials more congenial than abstract notions. In general, emblem — by which Bacon meant any sensible object — "reduces intellectual conceptions to sensible images . . . an object of sense always strikes the memory more forcibly and is more easily impressed upon it than an object of the intellect. . . ."[12] Bacon promptly illustrates his own precept: "you will more easily remember the image of a hunter pursuing a hare, of an apothecary arranging his boxes, of a pedant making a speech, of a boy repeating verses from memory, of a player acting on the stage, than the mere notions of invention, disposition, elocution, memory, and action."[13] What Bacon calls "places"

---

[10] *De Aug.* II, 1; *Works* IV, 292.   [11] *Ibid.*, p. 293.
[12] *De Aug.* V, 5; *Works* IV, 437.   [13] *Ibid.*

also makes for concreteness rather than abstraction. Places are not only concrete in themselves but they point specifically to the object of recall.

In referring to "places," Bacon is conscious of the rhetorical canon of memory and of the practice and advice of veteran speakers who believed that they had learned to control the processes of recollection. The classical practice of orators was to settle upon some object, such as an animal, a house, or a church, and to divide it up spatially and temporally into definite parts or places. A house might be readily arranged into the porch, front entry, first room on the right, second room, back exit, and so on, around the building. The places might be prominent features of such spaces, as, for example, doors, windows, niches, and the like. With his places fixed, and with his speech composed, the orator would select objects or images with which to associate the chief parts, the main arguments, and the striking details of his speech. He would then locate these images or objects in the places of his house. Thus the memory system was one that emphasized concrete, specific objects and images and the association of these with ideas. If it were possible, the orator would actually move through his house as he rehearsed his speech. Memory could be controlled, partly because the house and its places remained essentially the same for a large number of speeches, and partly because the images and figures, though they had to be newly invented to be "conformable" with the ideas of each speech, pinned the memory to specific details. "Such artificial places help the memory wonderfully, and exalt it far above its natural powers." [14]

Perhaps because memory prefers concrete experience to abstract ideas, it is particularly amenable to experience that strikes it intensely. So we find Bacon observing that "things which make their impression by way of a strong affection, as by inspiring fear, admiration, shame, delight, assist the memory." [15] Writing also intensifies ideas and their accompanying language. In "matters of much length and accuracy," it is absolutely essential. [16] Holding this conviction, Bacon insisted that scientific investigation must

---

[14] *Novum Organum* II, 26; *Works* IV, 162.
[15] *Ibid.*, p. 163.
[16] *De Aug.* V, 5; *Works* IV, 435.

include the preparation of tables in which observations were compared, contrasted, and classified. If done properly, the making of commonplace books, despite the belief of some critics that the practice invited the memory "to take holiday," promoted the retentive powers by contracting "the sight of judgment to a point."[17]

Memory behaves somewhat like a sense organ, for retention seemed to be particularly good when the faculty is fresh and undistracted. ". . . things which are chiefly imprinted when the mind is clear and not occupied with anything else before or after, as what is learnt in childhood, or what we think of before going to sleep, also things that happen for the first time, dwell longest in the memory."[18]

Memory likes order and organization. The effectiveness of "places" in recollection is due in part to order and repetition. Verse is remembered easier than prose because of its rhythm, and rhythm is a kind of order. Furthermore, the use of "topics" aids the memory by cutting off "an infinity of search" and directing the memory to where it had been before. In mentioning topics, Bacon is again drawing upon standard rhetorical practice and doctrine. Speakers often employed a system of topical heads to guide them in surveying the subject on which they were to speak. The heads were usually developed as an elaborate outline, and intelligent application of it frequently suggested ideas, materials, and arguments for the speech at hand. The rhetoricians thought of the process as one of invention, of finding or discovering arguments. Bacon believed that such a survey device was of little or no use in discovering something "new," as was the object of scientific discovery, but that it was of real value in recovering things old. He acutely observed that invention for writing and speaking was but a "*Remembrance* or *Suggestion*, with an application. . . ."[19]

It is probable, then, that the functions of memory are those of recording and remembering both mental and sensory experience. The organic or physical basis of memory is doubtless the spirit diffused throughout the body and extremely sensitive to stimulation from sources both without and within man.

---

[17] *Ibid.*

[18] *Novum Organum* II, 26; *Works* IV, 163.

[19] *Advancement of Learning*, II; *Works* III, 389. As a concept, invention is discussed most fully in *De Aug.* V, 2; *Works* IV.

Memory and the Internal Senses

Perhaps we can come a little closer to the nature of memory as Bacon understood it by looking at it in the company of its traditional associates, common sense and imagination. The internal senses, as they were called, were distinguished from the external senses. They were three in number: common sense, memory, and imagination.[20]

The common sense was the faculty that unified the data of the external or special senses. Each sense did what was "proper" to it, the eye seeing, the ear hearing, and the like. What was "common" to disparate sensations was organized into a whole by the common sense. The result was a shape or figure of an object. Common sense also gave meaning to successive affective aspects of experiences, such as pleasure and pain, and organized experience into things to be pursued and things to be avoided. To some philosophers, notably Avicenna, the evaluation of sensory experience was distinctive enough to furnish evidence of a separate power, the estimative faculty. The common sense, moreover, supplied the dimension of consciousness or awareness of experience. No sense was aware of its own activity, but the common sense identified the work of each sense. Hence, one "knew" that *he* as subject was undergoing or "receiving" the experience. In brief, common sense was the receiver, organizer, and evaluator of stimuli from the special senses. In the vocabulary of the Schoolmen, its products were the "common sensibles," as St. Thomas Aquinas said, or in modern parlance, perceptions. Its work dealt with the realities of concrete, everyday experience. In the system of communication among things mental and sensory, the common sense passed along its products to the memory for storage. The basic material of memory, then, was held to be a first-level classification of experience — possibly one could say, first-level abstrac-

---

[20] In the history of the internal senses, there were sometimes as many as seven, depending upon how finely the philosophers wished to discriminate. To the Greek tradition, Avicenna and Averroes added refinements. The interpreters most helpful to me have been St. Thomas Aquinas (*Summa Theologia*) and Harry A. Wolfson, "The Internal Senses in Latin, Arabic, and Hebrew Philosophic Texts," *Harvard Theological Review*, XXVIII (1935), 69–133. The complete lore was preserved in the English universities as late as 1678.

tion — that in character was much closer to the world of the senses than to the life of the intellect.

The imagination as an internal sense was the sole faculty having the power to handle images in the absence of the stimulation that originally gave rise to them. A man might look at London Bridge and go on about his business. Later his visions of it were the work of the imaginative faculty, imagination. It also made images of its own and in this, its creative role, it was often called fancy. In its reproductive capacity, say imagining London Bridge in the absence of the object, was the imagination responsible for recall or was the memory? Some theorizers, Descartes for example, held that common sense acted like a seal and impressed shapes on the imagination, which retained them, at least for a time.[21] If imagination remembered the shapes of things and recalled them, did memory in its proper role have nothing to do with images? Believers in Galen would quote him: "that part of the soul which imagineth, whatsoever the same may be, seemeth to be the selfe that also remembereth."[22] Followers of Aristotle maintained that sense images go directly to the imagination which transmits them to the memory.[23] There they are kept until wanted, whereupon the imagination returns and scans the record, behaving much like a person who writes something, lays it aside, and returns to read. In this account, some of the stuff of memory included images.

As the retentive faculty, memory also stored the products of the understanding and reason. These products were much more abstract than those of common sense and imagination, ranging from the less abstract forms only slightly removed from the sensory levels of experience to the highest abstractions man was aware of when he thought in terms mathematical, philosophical, and theological.

---

[21] Descartes, *Rules for the Direction of the Mind*, in *The Philosophical Works of Descartes*, I, 38. Cf. Wolfson, "The Internal Senses," p. 96.

[22] Juan Huarte, *Examen de ingenios. The Examination of Men's Wits*, trans. Richard Carew (London, 1594), p. 79. There were some fifteen editions of this work published on the continent and in England. Huarte was credited with being the first physician to deal convincingly with the identification and nurture of natural talents. Denis writes in NBG that "Huarte established on the foundations of physiology the influence of 'physique' on 'le morale.' "

[23] *Ibid.*, p. 78. Cf. Sir Kenelm Digby, *Two Treatises* . . . (Paris, 1644), pp. 283–284.

It seems clear, then, that in Bacon's times, as in other times, memory was the recorder, the storehouse, the treasury, of a man's entire experience. But it is not clear whether memory was held to be solely, or even primarily, responsible for recall and recollection. Especially in recovering and reinstituting a particular image from the past, one's imagination seemed to be chiefly involved in the effort and to be doing much of the remembering. In the seventeenth century keen analysts of human nature were less ready than the Schoolmen to draw neat borderlines among the psychological functions.[24]

When Bacon asserted that the senses respond to individuals only, that individuals pass entire into the memory, that individuals are impressions and images, he was implying that the end product of sensory activity is an image of a particular object — the sensory counterpart of a particular tree, a musical note, a spoken word. Sense experience involves selection and rejection among stimuli emanating from objects — and that is all. The forms and shapes of things are part of the data presented to the senses. The senses did not interpret their own movements as Hobbes maintained they did. Bacon would have accepted Pico's statement that whatever "the object of sensation . . . the object produces, in so far as it can, a likeness and image of itself, in imitation of incorporeal and spiritual nature."[25] But he went further. The immaterial copy of a material object was not merely that of a particular shape; upon it was impressed the species of the object as well. So what went into the memory whole was the shapes and species of things. Burton likewise thought that the memory recorded the species of things, "as a good *register*," ready when called for by imagination and reason.[26]

Among man's faculties Bacon found no place for a common sense. He never uses the term, nor does he allude to it. He never speaks of "common sensibles." Did he attribute any of the func-

---

[24] A good example is Joseph Glanvill, especially in his *The Vanity of Dogmatizing*. See particularly pages 27–39 (London, 1661) for the troubles of those who seek a "scientificall account of" the external and internal senses. With respect to common sense and memory, Glanvill sketches the views of Aristotle, Descartes, Sir Kenelm Digby, and Hobbes.

[25] G. Pico della Mirandola, *On the Imagination*. The Latin text, with . . . an English translation . . . by Harry Caplan (New Haven, Conn.: Yale University Press, 1930), p. 25.

[26] Burton, *Anatomy of Melancholy*, p. 140.

tions of this faculty to memory? As we have remarked, he seems to give memory the task of evaluating sense experience, because secondary objects — sense images — please or displease "but in memory." Possibly this is Bacon's way of saying that the affective and emotional aspects of experience are stored in memory and that in the storehouse through some process of association they become guides to decision and conduct.

Bacon seems to have found no spot for an estimative faculty. This power, responsible for evaluating sense-bound or practical experience as distinct from intellectual or contemplative activity, sometimes had another name, the cogitative faculty. *The French Academie*, for example, takes note of those who recognize "a knowing soule." All beings who possessed this power were not sensitive creatures merely, but showed a "certain vertue and vigour, as of cogitation, of knowledge and memorie, that they may have skill to preserue their life, and know how to guide and gouern themselues according to their natural inclination."[27] A cogitative power so understood must not be confused with Bacon's *vis cogitiva*, a power of thought fundamental to the functioning of all of man's faculties.

The passage in which Bacon announces that thinking goes on whenever man exercises any of his faculties is important to us here in two ways. First, the distinctions drawn among the mental faculties are broad ones in which Bacon is thinking in terms of genus and species. The genus of mental life is *vis cogitiva*; the species can be considered as "memory, imagination, reason . . ." and "the will and affections. . . ." On this basis, the faculties share in an activity that is substantial, not merely formal. The faculties can be designated in part by noting their most general manifestations. Indeed, in the passage under scrutiny, reason is taken broadly enough to include understanding, as it does when Bacon, classifying all knowledge in sweeping terms, relates philosophy to reason. Second, in employing broad language Bacon assigns to memory the functions of remembering and recollecting. It is evident that to him memory was something more than a repository of experience. In the human being, memory referred to a kind of thinking, possible only because experience of all sorts

---

[27] Pierre de La Primaudaye, *The French Academie* (6th ed., London, 1618), p. 403.

and from all sources of stimulation could be both retained and recalled. The materials of memory came from other kinds of thinking. At the higher levels of organized behavior, the materials were products of understanding, reason, and will; at the lower levels of behavior they were the experiences of the special senses, the affections, and the appetite. Among the qualities of affective states as they relate to memory were the pleasant and unpleasant. These became guides to future action; they gave meaning to expectation. In the middle of things, as it were, was imagination. This faculty, as we shall see in Chapter 5, not only created images of its own and revived sense images but translated abstract thought into objects of sense. These, too, were engraved in memory, and on demand of the other faculties they were summoned up again.

In recognizing an art of memory and placing it among the intellectual arts, Bacon was doubtless well aware that reasoning must presuppose memory. Reason typically isolates items of experience, analyzes them, and combines them into statements and patterns of statements of which the classic examples are deduction, induction, and analogy. Such intellectual activity is reducible to separate, sequential operations. Each must be held in mind until the full pattern is completed. So memory is involved in reasoning. It is not merely evident in each instance of reasoning, but it also provides a storehouse of materials upon which the intellect can draw whenever it wishes. On these matters Edward Reynoldes, a near contemporary of Bacon's, is more explicit. Memory "preserveth" each separate act of the understanding "untill a through [sic] concoction be wrought; so proportionably is the Faculty of *Memory* given to Reason, as a meanes to consolidate and enrich it." [28] In retaining experience, memory remembers not only the species of things brought to it by the senses, but it functions as "*Consors & co-operatrix Rationis* . . . a joynt-worker in the operations of Reason; which the Latins call *Reminiscentia*, or *Recordatio*; including some acts of the Understanding: Which is a reviewing, or (as wee speake) a calling to minde of former objects, by discourse, or rationall searching for them." [29] The dependence of intellectual life upon memory led Aristotle, so Reynoldes reminded his readers, to regard remembrance as the

---

[28] Edward Reynoldes, *A Treatise of the Passions and Facvlties of the Sovle of Man* (London, 1640), p. 453.
[29] *Ibid.*, p. 13.

remote ground of all the arts. Hobbes also linked memory to the
retention of sense experience and to the "cause" and "coherence"
of thoughts or conceptions. Sense always had "some memory ad-
hering to it. . . ."[30] Certain sequences or coherences of thoughts,
called reminiscence, experience, and expectation, were the chief
manifestations of memory.[31]

It is somewhat surprising to find that Bacon has nothing to say
about the physiological basis of memory. Another near contemporary of Bacon's, Sir Kenelm Digby, tried to explain remembrance
by postulating vibratory, undulatory behavior of atom-like particles in a "liquid vaporous" substance. The movements were
analogous to those of musical sounds. Similar and simultaneous
movements reinforced each other. A particular movement long at
rest was revived by a similar undulatory motion.[32] But Bacon's
interest in the phenomena of recall, the art of memory, and the
general nature of the faculty did not lead him into physiological
speculations.

In sum, Bacon regarded memory as man's power of recording
and recalling his experience. It received and stored images from
the external senses and it organized the affective accompaniments
of sensory life in ways that made them meaningful guides to
action. In common with man's other faculties memory at work appeared to be thinking; hence, remembering was memory thinking.
Memory kept the records of man's analytical, critical, and imaginative thinking which in its symbolic and imageful garb was
peculiarly the work of understanding, reason, and imagination.
It not only kept the intellectual record; it was essential to its
making. Man had to remember if he were to reason at all.

In reflecting on Bacon's treatment of memory and its relationship to other faculties, one becomes aware of two striking, possibly
unique, features. The explanation of man's behavior is being managed without recourse to as many "entities" and divisions of the

---

[30] Thomas Hobbes, *Elements of Philosophy* (London, 1656), p. 294; *Works*
I, 393. Man could never make judgments, said Hobbes, if motion did not
persist in the sense organ for some time and "make" the experience return.
[31] Hobbes, *Human Nature*, *Works* IV, 16–17.
[32] Digby, *Two Treatises*, especially pages 284–286. ". . . the same body
[i.e., atom-like particle] being in the same medium, must necessarily haue
the same kind of motion; and so consequently, must make the same impression
vpon the same subject." Digby had sense impressions moving first into the
imagination and then into memory.

soul as was the usual practice. The soul customarily had at least
three parts or levels of being: vegetative, sensible, and rational.
Bacon abandoned this vocabulary. The sensible soul was usually
divided into two parts: the external or special senses, and the
internal senses. Man's internal sensory powers had numbered as
many as seven, although common practice in the seventeenth
century reduced the number to three: common sense, memory,
and imagination. Bacon eliminated the common sense. As a result — or perhaps the cause — of the reduction in the number of
man's parts, a second important feature becomes evident. Man's
sensory functions are closely associated with his intellectual functions, and vice versa. Bacon found that the faculties overlapped
in their operations and that it was impossible to fix precise boundaries. The operations were often mutually dependent and the communication direct. Yet a rational act or a memorative act could be
recognized as such, and hence was subject to study and improvement, without knowing exactly where reason began and memory
left off. The operations of the faculties were "very different,"
asserted Juan Huarte, yet they were closely linked and so "nere
neighbored" that they could be discerned separately:

the understanding cannot worke without the memorie be present,
representing unto the same the figures and fantasies agreeable there-
unto, it behooueth that the understanding part busie it selfe in behold-
ing the fantasmes, and that the memorie cannot do it, if the imagination do not accompany the same . . . we shall easily understand,
that all the powers are united in euery severall ventricle [of the brain],
and that the understanding is not solely in the one, nor the memory
solely in the other, nor the imagination in the third . . . but that this
union of powers is accustomably made in mans body [as is the union
of the four natural abilities: digestive, retentive, attractive, and ex-
pulsive].[33]

---

[33] Huarte, *Examen de ingenios*, pp. 54–55.

CHAPTER 5

Imagination

The imagination was responsible for imagery of all kinds. In the *Sylva Sylvarum,* or Natural History, Bacon offers one description of imagination neatly and briefly. It is "the representation of an individual thought."[1] In other places in his works, notably where he discusses poetry and rhetoric, he speaks of two principal functions of imagination, that of reproducing images made originally by the senses or held in memory and that of creating images either in cooperation with reason or in its own right. These functions are in turn revealed in what Bacon called the "three kinds" of imagination, "the first joined with belief of that which is to come; the second joined with memory of that which is past; and the third is of things present, or as if they were present; for I comprehend in this, imaginations feigned and at pleasure; as if one should imagine such a man to be in the vestments of a Pope, or to have wings."[2] Examination of the three kinds of imagination discloses most of what Bacon has to say about the reproductive and creative roles of imagination, and about the force of imagery qua imagery, i.e., imagination intensive.

Representation of Thought

What is the representation of an individual thought? Bacon probably meant his descriptive phrase to be taken literally. At the level of understanding and reason, thought could be so abstract as to be impalpable. Imagination had the power of rendering abstract

---

[1] *Sylva Syvarum,* 945; *Works* II, 654.   [2] *Ibid.*

thought tangible. The tangible manifestation appeared most widely as words in speech and writing, for words were "the images of thought," the "images of cogitations." Thinking could occur in the absence of imagery, but if it were to be available to sense, it had to appear as auditory and verbal imagery. Bacon would have accepted Aristotle's statement that "thought images" serve as if they were the contents of perception, but he would have rejected the Peripatetic's belief that thinking did not take place at all without some kind of an image.[3] He implied what Locke said later, that the mind could frame a purely mental proposition "without the use of words."[4] So from the point of view of the mind that makes them, the imagery of speech and language was the concrete analogue of abstract thought. The imagination thus gave body to thought. A thought occurred, an image followed upon it. Imagery was in this sense a re-presenting of thought.

The objectification of thought as verbal imagery is strikingly perceived when one contemplates the context within which Bacon located speech and writing along with the communication, or transmission, of ideas among the rational or intellectual arts. He distinguished four "intellectual" or "logical" activities, and these gave their names to corresponding arts. Reason was the discursive movement of the understanding, and *logic* was a term applied

---

[3] See *De Anima*, 431 a 14–16. J. H. Randall, Jr.'s translation in *Aristotle* (New York: Columbia University Press, 1960), p. 96.

De Aug. VI, 1; *Works* IV, 439. The idea comes from *De Interpretatione*, 16 a 3–4 (trans. E. M. Edgehill, in *The Works of Aristotle Translated into English Under the Editorship of W. D. Ross*). Immediately following this passage Aristotle remarks also on the symbolic aspect of language. In Bacon's English in the *Advancement of Learning*, "words are images of cogitations. . . ." (*Works* III, 399.) Cf. "words are but the images of matter; and except they have life of reason and invention, to fall in love with them is all one as to fall in love with a picture." (*Ibid.*, p. 284.) By "images of matter" Bacon was probably referring to the sense image, which as a picture of an external object one may come to love as well as the object itself. Bacon was fully aware that any language event taken as a physical thing has different faces. From the point of view of a speaker, speech is the codification of thought, or, in Bacon's terminology, the image of thought. From the point of view of the listener, speech is an object to which he may respond in some appropriate way. ". . . the images of men's wits and knowledges remain in books . . ."; yet not merely images, because they generate thought and "cast their seeds into the minds of others." (*Ibid.*, p. 318.)

[4] John Locke, *An Essay Concerning Human Understanding*, collated and annotated by Alexander Campbell Fraser (2 vols.; New York: Dover Publications, Inc., 1959), IV, 5. 5; II, 246.

to the study of its modes of discursion as they appeared in discourse. There was invention—the finding and discovering of ideas; there was judging—the evaluation and criticism of the results of invention; there was memory—the retention of what was judged acceptable; and there was the transmission and communication of ideas. Bacon held the first three of these activities to be mental, or as we should say, psychological, processes. They were unavailable to our senses directly. To the extent that they became available as discourse, rather than through spirit (human or divine) or in other nondiscursive, immediate ways, they must appear as material and form. So Bacon placed under the transmission of ideas three other features of intellectual discursiveness: the *organ* of discourse, the *method* of discourse, and the *illustration* of discourse. The organ of discourse dealt with the smallest physical elements, and the smallest number of them, that can be used alone or in combination to depict thought and its processes. In ordinary languages these are speech and writing, though other kinds of characters have been used, such as hieroglyphics. Abstractly considered, the organ of discourse is grammar; concretely considered, the organ of discourse is speech and writing. The organ is so designated, Bacon would say, precisely because reason in its discursiveness needs an organ. On the other hand, the understanding as such, or "pure" reason, does not require an organ. In brief, the sound images of voice and speech and the visual images of language written are the simplest and most pervasive products of imagination. They are somehow bound in with thought. To Bacon, image and thought are two facets of a unitary whole. The whole may be a modulation of the spirit, whose nature we tried to indicate in Chapter 2.

Reproduction and Communication of Thought Internally

In conceiving of a psychological power that represented mental events Bacon was probably thinking of what his predecessors called the reproductive role of imagination. In this role its products were not representative in the sense that signs and symbols are representative. The meaningful, the symbolic aspects, of imagery were reserved to the imagination in its creative role. In its reproductive role, the imagination re-presented, i.e., revived sense images that had passed into the memory. If the senses perceived a rose and the experience lodged in memory, imagination could copy or imitate it. If reason thought, "treason involves conspiracy to depose a monarch," and the idea were lodged in memory, imagination could revive it and return it to reason for contemplation or pass it on to the will for acceptance.

The kinds of simple images representing thought, it is evident, were diverse: sound images, including the patterns of speech, visual images, including words as written and printed, and indeed all kinds or "copies" of sensory objects and experience. Thus Bacon was content to indicate the general character of the copy image. In producing it the imagination simply revived, probably with the help of memory, any and all experience deposited in the mind's storehouse. But other theorists, holding that sense experience was transmitted first to the imagination and then to memory, believed that imagery was more mindlike than sensory. Pico della Mirandola, for example, thought that imagination was "that motion of the soul which actual sensation generates. . . ." It was a power "which out of itself produces forms . . . a force related to all the powers. . . ." It fashions "all the likenesses of things, and . . . it is a faculty of assimilating all other things to itself. . . ."[5] Imagination detects the species of things. It purifies the objects of sense. It prepares for reason "the inferior nature" and puts it in shape "to be cognized."[6] Thus to Pico it is a bridge between body and soul, a mean between the material object and the immaterial form thereof. But to Bacon, the imagination did not detect the species of things, because the senses as reporters of external reality registered the species that was implicit in the object. Nor was the image any less material or more abstract than the sense picture. Rather, images were discrete materials that the understanding and reason could contemplate, compare and contrast, divide and combine, and in general manipulate much as if they were pieces that could be moved about.

Thomas Hobbes, on the other hand, regarded images, which he called *phantasms*, in two ways. There was the sense image, the product of sensory activity, and the more or less decayed, weak, and obscure residue of the sense image. This obscure

---

[5] Pico della Mirandola, *On Imagination*, p. 33.   [6] *Ibid.*, p. 41.

"conception," said Hobbes, is called *"Phantasie, or Imagination:
Imagination* being (to define it) *conception remaining, and by
little and little decaying from and after the act of Sense."* [7] It is
"nothing but decaying sense." [8] Fading out of the image were its
parts. Being retained — if there was retention at all — was a fuzzy
whole. The experience became obscure. Accordingly, "an *obscure*
conception is that which representeth the *whole object* together
but none of the smaller parts by themselves; and as *more* or *fewer*
parts be represented, so is the conception or representation said to
be *more* or *less* clear." [9] Concerned almost exclusively with imagination as the power responsible for reproducing sense experience,
Hobbes could hardly distinguish imagination from memory. Phantasms decay "in memory," and a man is said to have remembered
only when he knows he has had the experience before. Bacon has
nothing to say about degrees of clearness, or of cloudiness, of images. All images had shape or figure; and in so far as shape con-
tributes to clearness, images could hardly be obscure.

What Bacon has to tell us about the behavior of the imagination,
both in its reproductive and creative roles, can be drawn from
his references to the three kinds of imagination — imaginative
activity that illuminates things past, present, and future. [10]

---

[7] Thomas Hobbes, *Humane Nature* (London, 1650), p. 20.

[8] Hobbes, *Leviathan, Works* III, 4. Hobbes seems to have used *phantasm*
as a general term to cover both the terminal product of sense activity and
the preserved but fading record thereof. Phantasms perpetually arise "both
in sense and imagination. . . ." (*Works* I, 399.) His assertion that "all phantasms are not images" (*ibid.*, 396) prompts the question: Among activities
attributed to the senses and to imagination, what is imagery? what is not
imagery? Hobbes apparently thought that at some stage in the decaying
and fading of a sense image in imagination and memory, its shape or outline was lost; it became obscure. The obscure record could be called conception. If this interpretation be correct, then conception for Hobbes did
not imply abstraction; rather, abstracting activity was the mark of the
understanding.

[9] Hobbes, *Humane Nature*, pp. 26–27; *Works* IV, 12. Cf. *Leviathan*, ed.
Oakeshott, pp. 9–10; *Works* I, 396–399.

[10] Aristotle seems to have set the fashion for naming three kinds of practical discourse (if indeed he did not originate the three genre): deliberative,
forensic, and epideictic. Among other things, these dealt with things future,
things past, and things present. This kind of distinction occurs in the
Rhetoric and in no other work of Aristotle's. Bacon was familiar with some
of the chief ideas of the *Rhetoric*. In associating imagination with rhetoric, he
may have been mindful of the three divisions with respect to time and have
chosen to apply them to imagination rather than rhetoric. See Aristotle,

In linking imagination with memory and with things past, Bacon had in mind the imagination's role in making past experience available to reason for deliberation and judgment, and available to the will for satisfaction and action. Imagination took images directly from the senses or helped resurrect them from memory and presented them to reason whenever they became subject to analysis and judgment. To the senses and memory it was thus agent and messenger. To reason, on the other hand, it was like a lawyer who presented needed materials for judicial decision, and like a deputy who delivered reason's decree to the will for execution. Bacon has this function of imagination in mind in a passage in which he illustrates the working of his own imagination: "It is true that the Imagination functions as a go-between in both provinces, the judicial and the ministerial, assisting alike as messenger, agent and deputy, and attorney. For Sense gives up all kinds of idols [the forms and images it worships] to the Imagination for Reason to judge of; and Reason again when it has made its judgment and selection, sends them over to Imagination before the decree be put in execution. For voluntary motion is ever preceded and incited by imagination; so that imagination is as a common instrument to both — both reason and will. . . ."[11] Because of its association with reason when a prudential decision was at stake, the action of imagination could reveal qualities of truth and goodness. So Bacon remarked that the faculty could be Janus-like, showing two faces as sisters should, the face toward reason having the print of truth and the face toward action having the print of goodness.[12] In its role as messenger imagination was clearly subservient to sense, memory, and reason. It helped these faculties to communicate with each other; it worked with them without participating in creation, simply presenting the record of things past and done. The power of an image to incite voluntary movement is a view echoed later by Hobbes. Imagination, he declared, is "the first internal beginning of all voluntary motion."

The imagination as messenger, and the nature of its message,

Rhetorica, trans. W. Rhys Roberts, in *The Works of Aristotle Translated into English Under the Editorship of W. D. Ross*.
[11] *De Aug.* V, 1; *Works* IV, 405–406. The language here is based on translations by Spedding, Wats, and Dever.
[12] *Ibid.*, p. 406.

Edward Reynoldes makes somewhat clearer than Bacon. The imagination assisted understanding principally in "matter of Invention." It supplied a "varietie of objects whereon to worke." It assisted the will by quickening, alluring, and sharpening "its desire towards some convenient object . . . ," for "some plausible Fancie doth more prevaile with tender Wills, than a severe and sullen Argument, and hath more powerfull insinuations to *persuade*, than the peremptorinesse of Reason hath to *command*."[13]

Creation of Ideas and Images

The creative functions of imagination were evident in two ways. First, imagination could interpret and illustrate the work of reason and judgment. If Reason said, "This will be good for you," Imagination could say, "Your friends will applaud this." Second, imagination could create its own products. It could do what other faculties could not do. It could make the image, *the valley of tears*, and *the cow jumped over the moon*.

In linking imagination "with things present, or as if they were present," Bacon had in mind the creative functions he gave to imagination in poetry and literature, and in rhetorical discourse. He may also have been thinking of the role of imagination in divine revelation.

In literary and rhetorical behavior, man's thinking went beyond the bare record of experience. Poesy interpreted and illuminated experience for man's instruction and pleasure, and in so doing it brought things past into the present. Rhetoric illustrated man's reasonings when he was thinking about his future, when he deliberated about what he *ought* to believe or do, and in so acting it brought things future into the present. That these arts could do these things was due to the special nature of the imagination. The imagination was not simply the servant and messenger of the other faculties. It was "either invested with or usurps no small authority in itself, besides the simple duty of the message."[14] In poetry its creativity was seen as "a play of wit" or fancy and resulted in images that were beyond the limits of ordi-

---

[13] The quotations are from pp. 18 and 19; Reynoldes, *A Treatise of the Passions.*

[14] *De Aug.* V, 1; *Works* IV, 406.

nary credibility. In rhetoric its creativity involved a partnership with reason, for "the duty and office of Rhetoric, if it be deeply looked into, is no other than to apply and recommend the dictates of reason to imagination, in order to excite the appetite and the will." In such ways, imagination enjoyed considerable freedom; yet to Bacon this Janus of imagination, wanton as it might be, was never completely free. Part of its being was anchored in experience. "For of things that have been in no part objects of the sense, there can be no imagination, not even a dream."[15]

Said Bacon, in paraphrasing Aristotle, "the mind has over the body that commandment which the lord has over a bondman; but . . . reason has over the imagination that commandment which a magistrate has over a free citizen who may come to rule in his turn."[16] Reason divided and composed the items of experience in orderly ways. But left to its own inclinations imagination often did not abet reason; quite the contrary, it combined the materials of sense, memory, and intellect as it wished:

the several individuals [of sense that pass into the memory whole] have something in common one with another, and again something different and manifold. Now this composition and division is either according to the pleasure of the mind, or according to the nature of things as it exists in fact. If it be according to the pleasure of the mind, and these parts are arbitrarily [i.e., by art] transposed into the likeness of some individual, it is the work of imagination; which not being bound by any law and necessity of nature or matter, may join things which are never found together in nature and separate things which are never found apart. . . .[17]

At this point in the description one expects Bacon to endow imagination with absolute freedom. But he did not, for he maintained that the ultimate materials of imagination must consist of the "primary parts of individuals," that is, of sense images, and at least some of their components and qualities.[18] Imaginative activity was anchored in experience and restrained by experience.

Further insight into the activity of imagination may be obtained by briefly examining Bacon's treatment of poetry. In its style — the rhythms, cadences, and tones of its language — poetry is restrained, but in all other ways is "extremely free and licensed."

---

[15] Description of the Intellectual Globe, Works V, 504.
[16] De Aug. V, 1; Works IV, 406.
[17] Description of the Intellectual Globe, Works V, 504.
[18] Ibid.

In all things pertaining to its subject matter, it is dependent upon "the Imagination, which may at pleasure make unlawful matches and divorces of things."[19] In its poetical garb, imagination brings forth "feigned history," which is but "an imitation of history at pleasure."[20] In handling historical materials at pleasure, nevertheless, imagination works within those rational boundaries within which man believes nature may be enlarged and corrected. Man wants a more perfect nature than pure reason, operating alone, can discover. In perfecting nature, poetry may even take the mind close to something divine:

as the sensible world is inferior in dignity to the rational soul, Poesy seems to bestow upon human nature those things which history denies to it; and to satisfy the mind with the shadows of things when the substance cannot be obtained. For if the matter be attentively considered, a sound argument may be drawn from Poesy, to show that there is agreeable to the human soul [Spedding translates *animae humanae* as "the spirit of man."] a more ample greatness, a more perfect order, and a more beautiful variety than it can anywhere (since the Fall) find in nature. And therefore, since the acts and events which are the subjects of real history are not of sufficient grandeur to satisfy the human mind, Poesy is at hand to feign acts more heroical; since the successes and issues of actions as related in true history are far from being agreeable to the merits of virtue and vice, Poesy corrects it, exhibiting events and fortunes as according to merit and the law of providence; since true history wearies the mind with satiety of ordinary events, one like another, Poesy refreshes it, by reciting things unexpected and various and full of vicissitudes. So that this Poesy conduces not only to delight but also to magnanimity and morality. Whence it may be fairly thought to partake somewhat of a divine nature; because it raises the mind and carries it aloft, accommodating the shows of things to the desires of the mind, not (like reason and history) buckling and bowing down the mind to the nature of things.[21]

When the imagination thus acts, it creates what Bacon called narrative or heroical poetry. This species of verse makes its images "such as might pass for real," yet it "commonly exaggerates things beyond probability."[22] Bacon did not attempt to specify the standard of probability in artistic creation. Since he liked the logic of things, he might well have preferred, with Aristotle, a probable impossibility to an improbable possibility. He seems to imply that the imagination sometimes goes quite beyond reason

---

[19] *De Aug.* II, 13; *Works* IV, 315.   [20] *Ibid.*
[21] *Ibid.*, pp. 315–316.   [22] *Ibid.*, p. 315.

in dreams and visions. Perhaps it is acting irrationally also when it creates images like those of a centaur, unicorn, satyr, and Pan.

Bacon's observations on representative or dramatic poetry add but little to our understanding of imagination. This species of literature "represents actions as if they were present. . . ."[23] There may also be the implied observation that the imagination of a man in an audience is more easily stimulated or responds more intensely than is the case when he is alone. "And certainly it is most true, and one of the great secrets of nature, that the minds of men are more open to impressions and affections when many are gathered together than when they are alone."[24] Hence the stage play can be a powerful instrument in moving men to virtue.

In talking of imagination when it presents its images in the present, or as if they were present, Bacon may also have had in mind what the imagination was doing in parabolical poetry. It was seen at work in the fable, similitude, and parable. In these manifestations of inventive activity, the imagination seemed to function for the human being in the same way it functioned for the divine spirit. It made tangible that which was intangible. This kind of operation gave to parabolic poetry "a higher character," and an appearance of "something sacred and venerable."[25] This sort of poetry is thus colored because "religion itself commonly uses its aid as a means of communication between divinity and humanity."[26] Here, then, with the case of divine communication before him, Bacon found imagination manifested in poetry in two ways. First, one duty of poetry was to teach. This it could do only if imagination "illustrated" the work of reason. In olden times, particularly, "the inventions and conclusions of human reason (even those that are now common and trite) being then new and strange, the minds of men were hardly subtle enough to conceive them, unless they were brought nearer to the sense by this kind of resemblances and examples. And hence ancient times are full of all kinds of fables, parables, enigmas, and similitudes; as may appear by the numbers of Pythagoras, the enigmas of the Sphinx, the fables of Plato, and the like."[27] So "parables were before arguments," and the force of them is still excellent "because arguments cannot be made so perspicuous nor true ex-

---

[23] *Ibid.*   [24] *Ibid.*, p. 316.   [25] *Ibid.*   [26] *Ibid.*   [27] *Ibid.*, p. 317.

amples so apt."[28] So it is that the imagination translates the
abstractions of understanding and reason into images. Not only
does reason become palpable, but through the inventive activity
of imagination it is made fitting for an audience.

The second office of poetry was that of "infoldment" or allusion,
when the object is not to teach plainly but to teach darkly, "when
the secrets and mysteries of religion, policy, and philosophy are
involved in fables or parables."[29] Between 1605, the publication
of *The Advancement of Learning*, and 1623, the appearance of
De Augmentis Scientiarum, Bacon seems to have acquired greater
respect for mysteries than he had held earlier. In 1609 he devoted
great care to the explication of thirty-one fables of antiquity,[30]
and much later he greatly enlarged three of them — Pan, Perseus,
and Dionysius — which served him as illustrations of three of his
major divisions of philosophy: natural philosophy, politics, and
ethics. Fables revealed the earliest of human mysteries, extending back in time far beyond their narrators — e.g., Homer and
Hesiod — and by implication they bodied forth the shadows of
man's primitive imagination. Indeed, in the parable there is "invented the figure to shadow the meaning. . . ."

Imaginative Reason

Imagination also made absent things present at those times when
it was allied with reason in a distinctively creative function. The
unique cooperation with reason Bacon appears to have assigned
only to the province of rhetoric as the practical art of communication via both speech and written word. It is true, as we have
seen, that in poetry imagination joined with reason to produce
inventions and that it gave substance to things abstract. But in
its poetic activity it could at times indulge in play; it could join
and sever natural experience in unnatural ways, and escape the
strictest rules of reason. In rhetoric, on the other hand, imagination worked with reason in strictly rational ways. It engaged in
joint creation with reason yet it had to obey the "dictates" of
reason. This sort of action is directly revealed in Bacon's famous
characterization of rhetoric: "The duty and office of Rhetoric,"

[28] *Ibid.*   [29] *Ibid.*
[30] *The Wisdom of the Ancients, Works* VI.

he said, "is to apply Reason to Imagination for the better moving of the Will."[31] Rhetoric was one of the rational arts and imagination was to serve it. ". . . Rhetoric is subservient to the imagination, as Logic is to the understanding; and the duty and office of Rhetoric, if it be deeply looked into, is no other than to apply and recommend the dictates of reason to imagination, in order to excite the appetite and the Will."[32] Accordingly, said Bacon in one of his great moments of imaginative invention, the subject of rhetoric is none other than "Imaginative or Insinuative Reason."[33] Reason and imagination together created a credible object or an argument, and the effect was insinuative. In what manner there was insinuation we shall see later on.

In the cooperation of imagination with reason, imagination was under the control of reason, and reason was not at the beck and call of imagination. Such mastership was essential to rational life if reason through imagination were to command the will and affections:

if the affections themselves were brought to order, and pliant and obedient to reason, it is true there would be no great use of persuasions and insinuations to give access to the mind, but naked and simple propositions would be enough. But the affections do on the contrary make such secessions and raise such mutinies and seditions . . . that reason would become captive and servile, if eloquence of persuasions did not win the imagination from the affections' part, and contract a confederacy between the reason and imagination against them.[34]

Bacon realized not only that will and conduct should be under a man's voluntary control but that the decisions and products of reason acting alone were ethereal abstractions, difficult or impossible for the common mind to cope with. What is necessary, if reason is to prevail, is to transform the abstract into the concrete, the immaterial into the material, the nonsensory into the sensory: "it is the business of rhetoric to make pictures of virtue and goodness, so that they may be seen. For since they cannot be showed to the sense in corporeal shape, the next degree is to show them to the imagination in as lively representation as pos-

---

[31] *Advancement of Learning,* II; *Works* III, 409.
[32] *De Aug.* VI, 3; *Works* IV, 455.
[33] *Advancement of Learning,* II; *Works* III, 383.
[34] *De Aug.* VI, 3; *Works* IV, 456–457.

sible, by ornament of words."[35] "The method of the Stoics," said Bacon, "who thought to thrust virtue upon men by concise and sharp maxims and conclusions . . . to shew . . . Reason only in subtilty of argument," which has "little sympathy with the imagination and will of man, has been justly ridiculed. . . ."[36]

In working creatively with reason, what was imagination supposed to do? Doubtless there is no way of describing what is going on when imagination is working with reason. One can only be sure of the result. The nature of the operation itself can only be hinted at.

Bacon was confident that he could recognize an imaginative product. Suppose a person had been thinking about a problem of practical conduct, had been turning it over in mind, analyzing it for some time. Then, intending to advise someone else, he said: "This will be evil for you." For Bacon the speech would be that of reason. Suppose, furthermore, another statement emerged: "Your enemies will be glad of this." For Bacon the speech would be that of imaginative or insinuative reason. The entire difference between reason and imaginative reason is thus illustrated.

The case invites interpretation. In the first place, the idea or thought-aspect of the first statement is, strictly speaking, the work of reason, and the appearance of the statement to ear or eye is the work of imagination. We have already observed that the act of representing entails verbal imagery and that verbal imagery constitutes the sensory accompaniment of thought. Yet unlike the sense image, the image that imagination creates for reason, or with reason, is the embodiment of thought, not of sensations.

We must try to see what imagination was supposed to do when it did more than embody the work of reason, when it joined with reason and moved from "This will be evil for you," to "Your enemies will be glad of this." The *illustration* of discourse, assigned to the art of rhetoric, consisted in applying the dictates of reason to imagination. To illustrate reason is to illuminate it, for illustration as a concept originally bore the notion of illumination. When we illustrate something we illuminate it. So imagination may bring illumination to the support of reason, and in the case before us the second statement may be more illuminating

---

[35] *Ibid.*, p. 456.   [36] *Ibid.*

than the first in a literal, not figurative, way. The imagination, however, does more than light up abstractions. It fills out, amplifies, and ornaments reason. This it does, not as unneeded froth and embellishment, for fun and frolic, but as something necessary to aid communication and secure understanding. When Bacon applied *ornament* to the process of illustrating, he was using the word in the old sense of equipment. Clothes ornament the person because they render the body fit for civilized life. Imagination ornaments reason because it makes the organ, the body, of discourse fit to influence conduct. When teamed with reason, in inventive, creative activity prompted by rhetorical occasions, imagination is responsible for that feature of argument and example we recognize as fitting and appropriate. The effect of that which is fitting is insinuative; it opens men's minds, said Bacon, as if one were fitting a key into a lock. In teaming up with reason, the imagination also invents something that Bacon terms a type, fable, parable, and similitude. One kind of poetry, the parabolical, is typical history, and it, like rhetoric, teaches us by illustration. It is produced when imagination joins with memory. The implication is that when persuasion, rather than instruction, is at issue, imagination works with reason and produces the same kind of product. Accordingly, imaginative creativity in both poetry and rhetoric is the same in kind, though its consequences may be different.

In illuminating the creative role of imagination, we can be no more clear and precise simply because Bacon was not more descriptive and explicit. Nevertheless, he has proffered himself as an example of one who reasons imaginatively — or who imagines logically. He does not say how he did it, but he does say what he did.

As one of the appendices to the art of rhetoric, he was interested in providing what he termed a "Promptuary," a collection of recurring ideas, phrases, and imageful statements such as would help a speaker in moments of creativity marry reason and imagination. Aristotle had made a collection of aphorisms that expressed beliefs about things good and bad. This was laudable, said Bacon, for Aristotle suggested how they might prompt argument and proof. Yet the Greek could have gone farther:

For their use is not more for probation than for affecting and moving. For there are many forms which, though they mean the same, yet affect differently; as the difference is great in the piercing of that which is sharp and that which is flat, though the strength of the percussion be the same. Certainly there is no man who will not be more affected by hearing it said, "Your enemies will be glad of this" . . . than by hearing it said only, "This will be evil for you." . . . these points and stings of words are by no means to be neglected.[37]

Consider what has been said. In an abstract way, Bacon is saying that an idea may or may not evoke an emotional response, may carry different degrees of emotional response, may call out different kinds of emotion in different persons. In a concrete way, Bacon is observing that a sharp instrument pierces easier than a dull one, though the force exerted be the same. Consider the economy in phrasing the abstract conception and note that it is instantly illuminated by the image of piercing. The abstraction and the image have been related analogically. Reason has been put to work and so has imagination.

Even more interesting, because more subtle, is the pair of statements:

> This will be evil for you.
> Your enemies will be glad of this.

The base of both statements was probably suggested by the stock, popular generalization: What is good for the virtuous man is evil for the bad man, and what is evil for the virtuous man is good for the bad man. As reason has applied the idea to a specific person or audience, the outcome is a flat, literal statement: this will be evil for you. As imaginative reason has applied the idea — your enemies will be glad of this — concreteness of language and indirectness of reference have set up a context of allusiveness that might well lead a respondent to construct a clear, full image for himself. The allusion works through the principles of comparison and contrast, and so the intellect is served; the images are intimated, and so the imagination is invited to act. Bacon went on to present a total of twelve sophisms of good and evil in which imaginative reason is the creative mechanism. Then he broke off his list of examples with these words: "I have by me indeed a great many more Sophisms of the same kind, which I collected in my youth; but without their illustrations and answers, which I have not now the leisure to perfect; and to set forth the naked

---

[37] *De Aug.* VI, 3; *Works* IV, 458.

colours without their illustrations (especially as those above given appear in full dress) does not seem suitable."[38] Bacon never explained why his standard of style was "a sensible and plausible elocution." The reason now seems evident. The content, explanation, and argument of discourse must strike the recipient as plausible; that is, they must appear reasonable rather than unreasonable. At the same time the ideas must be accessible to sense; that is, they must be images of one kind or another that the recipient can "see."

The imagination was not always directed, restrained, and bound by reason. It could serve a higher power than reason. Bacon saw it as the instrument of faith and divine grace and as the faculty through which God communicated directly with men. In a key passage Bacon is quite explicit: "in matters of faith and religion our imagination raises itself above reason; not that divine illumination resides in the imagination; its seat being rather in the very citadel of the mind and understanding; but that the divine grace uses the motions of the imagination as an instrument of illumination, just as it uses the motions of the will as an instrument of virtue; which is the reason why religion ever sought access to the mind by similitudes, types, parables, visions, dreams."[39] Man could learn of things divine from two sources: from nature or from God directly. If from nature, there can be two avenues of knowing. One is that which "springs from sense, induction, reason, argument, according to the laws of heaven and earth."[40] One is that which "flashes upon the spirit of man by an inward instinct, according to the law of conscience; which is a spark and relic of his primitive and original purity."[41] Here, of course, Bacon is alluding to the almost universal belief of his times that when God drove man from the Garden of Eden he vouchsafed him a vestige of a knowledge of truth and goodness, a seed to which he could become sensitive and could learn to nourish. This kind of seed was in the citadel of the mind. But man also could learn of God directly. If he did, it would be through faith, a mysterious way that was based on Bacon's belief that "spirit is

[38] *Ibid.*, p. 472.
[39] *De Aug.* V, 1; *Works* IV, 406. Cf. *Advancement of Learning*, II; *Works* III, 479–480.
[40] *De Aug.* IX, 1; *Works* V, 113.
[41] *Ibid.*

affected by spirit." Imagination was that modulation of spirit that
was peculiarly sensitive to images and that was adept at reproducing and making them. So by nature imagination was a sensitive instrument, sensitive to its own matter, spirit, and sensitive
to its own kind, similitudes.

In matters of faith, God communicated with human beings by
stimulating the human spirit directly. The spirit put into motion
roused the imagination and the direct effects were visions, dreams,
parables, and similitudes. Like Bacon, Glanvill conceived of a
"Prophetick Spirit" that in communicating with man made "its
first Impressions on the *Imagination,* by *sensible* and *material
Representments.*"[42] The images thus inspired and revealed gave
the understanding something firm to grasp and the reason something to interpret and explain. The materials, furthermore, became luminous, a condition that helped the understanding, which
was weak and cast a dim light. The imagination, stimulated to
activity, made the light strong and clear. Such was the context
in which Bacon observed that "the informations of revelation and
of sense differ no doubt both in matter and in the manner of
entrance and conveyance; but yet the human spirit is the same;
and it is but as if different liquors were poured through different
funnels into one and the same vessel."[43] Adam fell from wisdom
and grace, but he kept the seed of perfect truth and morality.
"And in this latter sense chiefly does the soul partake of some
light to behold and discern the perfection of the moral law; a light
however not altogether clear, but such as suffices rather to reprove
the vice in some measure, than to give full information of the
duty."[44] Through his faculties, man makes available the full information for himself and for others.

So the intellectual movement from a product of reason to a
product of imaginative reason is illuminated somewhat by the
process of receiving a parable, a type, a similitude from on high.
In such forms God presented "his inspirations to open our under-

---

[42] Glanvill, *Plus Ultra* (London, 1668), p. 132. In the passage, Glanvill is
talking of prophetic inspiration. Two faculties are responsive to it, the imagination, as we have indicated, and the intellect. The inspiration through the
intellect is "from a Light *immediately infused* into the Understanding," as
when God spoke face to face with Moses.
[43] *Description of the Intellectual Globe, Works* V, 504.
[44] *De Aug.* IX, 1; *Works* V, 113.

standing."[45] The "Truth of Revelation," said an anonymous Restoration divine, "clear'd our Understandings. . . ."[46] This process was insinuative, as Bacon himself illustrated by similitude; it was "as the form of the key to the ward of the lock."[47] The parable was a key fitted to the understanding. The product of creative activity likewise fitted the understanding. Just as the divine spirit used the imagination to give body and shape to inspiration, reason and imagination transmuted an abstract idea into an image.

Among the men of his day and age Bacon was not alone in speculating what the mind was doing when reason and imagination united in invention. We can appeal to others to amplify somewhat Bacon's insights and illustrations. Edward Reynoldes, nearly contemporaneous with Bacon, was also concerned with the form and qualities of the image-thought phenomenon. When imagination worked creatively with reason it not only brought with it a multiplicity of object-images, but it quickened and raised "the Minde with a kind of heat and rapterie proportionable in the inferior part of the Soule, to that which in the superior, Philosophers called Extasie. . . ." That "strong delight," always attendant upon the discovery of something, stirs in imagination an anticipation or expectancy felt as restlessness and impatience. Such "motions" help give form to the response, or product. The "quicknesse of Apprehension," said Reynoldes, "though it may seeme to be the most peculiar worke of Reason, yet the Imagination hath indeed the greatest interest in it: For though the Act of Apprehending be the proper worke of the Vnderstanding, yet the forme and qualitie of that Act . . . namely, the lightnesse, volubilitie, suddennesse thereof, proceeds from the immediate restlessnesse of the Imagination. . . ."[48] Shakespeare may have been speaking

---

[45] *Ibid.*, p. 114. Cf. Hobbes, "sometimes the understanding have need to be opened by some apt similitude. . . ." (*Leviathan, Works* III, 59.)

[46] M.S., *A Philosophical Discourse of the Nature of Rational and Irrational Souls*, p. 1.

[47] *De Aug.* IX, 1; *Works* V, 114.

[48] Reynoldes, *A Treatise of the Passions*, p. 22. Reynoldes virtually identifies the operations of imagination with "thoughts." These seem to be different from "meditations" of the mind, which, relative to thoughts, seem to be "fixt, and standing . . ." (p. 22). The objects or matter involved in the operations are species derived from the "other faculties." Though the sources of objects are external to the human being, they are *objects of thought* only as images (*phantasmata*) (p. 23).

quite literally when he wrote that "imagination bodies forth the forms of things unknown. . . ."

For Glanvill the imagination joined reason in exercising judgment. At the propositional level of thought, the mind combines two "simple intellections," or apprehensions. If the apprehensions are of the "*distinctions* or *identities* of objective representations," i.e., if they are images of material objects, "the Judgment is made by the Imagination. . . ." If the apprehensions are "immaterial," the "*Understanding*" performs the operation.[49] In handling "simple Images" at the judgment level, the imagination, says Glanvill, is engaged in "*compositions, divisions*, and *applications*. . . ."[50] So in moving from the proposition, "This will be evil for you," to "Your enemies will be glad of this," Glanvill would attribute the translation primarily to the imaginative faculty.

Somewhat earlier than Glanvill, and later than Bacon, Descartes employed kinds of propositions to illustrate and comment on the operations of the understanding and imagination. The statement, "Paul is wealthy," has an image corresponding to it in the phantasy (imagination), but the sentence, "Extension is immaterial," evokes no image. It is the work of the "pure understanding."[51] The distinguishing feature of the image, observed Descartes, is magnitude. The magnitude which can "most easily and most distinctly be depicted in the imagination . . . is the real extension of a body . . . abstracted from everything else save only its shape," i.e., its figures "[*figuras*]."[52] Extension entails length, breadth, and depth; it involves dimension, number, and measurement. These the imagination becomes aware of only in real objects; it cannot grasp "philosophical entities." Sir Thomas Browne recognized what E. S. Merton calls a "philosophic" imagination and an "artistic" imagination. The first was held to work closely with the understanding, correlating ideas and abstract thoughts,

---

[49] Glanvill, *The Vanity of Dogmatizing*, p. 97.

[50] *Ibid.*, p. 99. Glanville is here more concerned with the "unwarrantable" compositive actions of the imagination than with the warranted.

[51] The quotations here and below are from Descartes, *Rules for the Direction of the Mind, Descartes' Philosophical Writings*, selected and trans. Norman Kemp Smith (London: Macmillan, 1952), pp. 87–96.

[52] The reason that shape is always associated with imagination is that "the phantasy, together with the ideas existing in it," is "a real body, extended and shaped." The real body was the pineal gland.

the second to be associated with the emotions and senses, "translating abstract ideas into concrete symbolism. . . ."[53]

Intensive Imagination: Fascination

We turn now to consider imaginative activity that, said Bacon, is "joined with belief of that which is to come. . . ." Up to this juncture we have been concerned with the essential work of the imagination and with the signs that identify it. Its unique product is the image. Bacon has said in effect: No image, no imagination; no imagination, no image. One type of image is that which reproduces the work of reason and the senses, and this type, linked with memory and things past, appears as verbal imagery and as depictive or pictorial imagery. The other type of image is the creative, in which imagination works with reason or on its own, and this type has the freshness and originality of being of the present or as if it were of the present. Now in looking at imagination as it is "joined with belief of that which is to come" Bacon directs our attention to the effect of imagery qua imagery. Does the faculty of imagination give a special touch to an image that has nothing to do with the coming into being of an image? Or, in logical terms, is there a property of the image that is not a defining property? Bacon apparently felt that the property was to be detected most surely, if at all, whenever a person believes in a prediction — a prediction that something will happen to him or to others, or that he will do or can be expected to do something. Take the case of two images, one involving the idea that man will cause his own destruction and the other the idea that Zeus hurled thunderbolts when he was displeased with man's doings. To Bacon, both images, one purely verbal, the other pictorial, are due to the power of imagination. But does the pictorial image more readily secure or enhance belief than the verbal image? If it does, what property or feature of it is responsible?

This phenomenon Bacon referred to as "the power and act of imagination intensive," and called it also by a more intriguing

---

[53] Merton, *Science and Imagination in Sir Thomas Browne*, p. 61.

name, *Fascination*.[54] Bacon believed in the imagination intensive because he had observed something similar in sense phenomena and these participated in the power of things in fact. Accordingly, "those effects which are wrought by the percussion of the sense, and by things in fact, are produced likewise in some degree by the imagination."[55] The image of a man eating a sour pickle may be just as effective in setting one's teeth on edge as does the act of eating the pickle itself. Bacon seems to mean here, as the context and similar examples suggest, that the effect is due not only to the figure but to the force and intensity of it. He was very close to an ideo-motor theory of voluntary movement and to the role imagination played in it. Indeed, "the imagination is as it were the director and driver of this motion [voluntary motion], insomuch that when the image which is the object of the motion is withdrawn the motion itself is immediately interrupted and stopped (as in walking, if you begin to think eagerly and fixedly of something else, you immediately stand still). . . ."[56] Again, "stamping, and bending of the fist, are caused by an imagination of the act of revenge."[57] If the image thus affects action, why should it not affect belief? And would not a striking feature of the experience be responsible for its impact? Bacon thought so.

That Bacon recognized force or intensity as a special property or dimension of the image is nowhere more evident than when he talks of strengthening or exalting or fortifying the imagination. To strengthen the imagination is not to help in the making of images but to increase the effectiveness of them. Authority, for example, will fortify an image, whether verbal or pictorial, but it will do nothing to produce the image. If a man believes that a ring or charm will bring him good luck, he may hold to the belief — and act upon it — because of his faith in the art of magic, or a practitioner thereof, not because of experience or of logic. Authority carries weight, as it were, and imparts weight.[58] Various kinds of objects enhance imagery in the same way, and Bacon

---

[54] *De Aug.* IV, 3; *Works* IV, 400. The subject is discussed principally in this chapter of the *De Augmentis*, and in *Sylva Sylvarum, Century* X; *Works* II.

[55] *Sylva Sylvarum*, 795; *Works* II, 598.

[56] *De Aug.* IV, 3; *Works* IV, 401.

[57] *Sylva Sylvarum*, 716; *Works* II, 569.

[58] *Sylva Sylvarum*, 947; *Works* II, 656.

produces quite a list of them drawn from "natural" magic. Rituals and ceremonies are not only imageful but they carry the authority of their sources. Scriptural words have the authority of God. Words of similitude — that is, pictorial images produced through words — are stronger than verbalizations without pictures.

Bacon seems to have detected another quality of the image, possibly associated with intensity and certainly contributing to the strength of imagery. He called it a binding or limiting effect. He observed it when he was speculating about ways of strengthening the memory. "We find in the art of memory, that images visible work better than other conceits; as if you would remember the word *philosophy*, you shall more surely do it by imagining that such a man (for men are best places) is reading upon Aristotle's Physics; than if you should imagine him to say, *I'll go study philosophy*." The reasons are two: "the more lustrous the imagination is, it filleth and fixeth the better," and there is a "binding of thoughts."

The remainder of Bacon's writing about the imagination intensive is devoted to suggestions, directions, and hints for systematic and experimental investigation into the phenomenon. He aimed to prepare the way and clear the ground. If serious study were to be undertaken the chief problem would be that of disentangling a maze of causes and effects. It would be proper to focus on two matters: the effect of imagery on the imaginant himself, and the effect of one man's imagery on another. But the whole enterprise had been confounded and confused by those who merely desired to exploit it for the ends of magic, witchcraft, myth and mystery, dreams and visions. Three established studies could make contributions if they would, for those "sciences . . . which have had better intelligence and confederacy with the imagination of man than with his reason, are three in number; Astrology, Natural Magic, and Alchemy; of which sciences . . . the ends or pretences are noble." [59]

Although Bacon made no substantive contributions to our knowledge of imagination intensive, his attempts to sort out relationships among similar phenomena help us to see what he thought imagination was not. We shall offer but a few instances.

The imagination may become hyperactive in eloquence. It is

---

[59] *Advancement of Learning*, I; *Works* III, 289.

"no small dominion which imagination holds in persuasions that are wrought by eloquence; for when by arts of speech men's minds are soothed, inflamed, and carried hither and hither, it is all done by stimulating the imagination till it becomes ungovernable, and not only sets reason at nought, but offers violence to it, partly by blinding, partly by incensing it."[60] Such effects may be due in part to the agitation of the spirit or of the affections. There is no doubting that both "imagination and vehement affection work greatly upon the body of the imaginant. . . ."[61] In undertaking any analysis and experiment of the "emissions of spirits" and their effects, one focuses on "the operations of the spirits of the mind of man upon other spirits: and this is of a double nature; the operations of the affections, if they be vehement; and the operation of the imagination, if it be strong. But these two are so coupled as they should be handled together; for when an envious or amorous aspect doth infect the spirits of another, there is joined both affection and imagination."[62] The sudden news of good fortune, or the sight of a much desired object, so stimulates the imagination and in turn so "wonderfully dilate[s] the spirits of animals" that it "sometimes endanger[s] a sudden fainting fit or death. And imagination produces the same effect in the sexual passion."[63] Imagination may be the instigator of both spirit activity and emotional behavior.

The force of imagination was probably something quite different from the cosmic forces — if any — that some men thought to obtain between man, the microcosm, on the one hand, and a perfect, living world, the macrocosm, on the other. Such a "monstrous imagination" Bacon attributed to the school of Pythagoras, was cultivated by Platonists, and made the basis of Paracelsian magic that "exalted" the imagination "with the power of miracle-working faith." Bacon's explanation of the macrocosm-microcosm rationale is worth quoting in full:

if the world were a living creature, it had a soul and spirit; which also they held, calling it *spiritus mundi*, the spirit or soul of the world: by which they did not intend God (for they did admit of a deity besides), but only the soul or essential form of the universe. This foundation

---

[60] *De Aug.* V, 1; *Works* IV, 406.
[61] *Sylva Sylvarum*, 902; *Works* II, 642.
[62] *Ibid.*, p. 644.
[63] *History of Dense and Rare, Works* V, 376.

being laid, they might build upon it what they would; for in a living creature, though never so great, (as for example, in a great whale,) the sense and the affects of any one part of the body instantly make a transcursion throughout the whole body: so that by this they did insinuate, that no distance of place, nor want or indisposition of matter, could hinder magical operations; but that (for example) we might here in Europe have sense and feeling of that which was done in China; and likewise we might work any effect without and against matter; and this not holpen by the co-operation of angels or spirits, but only by the unity and harmony of nature. There were some also that stayed not here; but went further, and held that if the spirit of man (whom they call the microcosm) do give a fit touch to the spirit of the world by strong imaginations and beliefs, it might command nature. . . .[64]

These ideas, said Bacon, are "vast and bottomless follies. . . ." Nevertheless, the scientist will examine them critically. If there be communication between the spirit of the world and the spirit of man, it is probably directly from spirit to spirit, rather than by imagination, for "the spirit is above all other things both strenuous to act and soft and tender to be acted on. . . ."[65] Furthermore, if there be magical communication among men, it is probably from spirit to spirit and directly from one man to another and well within the range of the human sense. Finally, there may be still other explanations of what seems to be the magic of nature. There are, indeed, the natural consents and sympathies of things, and the appetite of things to give and receive.[66]

In studying the force of imagination and its effects on the belief

---

[64] Sylva Sylvarum, Works II, 640–641.

[65] De Aug. IV, 3; Works IV, 400.

[66] The possible role of imagination in magical and mysterious phenomena is considered chiefly in the De Augmentis, IV, 3, and in Sylva Sylvarum, Century X. In place of the Pythagorean model, Bacon would seem to favor an Aristotelian one, whose figure is the pyramid. ". . . the whole frame of nature rises to a point like a pyramid. For individuals are infinite: these are collected into species, which are themselves also very numerous; the species are gathered up into genera, and these again into genera of a higher stage; till nature, contracting as it rises, seems to meet at last in one point . . . the summits, or universal forms, of nature do in a manner reach up to God; the passage from metaphysic to natural theology being ready and short." "Man has something of the brute; the brute has something of the vegetable; the vegetable something of the inanimate body; and so all things in truth are biformed and made up of a higher species and a lower." (The Wisdom of the Ancients, Works VI, 710–711; cf. De Aug. III, 4; Works IV, 360–362.) There might be some kind of pervasive, occult influence between species or genera of different things, but not between individuals. (Sylva Sylvarum, 910; Works II, 645.)

and action of others, one should not mistake an effect on oneself for that on another. "The problem . . . is, whether a man constantly and strongly believing that such a thing shall be, (as that such an one will love him, or that such an one will grant him his request, or that such an one shall recover a sickness, or the like), it doth help any thing to the effecting of the thing itself." [67] An imaginant can be primarily influencing himself: "if a man carry a planet's seal, or a ring, or some part of a beast, believing strongly that it will help him to obtain his love, or to keep him from danger . . . it may make him more active and industrious, and again more confident and persisting than he would otherwise be. . . ." [68] Furthermore, if repetition of imagery strengthens it, the impact could be principally on the imaginant rather than on his subject: "the state of human affairs is so variable, that to try things oft, and never to give over, doth wonders: therefore it were a mere fallacy . . . to ascribe that to the force of imagination upon another body, which is but the force of imagination upon the proper [one's own] body. . . ." [69]

From Bacon's point of view, then, imagination is the power of representing thought. It is the power of reproducing and creating images, verbal and pictorial, from the products of sensory experience and the products of the understanding and reason. Its images have a kind of force or strength that can stir the human spirit and rouse the affections. By and large, the imagination serves rational life. It illuminates and illustrates abstract thought in much the same way it lights up divine spirit and grace in moments of revelation and inspiration. If understanding and reason may be said to form experience, imagination may be said to give it body and shape. Reason and imagination join in creative activity that bears the marks of both faculties, reason rendering the product plausible, imagination rendering it sensible. Together they give rise to the fitting and the appropriate. Yet in their creativity, neither reason nor imagination works independently. Imagination is not merely processing the work of reason; it is not translating. Rather, there is a sort of transmutation, perhaps transubstantiation, going on between them. The color of imagination and the color of reason are present, but one sees neither distinctly;

---

[67] *Sylva Sylvarum, Works* II, 654.
[68] *Ibid.*, p. 642.   [69] *Ibid.*

they are blended in any creative product that man judges to be fitting and appropriate. In rhetorical and poetical creativity, as distinguished from scientific creativity, the imagination is responsible for, is the immediate cause of, that quality of argument, example, and style that we label "appropriateness."

The roles of understanding and imagination in creativity may be suggested in another way. From the point of view of modern semiotics and psycholinguistics, signs are said to elicit different kinds of responses, or "meanings." They may have a real referent: the word "pencil" refers to the object thus conventionally designated. They may appear in other sign contexts: "My pencil needs sharpening." The context here refers to an act that involves an object and a quality, sharpness. Signs may also appear in "statements" such as these: two plus two equals four $(2+2=4)$; and one thing relates to a second thing in the same manner that a third thing relates to a fourth $(1:2::3:4$, or $A:B::C:D)$. In these statements a *relationship* is indicated, or symbolized. It is not said, nor can it be said. Bacon would have held that imagination always joins with the understanding and reason in sign activity, i.e., in the sayables. The understanding — the faculty responsible for abstracting and forming — works independently in the nonsayables. The "content" aspect of a sign or statement is due to the imagination and the formal aspect to the understanding.[70]

---

[70] The interpretation offered here accounts in large part, I believe, for the treatment of poesy in the *Advancement* and the *De Augmentis*. As one of three coordinate divisions of learning, it receives scant space. Bacon's explanation is twofold. Poesy has much in common with history, for with respect to its matter, it is "but an imitation of history at pleasure"; it is "feigned history." Further, poesy has much in common with rhetoric, a verbal art, which has been "well laboured." Yet another reason, advanced by Bundy and others, is said to be Bacon's "distrust" of the lawless and nonrational behavior that imagination is capable of and that in modern literature is often called the fanciful. A better reason for the summary treatment is evident when one sees that the imagination brings forth the content aspect of utterance. Man's utterances, like any experience, pass into memory, and if preserved become history and the potential subject matter of subsequent utterances. With this idea in mind Bacon classifies literature according to its content, not its forms. Some literature deals with individual events and ideas whether in fact (history) or in imitation (poesy), or with universals (philosophy). Bacon respected the imagination, particularly what he called its fascinating and binding effects. What he distrusted and feared were the imaginations of bad men as exemplified by some Paracelsians, practitioners of "artificial" magic and alchemy.

Bacon assumed that matter possessed the rudiments of form and the "principles" of motion; hence "these three [matter, form, and motion] are by no means to be separated, only distinguished. . . ." (*On Principles and Origins, Works* V, pp. 467, 468.) For the classical view, see pp. 17–18. The rudiments of form were probably those of length, width, and breadth or depth. So imagination always had something to work with, whether the sayable simply made the work of understanding and reason accessible to sense or was the product of reason and imagination's creating something appropriate.

CHAPTER 6

Understanding and Reason

We continue with Bacon's account of man's powers — the faculties of understanding, reason, imagination, memory, appetite, and will. As we have seen, the faculties were distinguished from one another because they functioned in special ways. The senses were responsible for experience and kept man in touch with his environment, physical and social, external and internal. They also fed information to the inner man. Organizing man's restless, dynamic spirit in distinctive ways, the senses with the help of memory built states of mind and being that were essential to the functioning of understanding, reason, and imagination. These three faculties, setting *homo sapiens* off from his relatives in the animal world, drew upon materials stored in memory, contributed rational experience, states, and habits to the storehouse, and used the complex of experience in ways that made it possible for man to control himself and the forces of physical reality, and even at times to bring his spirit in touch with the divine spirit. The imagination in its own right afforded images of accumulated experience that memory alone could not produce and it afforded rational imagery that reason alone could not create. Now we are to see how Bacon regarded the powers of understanding and reason. Exposition will be aided by a short account of these powers as they were traditionally viewed.

The Setting

In sixteenth- and seventeenth-century English thought, *understanding* in its precise meaning always referred to man's power of discerning and using the *forms* of experience. The faculty was sometimes called a "wise and subtile Ulysses. . . ."[1] The understanding enabled man to abstract and isolate items from the rush and surge of immediate behavior. It enabled him to stop experience, consider it, interpret it, account for it, and "reason" about it. In a word, the understanding was the power of dealing with the forms of experience. It was often said, in figurative language, to be the "place" or home of forms. The more abstract, the more formal, one's thinking, the nearer it was to "pure" understanding. The power was known also under a Latin term, *intellect*, but beginning with Elyot the English preferred their own word, *understanding*.[2] The preference became so fixed that the translators of *De Augmentis Scientiarum* and of the *Novum Organum*, first published in Latin in 1623 and 1620, almost invariably rendered *intellectus* as *understanding*. In the *Advancement of Learning* (1605) Bacon's English used *intellect* and *understanding* to mean the same thing.

The understanding manifested two kinds of motion. It seized upon and gathered unto itself a unit of formal experience. This movement can be compared to the simplest and fastest of stimulus-response events. It was the *element* of intellectual movement. It was intellect behaving nondiscursively. On the other hand, reason, so far as it was separate from understanding, was the intellect moving discursively. This kind of movement was most evident when man combined symbols, such as words, in various ways. Speaking and writing were constant illustrations of discursive reason. Grammar and logic dealt with the forms of reasoning. The term *discourse* was intended to denote the manifest activity of reason, and man was a rational animal because he used speech. Burton could report that the actions of "the mind," i.e., primarily understanding and reason, were "generally considered to be *apprehension, composition, division, discoursing, reasoning, memory*, which some include in *invention*, and *judgment*."

Intellectual movement was explained by postulating three as-

---

[1] Richard Brathwait, *Essaies upon the Five Senses* . . . (London, 1620), p. 32.
[2] In *The Book Named the Governour* (1531), Sir Thomas Elyot wrote that the understanding, the "most pure part of the soul," is "in Latin, Intellectus, whereunto I can find no proper English, but Understanding." (Ed. Arthur T. Eliot [London, 1834], p. 258.)

pects of mental life and a characteristic function. One aspect was the passive, and Schoolmen referred to it as the passive intellect. It was passive in the sense of being acted upon, of being affected. At birth man's intellect was like a clean slate or sheet of paper or tablet. A condition of being acted upon implied a change or alteration of the condition, and this implied, in turn, that something could be taken away. Hence change in the passive state was sometimes said to be that of suffering. There was a further implication: if something could be taken away, something could be added. Accordingly, passivity entailed both receiving and giving up. The passive understanding was that state of mind that receives and yields.

Another aspect of mental life was called the possible understanding. It was that which was potential to receiving and giving up. The mind could not receive and yield without establishing the potentiality to behave thus. In this way the ideas of passivity and potentiality of intellectual action were coupled by philosophers in the Aristotelian tradition. It must be noted that potentiality was employed in two senses, first in the sense of the capacity to receive, and second in the sense of a capacity to use what had been received. The mind had both the power to learn and to use what it learned.[3]

The third aspect of mental life was named the active intellect, or the agent intellect. It was that which rendered actual the potential. Passivity, possibility, and potentiality were states or conditions of mind which set up a readiness to act; the agent intellect was the mind acting. The agent intellect is like light, for it is as essential to mental activity as light is to vision. Mind is what it is, said Aristotle, "by virtue of becoming all things," and "by virtue of making all things"; and the power of making things is "a sort of positive state like light; for in a sense light makes potential colours into actual colours."[4] The active intellect appears to have been called in Latin, *ingenium*, and in English, wit or intelligence. One notes, in passing, that grammarians, knowing that words and speech are of the mind, referred to language behavior as having an active voice and a passive voice.

---

[3] Cf. *De Anima*, 429 b 8 (trans. J. A. Smith).
[4] *Ibid.*, 430 a 14–17.

Again it is Burton who reports the general belief of educated men of his day:

The *agent* is that which is called the *wit* of man, *acumen* or *subtlety*, *sharpness* of invention, when he doth invent of himself without a teacher, when he learns anew, which abstracts those intelligible species from the phantasy, and transfers them to the passive understanding. . . . That which the imagination hath taken from the sense, this *agent* judgeth of, whether it be true or false; and being so judged he commits it to the passible [passive intellect?] to be kept. The *agent* is a doctor or teacher, the passive a scholar; and his office [i.e., the passive intellect's office] is to keep and farther judge of such things as are committed to his charge: as a bare and raised table at first, capable of all forms and notions.[5]

As the passive understanding grew and developed, its contents were thought of as *states* or *conditions*. Memory played its part in maintaining them. Five states were usually recognized: Intelligence, Wisdom (*sapientia*), Knowledge (*scientia*), Prudence (*prudentia*), and Art (*ars*). Fully developed in the mature man who had been properly educated, they produced, under proper stimulation, statements marked by truth rather than falsehood, and as a result yielded acts accepted as good rather than bad. Hence these states of mind were often called the intellectual virtues, or intellectual habits. Two additional states were sometimes identified, Opinion (*opinio*) and Suspicion or Doubt (*suspicio*), which were thought of as sources of false statement and bad conduct. The two were occasionally called habits, but never virtues. The states taken together constituted the possibility and potentiality for thinking and acting.

Roughly paralleling the vocabulary of the states and conditions of intellect was a vocabulary referring to the intellect when it was moving and acting (the intellect-in-act): *ingenium, experientia, apprehensio, conceptio,* and *ratiocinatio.* An intellectual act involved intelligence (the doing of what only intellect could do). It carried the certainty of sensory-derived materials, and the certainty or "acceptance" of the intellectual act itself, as in apprehension, when the species of a thing embedded in an image is recognized as man, or ox, and reflected by the common concrete noun. Involved, also, was the generalization of intellectual acts

---

[5] Burton, *The Anatomy of Melancholy*, p. 145.

into the idea reflected by the abstract noun, e.g., *animal*, or *animalness*; and the discursive action of the intellect, seen when intellectual objects were combined, as in the proposition and the syllogism.

Beginning at least as early as Boethius, so Professor Harry Caplan believes,[6] ratiocination or reasoning was distinguished from understanding and assigned to a separate power or ability, the reason. Nevertheless, understanding continued to carry three meanings. It meant the state or condition of man built up as a result of rational acts and experience. It meant the power of abstracting and of forming apprehensions and conceptions. It meant the power of supplying both intellectual materials and first principles with which reason worked.[7]

In the long tradition behind Bacon and his age, it was customary to speak of the "exercise" of the intellect. The word referred to the working intellect, specifically to two chief modes of activity recognizable when the understanding and reason, either alone or in concert, engaged in sustained endeavor. Involved more or less prominently were all actions of the passive, potential, and active aspects of the mind. The two modes of activity were labeled *invention* and *judgment*. They comprised searching, exploring, and finding on the one hand, and judging, accepting, and rejecting on the other. The mind moved from one state to another, the end of the movement being different from the beginning and depending upon it. The mind would consider what it invented, comparing the product with its criteria of truth and goodness. Invention and judgment thus embraced the mind creative and the mind critical.[8]

---

[6] Pico della Mirandola, *On the Imagination*, p. 28n.

[7] The domain of intellectual behavior and the vocabulary applied to it are readily seen in Nani Mirabelli, *Polyanthea* (1552). See particuarly the chart of the intellectual soul (Cologne, 1567), p. 96. The system and the vocabulary, elaborated from time to time and refined somewhat, were maintained in the English universities well through the seventeenth century. See, for example, M. Joanne Stierio, *Praecepta Physicae*, Tabulis inclusa . . . London, 1678), bound with *Praecepta Doctrinae* . . . (8th ed.; London, 1679); and Harris Francis Fletcher, *The Intellectual Development of John Milton* (2 vols.; Urbana: University of Illinois Press, 1956–61). The vocabulary of intellectual states appears exactly in Everard Digby, *Theoria analytica, viam ad monarchiam scientiarum demonstrano* . . . (London, 1579), p. 355. Among logicians in the Aristotelian line, Thomas Blundeville's *The Art of Logike* . . . (1598) prefers *habits* to *states* (ed. 1619, p. 29).

[8] Another distinct activity of the intellect was called "interpretative." It

An intellect thus constituted had a characteristic function — that of abstracting. It abstracted qualities from the experience supplied by imagination, memory, and the senses, and combined them into *forms*. The process of abstracting and forming was said to make experience *intelligible*. A particular act of the mind produced what was called an "intelligible species." An act of the senses produced, in contrast, "sensible species." Using modern terms, we would speak of conceiving and perceiving.

Understanding: Abstracting and Apprehending

Bacon's view of the understanding was more dynamic and somewhat less complex than the view he inherited. He accepted some of the traditional doctrine and vocabulary and hence in his writings he seldom offers neat characterizations. He alludes rather than explains. Nevertheless, a clear and credible picture can be discerned.

The power to abstract belonged to the understanding. It is "of its own nature," he declared, "prone to abstractions. . . ."[9] Time and again he complained that the understanding was only too ready to abstract. It had no organ and needed no organ, as did the senses. Characteristically, it was most active when it was not restrained by sensory data. It loved to fly upwards to the highest generalities. Its unfettered movement was often evident in language behavior when the notions behind words became "confused" and were "over-hastily abstracted from the facts. . . ."[10] Indeed, the understanding, enjoying "the serene tranquility of abstract wisdom," often left the real world so far away that the intellect seemed so insubstantial as to be deemed immortal: "we see some of the philosophers which were least divine and most immersed in the senses and denied generally the immortality of

holds a special interest for modern students of the communication process. The intellect started interpreting the moment man communicated. In communicating there were two acts, *excogitatio* and *significatio*. The former, which *Polyanthea* related to the *configuratio* or the *confirmatio* of knowledge, was the act of expressing outwardly the inner experience. Signification carried the sign and symbol aspect of utterance and revealed the speaker's knowledge and meaning. Mirabelli, *Polyanthea*, p. 96.

[9] *Novum Organum* I, 51; *Works* IV, 58.
[10] *Novum Organum* II, 14; *Works* IV, 49.

the soul, yet came to this point, that whatsoever motions the spirit of man could act and perform without the organs of the body they thought might remain after death; which were only those of the understanding, and not of the affection. . . ."[11]

The power of abstracting enabled and accompanied another characteristic activity of the understanding, namely, that of apprehending. This process seemed to be to the understanding what sensing was to the sensorium. Abstracting and apprehending, mutually supporting each other, enabled the human being to handle the forms and the formal aspects of things and to deal with the relationships among natural objects and events and among manmade things, including speech and language. The senses produced organized bits of experience that in an older vocabulary were called "sensible species." But to Bacon every sense package went into the memory whole, as individuals, to be used as the materials of imagining and thinking. The understanding produced what an older terminology labeled "intelligible species." But Bacon saw the understanding producing "forms" and "natures." He never talked of the intellect-in-act. Although the words used to describe it occur singly through his writings, they never seem to imply the hierarchial functions of the Schoolman's intellectual system.[12]

Bacon undoubtedly thought of experience as a continuum ranging from the concrete, particular individual bit of behavior to the most abstract and general of ideas. One of his divisions of physics was into the concrete and abstract, the abstract dealing with the "natures" of things and actions. In describing these divisions Bacon, lacking an appropriate psychological vocabulary, had to employ logical terms. Concrete physics "inquires concerning substances, with every variety of their accidents," and abstract physics inquires "concerning accidents, through every variety of substances. For example, if the inquiry be about a lion,

---

[11] *Advancement of Learning*, I; *Works* III, 318. Huarte referred to the understanding as "a Spiritual Faculty. . . ." Huarte, *Examen de ingenios*, author's supplement to Proem (London, 1698).

[12] It is worth noting that Robert Burton associated *apprehending* with both rational and sensitive functions. The understanding, a faculty of the rational soul, referred to both the power and the act of apprehending. The "sensible soul" also was assigned an "apprehensive" power by which "we perceive the species of sensible things, present or absent, and retain them as wax doth the print of a seal." Burton, *The Anatomy of Melancholy*, pp. 144, 137.

or an oak, these support many different accidents; if contrariwise, it be about heat or gravity, these are found in many different substances."[13] In his "Ladder of the Intellect" Bacon was aware of levels of intellectual abstraction. In his method of inductively inquiring into nature's behavior, apprehending and abstracting were illustrated when the mind formulated a first-level axiom and thus revealed the "form" of the thing being observed.

Bacon implied a progression of behavioral events from sense to understanding when he pointed out as examples of "our notions of less general species," man, dog, dove, and as examples of "the immediate perceptions [*prehensionum*] of the sense," hot, cold, black, white.[14]

Bacon's Latin term, *prehensio* (*prehendo*), meant a going out to something and a gathering in. This is what the senses did, the result being sensory images. The experience of hot, cold, black, and white, modern psychology would call sensations. I believe Bacon regarded them as images of simple physiological changes.[15] His reference to species here and his examples, man, dog, and dove, show that he was aware of classes of things arrived at by employing the notions of genus and species. In fact, his university education would have made these notions as familiar as his A B C's. The difference between genus and species was a difference not of material or substance, but of form. Man and animal, of the same stuff, were different in form. Hence, when human behavior was organized on an ascending scale of responses, it seemed to present lesser forms and higher forms, lower and higher degrees of abstraction.

In the process of abstracting Bacon certainly felt that the material aspect of experience had become less material. Yet to him there could not be a complete transmutation from the material to the immaterial; for he believed, as we have explained elsewhere, that the living spirit consisted of particles in motion, and spirit permeated all modes of man's behavior. But to the degree that abstracting was more breathlike than sensing, the result was due to the understanding. Pico, on the other hand, who clung to the notion of species, thought that the shift from sensible species to

---

[13] *De Aug.* III, 4; *Works* IV, 347.
[14] *Novum Organum* I; *Works* IV, 49.
[15] Hot and cold were usually regarded as qualities of the element fire.

intellectual species was due in part to imagination. Phantasy was a mean between extremes, rational soul and physical body, partaking of both. It prepared "inferior" natures, rendering them "more pure" than they were in sense experience, and thus ready for the active intellect to grasp.[16] Among Bacon's contemporaries Sir John Davies used the Schoolmen's account. The soul turns

> Bodies to spirits by *sublimation* strange,
> As fire conuerts to fire the things it burnes,
> As we our meats into our nature change.
> From their grosse *matter* she abstracts the *formes.* . . .

This occurs, Davies continued:

> . . . when from things *particular,*
> She [the soul] doth abstract the *universall kinds*
> Which bodilesse and immateriall are,
> And can be lodg'd but onely in our minds. . . .[17]

Although the understanding found abstracting and forming mental materials congenial to its own nature, it could not abstract to the point of apprehending form as form. Bacon believed that Plato had let himself be led off into unproductive channels of thought "by considering and trying to apprehend Forms as absolutely abstracted from matter."[18] Form can only be a sort of dimension that makes matter and experience determinate. Bacon would have agreed with Ramus that "the forme is the cause, by which the thing is that, which it is." Even the first matter had some form.[19] The understanding characteristically responded to the formal aspects of nature and mind, yet it could not grasp pure form. Only "to God, truly, the Giver and Architect of Forms, and it may be to the angels and higher intelligences, it belongs to have an affirmative knowledge of forms immediately, and from the first contemplation. . . . this is assuredly more than man can do. . . ."[20]

---

[16] Pico della Mirandola, *On the Imagination*, pp. 33, 41.

[17] Sir John Davies, *Nosce teipsum* (London, 1619), pp. 22–23.

[18] *De Aug.* III, 4; *Works* IV, 360. Cf. *Works* I, 565, where the Latin for *considering* and *trying* is *contemplando* and *prensando* (*prehendo*).

[19] Pierre La Ramee, *The Art of Logick, gathered out of Aristotle and set in due forme according to his instructions, by Peter Ramus* (London: Anthony Wotton, 1626), p. 27. For the relationships that obtain among matter, form, and motion, see "On Principles and Origins," *Works* V, especially 467–469.

[20] *Novum Organum* II, 15; *Works* IV, 145.
The ideal world — real world relationship embraced by the Neoplatonists is

How did the understanding abstract and apprehend the qualities necessary to realize form and structure? In part because of its original nature, and in part because of categories of thought it had abstracted from its own activity. At the beginning of one's life, the understanding was not quite a blank tablet.[21] The human soul at birth was a product of divine inspiration, not the outcome of natural laws. As the highest part of the rational soul, the understanding contained the seed of conscience from which it developed notions of good and evil, and the vestige of Adam's perfect wisdom on which it grafted knowledge. As it matured it formed its own ideas; and though it derived information directly from the senses as well as from its own experience, Bacon was sure that it was always mixing up "its own nature with the nature of things."[22] The materials that were "laid up" in the understanding, as a result of its own action and that of reason, were materials

---

concisely sketched in *The Zodiake of Life,* a work reprinted thirty times in the sixteenth century and translated into English by Barnaby Googe. Man's world presents the "shadows" and "counterfeits" of an ideal world, if such there be. "Our World is but a figure plaine, of . . . princely powrs." It is seen with "minde alone." Either mind is nothing, or "nature" has wrought a world in agreement with a suprasensible world. "This same just framed world doth passe the world that senses see, as much as minde excelles the sense in perfecter degree." The more perfect world, with God, saints, angels, and stars, contains "the causes of each thing," which, contrary to Bacon's belief, the mind can grasp.

> The world the senses may perceiue: from this same world
>   doth spring
> And seemeth here a figure sure, and shadow of that thing.
> All things more sound and perfect there, and all things
>   whole appeare,
> We haue but portions of the same which are increased
>   here.

M. Palingenius, *The Zodiake of Life by Marcellus Palingenius,* trans. Barnaby Googe, with an introduction by Rosamond Tuve (New York: Scholars' Facsimiles and Reprints, 1947), pp. 117–118.

[21] Like Bacon, Pierre Charron could not accept Aristotle's teaching that the understanding was like a blank tablet on which nothing was written. Rather, "the seeds of all sciences and vertues are naturally dispersed and insinuated into our spirits" and only want tillage. Charron, *Of Wisdome,* p. 54. Cf. John Woolton, *A Newe Anatomie of the Whole Man,* fol. 2, and *A Treatise on the Immortalitie of the Soule,* esp. fol. 63: in man's reason there are "Notices, or the vnderstanding of thinges ingraffed, and as it were bredde in men naturally. . . ." The "Notices" are evidence of the divine origin of reason; so "intelligence or reason" is "as it were certayne beames of the heauenly lighte. . . ." Cf. fol. 9.

[22] *Plan of the Work, Works* IV, 27.

"altered and digested" from the stimuli that prompted them.[23] The processes of understanding, Bacon seems to say, are in part creative.

Bacon did not speculate long on the "nature" of the understanding. In its nature, as he said, it was prone to abstractions and forms. Some of the sources of forms were sense experience and images. So he could well say that forms, forming, and abstracting were mixed up with the nature of things. In speaking of materials laid up in the understanding, he may have been thinking of the passive intellect, which was held to receive materials from all kinds of sources, sensory, imaginative, and intellectual. He may have been thinking, too, of a memorative power of understanding, a power that understanding shared with memory and memory with understanding. This property of the intellect Robert Mason referred to as "the memorie of vnderstanding, or of mindefull vnderstanding" sometimes considered as "an aboundance of reason, and as it were a hoorder vp of the continuall influences of the minde [sometimes called] a workefull minde, which is, a power, or force, that can skill [i.e., knows how] to extend reason from one thing to an other. . . ."[24]

Overrefined speculation and spun-out subtleties about the nature of understanding Bacon did not pursue. To see what he did not, and would not do, one has only to read Lewis Bryskett, friend of Sidney, who translated or paraphrased a dialogue of Cinitio Geraldi's dealing with politics.[25] The work reveals a picture of the understanding as complicated as that of St. Thomas Aquinas. There is set out a "passible," or passive, understanding chiefly identified with what is labeled fantasy and considered as an imaginative and cogitative power, which "as an inward sense depending vpon the bodie, receiueth the sensible kindes from the common sense, and presenteth them to the possible understanding, which is the place of the intelligible kindes or formes. . . ."[26] The possible understanding is not only the "place" of forms, but it exhibits an agency which is responsible for the understanding in action. The agency is termed the "agent understanding," probably equivalent to what others called the active

---

[23] *Novum Organum* I, 95; *Works* IV, 93.
[24] Robert Mason, *Reason's Monarchie* (London, 1602), p. 54.
[25] Lewis Bryskett, *A Discourse of Civill Life* . . . (London, 1606).
[26] *Ibid.*, p. 270.

understanding. Its function was the illumination of forms. The relationships involved may be expressed in a proportional analogy:

Possible understanding: agent understanding:: potentiality: actuality:: darkness: light

Intellectual experience creates a potentiality that is made actual only through an agency that is comparable to what occurs when darkness is made light. The relationships entailed are meant to suggest mental activities so interdependent as to be inseparable. The act of understanding and what is understood become one; they are more closely bound together than matter and form.[27] To Phineas Fletcher in *The Purple Island*, or *Isle of Man*, "the active faculty," or intellect-in-act, fits itself to the form of an object or image; there is an accommodation between that which responds only to form and that which has form. Accommodation is so complete that subject and object appear to be the same:

> . . . the Active Facultie . . . cunningly
> Changing it self, the object soon perceives:
> For straight it self in self same shape adorning,
> Becomes the same with quick and strange transforming;
> So is all things it self, to all it self conforming.[28]

When the understanding operated on natural things, said Bacon, it encountered the "Essential Forms of things."[29] Some of these were extremely abstract. They occurred with "configurations of matter," and with matter in motion. They appeared also in the motions of living things, and these of course included the motions of the mind and senses. In order to understand itself and nature, the understanding applied categories to physical movement and

---

[27] ". . . some haue said this possible vnderstanding . . . to be such a thing, as out of it all things should be made as if it were, in stead of matter; and the other agent vnderstanding to be the worker of all things, and as it were the forme, because this part which before but in power to things intelligible, becometh through the operation of the agent vnderstanding to be now in act." Hence, "the vnderstanding, and things vnderstood, become more properly and truly one selfe same thing, then of matter and forme it may be said. For it is credible, that both the formes of things and the vnderstanding being immateriall, they do the more perfectly vnite themselves, and that the vnderstanding doth so make it selfe equall with the thing vnderstood, that they both become one." *Ibid.*, pp. 124–125. There are indications that these views were considered Aristotle's as interpreted and amplified by Averroes and St. Thomas Aquinas.

[28] Phineas Fletcher, *The Puple Island* or *Isle of Man* (London, 1633), p. 86.

[29] *De Aug.* III, 6; *Works* IV, 370.

human behavior. Metaphysicians and logicians had evolved two sets of categories over the centuries. These Bacon recognized and used widely in his analysis of nature and man. First was the general notion of causation (effect and cause) that grew out of the study of motion and change. Four principal "kinds" of causes were isolated: material, efficient, formal, and final. The second set comprised two subclasses: the "Predicaments" and the "Predicables." These reflected two different levels of abstraction, one being that beyond speech or any kind of sign and manifest symbol, yet appearing simultaneously with speech and language. It was supposed that men had ideas in the absence of signs, that they thought first and spoke afterwards. Bacon had his own list of categories by which men thought at the highest level of abstraction. It is a list termed "transcendentals." These were "Greater, Less, Much, Little, Before, After, Identity, Diversity, Potential, Actual, Habit, Privation, Whole, Parts, Active, Passive, Motion, Rest, Entity, Nonentity, and the like."[30] The list of traditional categories need not be cited here. It is sufficient that Bacon acknowledged the predicaments as a general class of categories. ". . . the Predicaments, if rightly managed, relating to cautions against confounding and transposing the terms of definitions and divisions, I hold to be of principal use. . . ."[31] We observe only that one of the predicaments, that of quantity, Bacon regarded as a natural form. The understanding in its love for things abstract displayed a preference for it:

of all natural forms. . . . Quantity is the most abstracted and separable from matter; which has likewise been the cause why it has been more carefully laboured and more acutely inquired into than any of the other forms, which are all more immersed in matter. For it being the nature of the human mind . . . to delight in the open plains (as it were) of generalities rather than in the woods and inclosures of particulars, the mathematics of all other knowledge were the goodliest fields to satisfy that appetite for expatiation and meditation.[32]

The mind could well be a place of forms, that area in the head where abstractions went on, where the motions of spirit were most lively and free when they were not immersed in image and

---

[30] *De Aug.* V, 4; *Works* IV, 430.
[31] *De Aug.* V, 4; *Works* IV, 431.
[32] *De Aug.* III, 6; *Works* IV, 370.

sense. Bacon commended Aristotle for his aptness and elegance in saying that *"the mind is the Form of Forms. . . ."* [33]

The activity of the understanding was inferred from the behavior of language. Speech and words gave evidence of the intellect's abstracting action and in particular of its power to make concepts. In a general way, words and discourse were "analogous" with things, things analogous with reason, and reason analogous with words and discourse.[34] On the one hand, things became objects of intellect through signs, the common kinds of which were words, letters, "real characters," hieroglyphics, and gesture. These were "the currency (so to speak) of things intellectual. . . ." On the other hand, "words are the images of thought." [35] Speech and language made ideas tangible to sense, and linguistic objects were regarded as responses to mental activity. Inner activity thus became known through outward behavior. A process opposite in direction took place when the senses reported natural things and linguistic behavior. Mental events were transformations. The tangible and real were transformed into mental events — the intangible and "ideal." Sense experience thus became available to understanding, either directly, or through memory. Because of his great interest in controlled, methodical investigation of nature, Bacon had considered the relationship of ideas to objects a long time. If the edifice of science were to be built soundly, the understanding must produce clear and accurate ideas. ". . . words are the tokens and signs of notions. Now if the very notions of the mind (which are as the soul of words and the basis of the whole structure) be improperly and overhastily abstracted from facts, vague, not sufficiently definite, faulty in short in many ways, the whole edifice tumbles." [36]

For further insights into the activity of the understanding — and for that matter into the nature and action of reason — one can appeal to sixteenth- and seventeenth-century writers on logic, grammar, and rhetoric. They analyzed, classified, and described linguistic events, and they thought they were close to the hidden processes of mind. Bacon wrote no formal treatise on logic. He

---

[33] *Advancement of Learning*, II; *Works* III, 383. Cf. Aristotle, *De Anima* III, 8.
[34] *De Aug.* VI, 1; *Works* IV, 441.
[35] *Ibid.*, p. 440.
[36] *Plan of the Work*, *Works* IV, 24.

seemed to be as much interested, perhaps more interested, in mental processes themselves as in their manifestation as language. Indeed, he built his system of knowledge on psychological categories, not on logical ones. It is well known, of course, that Bacon objected to the received systems of logic, whether they were founded on Aristotle or on Ramus, because they encouraged the mind to deal only with words and this in effect habituated the mind to study only itself rather than nature. Nevertheless, the traditional approach to mind was a sound one so far as it went, and the arts of thinking and communicating about everyday affairs and about business and public life could be entrusted to the arts of grammar, logic, and rhetoric. So in training the intellect, youth studied and was exercised in language and literature, to which were applied knowledge and techniques learned from grammar, logic, and rhetoric.

The logicians in Bacon's times add but little to what has already been said about the nature of apprehending and abstracting. Yet apprehension was given an additional attribute, and the language of the logicians leads us toward the nature of reason and reasoning.

We take an example or case of apprehending ideas: "Man is a rational animal." This sort of thing, a *statement*, was usually called a judgment, sometimes an "enunciation," although Bacon and the Ramists seem to have preferred "axiom." After the custom of logicians, the statement was said to consist of two "terms," separate and distinct, which seventeenth-century writers called by a variety of names, *themes, speeches, arguments.* "Man" and "a rational animal" are here the two terms. Each was the result of the apprehending, abstracting process, and the statement that combined two terms was either wholly or partially the result of the same process. The idea giving rise to a statement, then, was a swift, unitary, mental event, clear and distinct. Producing a term seemed so short in duration as to be flashlike. Producing a statement took a split second longer. Descartes called the same experience an "intuition," if it bore a feeling of confidence and held no trace of doubt.[37]

---

[37] See Descartes, *Rules for the Guidance of Our Mental Powers*, probably composed about 1628. I have used the version in *Descartes' Philosophical Writings.* "By intuition I understand, not the fluctuating testimony of the senses, nor the misleading judgment of a wrongly combining imagination,

Involved in a statement was a feature of apprehension that implies the truth of the statement. Bacon alludes to this feature when he points out the nondiscursive character of inductive thought and the judgment of it: "the same action of the mind which discovers the thing in question judges it; and the operation is not performed by help of any middle term, but directly, almost in the same manner as by sense. For the sense, operating on its primary objects, at once perceives them and consents to the truth thereof."[38] The meaning of Bacon's Latin is somewhat clearer than the translator's English. A completed sense experience — in modern terms a perception — testifies to its own reliability and validity. A perception implies the existence of the object that prompted it and it implies *that* object, not some other. Similarly, apprehension testifies to its own truthfulness. Some English writers were more explicit than Bacon. Sir Kenelm Digby declared that apprehensions were responsible for our notion of being, as opposed to nonbeing, our notion of "thing" and "something," i.e., "that which hath being," and our notion of "respect" or relation, the *in* or *of* or *among* things.[39] Apprehension tells us that our ideas are real. It gives force to "is" and to other linguistic elements that connect terms. Bacon could hardly have been unaware of such views, but he may have assigned to spirit activity, the vehicle of all movement, mental and sensory, the most tenuous and ethereal functions and properties. Certainly there was some distinct process, some movement, common to the rational faculties.[40] Thomas Granger in his logic for divines spoke truly for those logicians who were conscious of Psyche as well as Logos: "Every thing is apprehended of us either simply, or with respect.

---

but the apprehension which the mind, pure and attentive, gives us so easily and so distinctly that we are thereby freed from all doubt as to what it is that we are apprehending . . . intuition is that non-dubious apprehension of a pure and attentive mind which is born in the sole light of reason . . ." (p. 1).

[38] The rendering is in part mine. In the Latin the last sentence is: Quippe sensus, in objectis suis primariis, simul et objecti speciem arripit et ejus veritati consentit. *De Aug.* V, 4; *Works* I, 640, IV, 428. I think Bacon's meaning would be clearer if put this way: The sense draws out (or grasps) the "sensible species" from its primary objects.

[39] Digby, *Two Treatises*, pp. 357–360. Cf. Reynoldes, *A Treatise of the Passions*, pp. 23, 452, who views apprehending as "the proper worke of the Understanding," and as having a receiving function. It is peculiarly responsive to "the right and distinct Notion of Things" represented to it.

[40] See Chapter II, pp. 29–30.

Simple apprehension is of the essence, existence, or being of things and truths without discourse, which more resembleth the Divine nature. In this respect they are called *entia*, beings. Respective apprehension is of things relatively and considered in the discoursive faculty, or reason, and therefore are they called *Rationes*, and *argumenta*, that is, reasons, and arguments." [41] Bacon himself associated traditional logic with reason: "I do not doubt but that common notions which we call reason, and the knitting of them together which we call Logique or the arte of reason, may have use in popular studies. . . ." [42]

We conclude that the understanding was the apprehending and abstracting mechanism by which man formed his experience and had ideas about it. We conclude, too, that the understanding formed and structured its behavior by means of — or perhaps we should say *in* and *through* — certain psychological conditions, partly innate, partly acquired, that seemed to transcend experience. These were associated with ability to abstract and to apprehend. These the understanding discovered when it analyzed its own products in moments of self-awareness. These were what the logicians were talking about when they spoke of predicaments, predicables, and post-predicaments.

Understanding: Inventing

For Bacon's view of reason and for further insight into the nature of understanding, one must see rational activities as they were supposed to function. This is to view them with reference to their uses and objects. These Bacon handles under his own notion of logic, which he offers under the caption Artes Logicae, or Logical Arts.

The logical arts are four in number: the art of invention in which man systematizes ways of finding or discovering that which he seeks; the art of judgment, in which man arranges and disposes what he has found so as to weigh its relevance and consistency with respect to the requirements of truth; the art of

---

[41] Thomas Granger, *Syntagma Logicum: or the Divine Logike* (London, 1620), p. 12.

[42] *A Conference of Pleasure*, ed. James Spedding (Lonon, 1870), pp. 13–14. Spedding believed that this ceremonial piece was Bacon's work.

memory, in which man trains himself to retain what he has learned; and the art of transmission or communication, in which man discourses for and with others. Discourse requires an organ of thought, i.e., speech sounds, words, and their management in grammatical forms; requires methods of structuring discourse in unified wholes that all may be clear and appropriate to the many purposes of communication; and finally, calls for ways of illustrating discourse, in which imagination is applied to ideas that they may be rendered vivid and acceptable. In brief, there are ways in which understanding, reason, memory, and imagination behave when they are dominated by certain ends: invention, judgment, remembrance, and communication.

The logical arts were so named because first, they were methodological in nature. They engaged the mind when it was directed to useful tasks. Second, they involved a number of faculties working in close concert or sequence, the dominant ones being understanding and reason. Early, in *The Advancement of Learning*, Bacon used the name "Intellectual Arts,"[43] and in one place he referred to them as the "Arts of Reason."[44] Later in the expanded, revised version of the *Advancement*, he allowed his translator to use *Artes Logicae*, thus suggesting that methodical and purposive behavior of the mind involved more than one faculty. Memory is recognized because the mind must draw upon its past experience. Imagination is mentioned because in discourse and communication the thought of a speaker is made tangible to others as words and speech sounds, which are images of thought. In communication, also, imagination joins with reason in producing images whose meanings are fitting and appropriate to the audience addressed.

Bacon's conception of the logical arts probably was derived from traditional analyses of the mind when it was said to "exercise." When it worked, or was "in act," it was inventing, judging, remembering, or interpreting. *Interpretatio*, i.e., the transmission or communication of ideas to others, referred to *excogitatio*, the physical basis, the events or carriers, necessary for the transmission of thought, and to *significatio*, the signs of thought associated with codes and symbols and affording meanings for him who listens. It is immediately apparent that the vocabulary of

---

[43] *Works* III, 383.   [44] *Ibid.*

Bacon's logical arts directly reflects the vocabulary customarily employed to describe the mind at work. His analysis of mind transmitting its experience, however, seems to be a refinement upon tradition.

When it is engaged in invention, the understanding searches around in available materials and in likely "places." From them it abstracts and apprehends and comes up with ideas. As we have indicated, ideas are revealed in phrasal terms and statements if they reach the level of imagery and logical scrutiny. In his desire to improve the ways of interpreting nature, Bacon laid great emphasis on two modes of searching. He labeled one, "*Remembrance* or *Suggestion*, with an application,"[45] where the end was to find arguments for speeches and popular discourse. The sources of search lay in one's own experience and in books and literature.[46] Guides for rousing expectancy and directing attention to likely places of search were the topics and categories of invention that had been built up for centuries by rhetoricians and logicians. Bacon said that this mode of search amounted to a systematic prodding of memory, heightened by some expectation that one would find what he was looking for. The mind ranged comfortably over materials that the understanding itself had made and that imagination presented to it. They were the materials of "every man's reason."[47] What was sought was in a sense familiar, and direct experience with nature was easily ignored. In fact, literary materials were once or twice removed from natural phenomena. As "letters" they were but "a degree and rudiment" of nature.[48] So traditional guides and habits of invention were useless in discovering the truths of nature.

The nature of the inventive process in remembrance or suggestion Bacon does not stop to speculate about. His insistence that ordinary methods of invention did not — and could not — yield new knowledge reminds one of Descartes' belief that when reason and imagination team up in creative endeavor, their product is not really new. Since images by their nature involved shape and magnitude, and compared with apprehensions were concrete, the understanding was being "aided by the species [of things] de-

---

[45] *Advancement of Learning, Works* III, 389.
[46] These were *Experientia literata. Ibid.*
[47] *Of the Interpretation of Nature, Works* III, 244.
[48] *Ibid.*

picted in the phantasy; and . . . nothing can be asserted of magnitudes *in genere* save what can be found to hold true of some magnitude *in specie*. . . ."[49] Again: "When something hitherto unknown is deduced from something previously known, we are not thereby discovering some new kind of entity: all we are doing is to extend our total knowledge in such a way that we are enabled to see that the thing sought participates in this or that way in the nature of the data being provided in the question which is being asked."[50] What is discovered is a sort of equality of ratios. Bacon's complaint that syllogistic reasoning was useless in scientific discovery rests on the perception that the minor premise reveals psychologically two ratios which are identified in accord with the context, or concrete question, which prompted them. Is Socrates mortal? He is, because he is a man. The ratios involved are:

Men:individual man::men:Socrates

Men in general are related to man in particular in the same way that men in general are related to Socrates. To see these ratios is to allow the possibility of transferring whatever is familiar and known about all men, or about most men, to the object posed by the question, namely Socrates. The operation thus had so much of the old and familiar imbedded in it that Bacon could not regard the product — the conclusion — as being new in the same ways that the product of scientific thinking was new.

Inventive activity of the understanding was marked by searching movements, by a flitting to and fro of the spirit stuff when one looked for something. The materials explored were the materials of memory; hence whatever was found always felt familiar.

The second mode of search was what Bacon called his "new logic" or new induction. He deliberately tried to hook the understanding directly to sensory data, and to control and restrict the abstracting process, to sharpen and make accurate the apprehending of comparable qualities of experience, and to discipline such conceptualization as went on in the production of an axiom. Thus the mind was to discover what no man had known before. Bacon talked of either mode of invention as "the ordinary use of the understanding in inquiring and discovering."[51]

---

[49] Descartes, *Rules, Philosophical Writings*, p. 82.
[50] *Ibid.*, p. 80.   [51] *Plan of the Work, Works* IV, 31.

Reason and Reasoning

Reason and reasoning were at work whenever one analyzed, compared, contrasted, and combined items of experience. These activities always involved the handling of ideas and images in a time sequence, and sequential activity always entailed ordering and placing. In a word, the activity was discursive. Bacon believed that this sort of mental behavior was sufficiently different from other mental activity to warrant naming it as a distinct faculty. Of course apprehending involved movement. But the movement was lightning fast, and if one could detect it at all it was only at its end point, the sign or word. One never knew the beginning of inventive activity, it was buried so deeply in experience. In contrast, reasoning was slow motion. One knew its beginning and end, and when one wished he could deliberately retrace the movement. Evidence of such motion and some indication of its nature was to be seen in the art of judgment and in the method or disposition of discourse.

The ends of judgment were validity and truth. To achieve them was to submit one's inventions to standards of validity and truth; to judge was to measure the uncertainties of present experience by the certitudes of past experience; and to conduct measurement was systematically to compare, contrast, and look for regularities and consistencies. Two processes of judgment were available, the deductive or syllogistic, and the inductive. Now "judgment by Syllogism," Bacon averred, "is but the reduction of propositions to principles in a middle term; the principles being understood as agreed upon and exempted from argument. . . ."[52] The proposition or axiom to be tested — in logic, the conclusion of a syllogism — was brought within the meaning of an accepted, or true, principle — the major premise — by connecting the two through another relevant proposition — the minor premise. To conduct the operation validly, the mind consciously applied rules of correct inference. The rules Bacon called "monitors" of reason. The mind also developed the ability to detect its mistakes, or fallacies, among which Bacon classed his famous Idols. The entire operation of judgment by syllogism was deliberate, sequential, and constrained by boundaries. Compared with the darting, explora-

---

[52] *De Aug.* V, 4; *Works* IV, 429.

tory, ranging activity of its inventive moments, the mind seemed at rest.[53] In judgment, the mind stopped, as it were, to look at and to criticize its own processes. Accompanying judgment was always the quality of deliberation, or calculation. Bacon hinted that it was this qualitative aspect of the movement, not its syllogistic character, that distinguished human beings from animals. When he proposed that the nature of *discourses ingenii* be studied, he cautioned: "The distinction between human reason and the sagacity of brutes appears to be a perfectly correct one. Yet there are certain instances of actions performed by animals, by which it seems that brutes too have some power of syllogising; as in the story of the crow which, in time of great drought being half dead with thirst, saw some water in the hollow trunk of a tree; and finding it too narrow to get in, proceeded to drop in a number of pebbles, till the water rose high enough for it to drink. . . ."[54] The modern reader might take Bacon's point half-humorously were it not for present-day experimentation on the reasoning ability of rats, doves, and chimpanzees. If we may take Bacon seriously, the hallmark of reason is mental activity, deliberative and evaluative. This kind of mental movement, moreover, appeared in judging the appropriateness of means with respect to ends. What kind of proofs — and by implication, what kinds of methods and materials — were deemed appropriate to what kinds and occasions of discourse? Though judging the logical validity of a process may not be quite the same kind of thing as estimating the fitness and propriety of behavior, the movement entailed in each case is deliberate and critical. In this sense, among others, the artist and the critic can be said to reason.[55]

The inductive process reveals reason at work whenever the mind passes on the "truth" of what it has invented or discovered. The process is the same as that in discovery, for "the same action of the mind which discovers the thing in question judges it. . . ."[56] Yet the faculties are different, for the understanding invents, the reason judges. Moments of discovery are not attended by deliberation and evaluation; moments of judgment are. In classifying its

---

[53] *Ibid.*, p. 428.

[54] *Novum Organum* II, 25; *Works* IV, 179.

[55] See *De Aug.* V, 4; *Works* IV, 434, "the doctrine of the judgment of judgments," the "Appendix" to the art of judging.

[56] *Ibid.*, p. 428.

apprehensions, the understanding is looking for the general idea among particulars, and in apprehending the causes of things it is looking for the presence or absence of a particular quality in recurring events. It is concerned with nothing else. In judging, on the other hand, the mind retraces its inventive behavior dominated by concern for truth and for accuracy of the conclusion. Are the mental events faithful to experience? Has the proposition or axiom sprung *directly* from the particular items of experience? Since in induction there is no mediating movement, no middle term or symbol, between particulars and conclusion, judgment is less complicated and the guides fewer than is the case in judging deductively. "With regard . . . to judgment by induction there is nothing to detain us . . . the operation is not performed by the help of any middle term, but directly, almost in the same manner as by the sense. For the sense in its primary objects at once apprehends the appearance of the object, and consents to the truth thereof."[57] As the *Novum Organum* shows, the guides for the critical appraisal of inductive processes may be found in disciplined, repeated observation and in the delay of abstraction.

The appearance of reason could also be plainly seen in the "method" of discourse. Method referred to the disposition, arrangement, structure, organization, and order of the propositions and statements of discourse, and not to the narrow aspects of style and linguistic detail. In general method referred to the activity of reason when a communicator was engaged in forming his composition. Whether he was shaping up poetical, didactic, or rhetorical discourse, he selected and rejected materials according to their relevance for his purpose and their appropriateness to audience and occasion. He then ordered and disposed his propositions into units and subunits with a view to securing clearness and special effects. Thus he worked until he had fully formed his discourse, his first and final guide being the dictum, "the end rules the method."[58] Judgments and evaluations went on until all was shaped into the final whole — a whole that Bacon and his contemporaries referred to as a "discourse of Reason."

When the discourse was conducted in the name of philosophy, reason was again at work. As a department of knowledge, philoso-

---

[57] *Ibid.*
[58] *Aphorisms on the Composition of the Primary History*, Works IV, 254.

phy selected propositions of the highest generality, judged of
their truth, submitted them to rigorous analysis, and built them
into a logical whole. These operations were certainly due to
reason. As we know, Bacon singled out philosophy as the work
of reason: "Philosophy discards individuals; neither does it deal
with impressions immediately received from them, but with abstract notions derived from these impressions; in the composition
and division whereof according to the law of nature and fact its
business lies. And this is the office and work of Reason."[59] That
these things are so, said Bacon, "may be easily seen by observing
the commencements of the intellectual process." After sense
images have passed into the memory, the mind proceeds "to
review and ruminate" upon them; "and thereupon either simply
rehearses them, or plays upon them imaginatively (*lusu quodam
imitatur*), or analyzes them and classifies them. Wherefore from
these three fountains, Memory, Imagination, and Reason, flow
these three emanations, History, Poesy, and Philosophy. . . ."[60]
The movements required in analyzing, classifying, and synthesiz-
ing apprehensions produced discourse; hence discourse was the
external sign of reason, and so reason was, as it were, "the soul
of discourse."[61]

Bacon's language and the broad context in which it appears
suggest strongly that reason is discursive intellect, self-conscious
and critical of itself. On the other hand, abstraction and apprehension, separable from reason, are nondiscursive operations of
the intellect. These operations, as we have suggested, either yield
separate ideas or concepts which are manifested in the terms
of propositions, or they yield propositions and statements in
which two concepts have been connected through the categories
of thought. Abstracting and forming are obviously present in
both discursive and nondiscursive processes. The putting together
of the terms of a proposition, accordingly, is recognizable as a
motion having a beginning and end. The movement, moreover,
can become the object of critical analysis. Would Bacon have
said that the proposition was made by reason, and judged by
reason, and was therefore the smallest unit of thought attributable

---

[59] *De Aug.* II, 1; *Works* IV, 292.
[60] *Ibid.*, pp. 292, 293. Cf. *A Description of the Intellectual Globe, Works*
V, 504.
[61] *De Aug.* VI, 1; *Works* IV, 439.

to the faculty of reason? If he were following the footsteps of either the Aristotelian or the Ramean logicians, he would have so held. The Rameans in particular always treated the proposition or enunciation as the first and simplest case in which judgment and disposition were involved. Whether Bacon so intended must remain a problem.

Some of what Bacon said of reason as discursive thought is compressed into Ramus' ultra-simple description, "Discourse is when one Axiom is drawn out of another, and it is either syllogism, or Method." [62] But Bacon would have included induction as a mode of judgment; he would have recognized a number of methods rather than one; and he would have called attention to the deliberative and evaluative qualities of reasoning.

Bacon did not intend to confuse reason and understanding. That their mechanisms were different was evident whenever man seemed to be in touch with things divine. Most spirit-like and most abstract were the "mysteries of God," but the understanding might lay hold on them. "The use of human reason in religions is of two sorts: the former, in the conception and apprehension of the mysteries of God to us revealed; the other in the inferring and deriving of doctrine and direction thereupon. The former extendeth to the mysteries themselves . . .";[63] the latter were from "the light of nature," that is, the light that "springs from sense, induction, reason, argument, according to the laws of heaven and earth. . . ."[64] The Scriptures were God's word and God revealed. They were fit objects of apprehension, but reason did not enter in until the mysteries of the Word were intelligible and accepted. Once the mysteries were revealed, man could reason about them. So it was that sacred theology — one of Bacon's departments of knowledge — ought to be derived "from the word and oracles of God, and not from the light of nature, or the dictates of reason." [65]

---

[62] Ramus, *Art of Logick*, p. 148. When "method" was written with a capital "M," the reference in the late sixteenth and early seventeenth centuries was always to Ramus' "one and only" method. This appeared in systematizing the materials of an art or science. The propositions were ordered from that of the highest generality, standing first, to that of the lowest generality, standing last. Each proposition, in addition, met Ramus' three famous tests: truth, justice, and wisdom.

[63] *Advancement of Learning, Works* III, 479.

[64] *De Aug.* IX, 1; *Works* V, 113.

[65] *Ibid.* Cf. *Advancement of Learning, Works* III, 479–481.

During the sixteenth century and extending into the early years of the seventeenth century, some thoughtful writers did not perceive understanding and reason as two distinct faculties. Rather, they spoke of one faculty as including the other. John Woolton, Juan Luis Vives, and Juan Huarte furnish ready examples. About the 1550's, Woolton, a bishop interested in anatomy, used the "Reasonable" soul as his generic term. It embraced "the minde vnderstanding" and "the Will working voluntarely. . . ." Reason thus encompassed all intellectual events, all "Actions and operations of the minde. . . ."[66] Vives, friend of Erasmus and More, an editor and interpreter of St. Augustine, a respected figure among English humanists in the middle years of the sixteenth century, appears to have adopted intellect (*intellectus*) as his general name. Its presence was manifested in three ways, as reason, as judgment, and as contemplation.[67] Like Woolton, Juan Huarte, a Spanish physician whose *Examen de ingenios* received at least four English editions in translation between 1594 and 1616, preferred to talk of the reasonable soul whose "proper operations" were "to vnderstand, to imagine, and performe actions of memorie. . . ."[68] Here one observes an interesting parallel between Huarte and Bacon. Both men were willing to bring memory and imagination within the orbit of things rational and intellectual.

Sir John Davies and Thomas Hobbes appear to restrict the understanding in ways that Bacon took no note of. Both pointed out that understanding appears upon the conclusion of reason's work. A man is said to understand when he apprehends the products of reason. Thus Davies:

When she [wit — perhaps intelligence?] *rates* things, and moves
   from ground to ground,
The name of *Reason* she obtaines by this.
But when by reasons she the truth hath found,
And *standeth fixt*, she *Understanding* is.[69]

---

[66] Woolton, *A Treatise on the Immortalitie of the Soule*, fols. 9–10.

[67] Walter A. Daly, "The Educational Psychology of Juan Luis Vives," unpublished Ph.D. dissertation, Catholic University of America, Washington, D.C., 1924, p. 35.

[68] Huarte, *Examen de ingenios*, p. 40; trans. Edward Bellamy (London, 1598), p. 112.

[69] Davies, *Nosce teipsum*, p. 49.

Thus to Davies the understanding is known by a special quality, truth, that emerges when one contemplates a reason, or reasons. One may need "many reasons" before understanding is gained, in the same way that one may require "many understandings" to secure knowledge, and "much knowledge" to achieve wisdom. Hobbes takes a tack different from that of Davies. The understanding comes into play only when language signs, or what Hobbes termed "names," are the stimuli or objects. The immediate results of sense activity are *concepts, images, ideas*, and *notices*, all four terms having the same meaning. To handle his concepts man attached names to them and "invented" language. And man "out of the words, contexture, and other circumstances of Language, to deliver himself from Equivocation, and to finde out the true meaning of what is said . . . this is it we call *Understanding*." [70] "When a man, upon the hearing of any speech, hath those thoughts which the words of that speech and their connexion were ordained and constituted to signify, then he is said to understand it; *understanding* being nothing else but conception caused by speech." [71] In discussing the kinds of responses that involved the understanding, Hobbes mentions some that are "according to Reason." Reasoning is "nothing but *reckoning*, that is adding and subtracting, of the consequences of general names agreed upon for the *marking* and *signifying* of our thoughts; I say *marking* them when we reckon by ourselves, and *signifying*, when we demonstrate or approve our reckonings to other men." Included in reasoning are ratiocination as seen in the syllogism, knowledge of the causes of things, and translation of the discourse of the mind into speech, that is, into discourse of the tongue. [72] So for Hobbes, as for Bacon, reason seems to be the understanding discursive.

---

[70] Hobbes, *Humane Nature*, p. 51. Cf. Science, "or knowledge of the *truth* of *Propositions*, and how things are called" is "derived from *Understanding*." (*Ibid.*, pp. 60–61.) "The imagination that is raised in man . . . by words, or other voluntary signs, is that we generally call understanding. . . ." *Leviathan, Works* III, 13. In *Humane Nature*, Chapter 5 and most of Chapter 6, Hobbes deals with what the understanding *does*.

[71] Hobbes, *Leviathan, Works* III, 28.

[72] See Hobbes, *Humane Nature*, Chap. 5; *Leviathan, Works* III, 30. Hobbes thought of *discursion* as the orderly handling of concepts, and distinguished it from *discourse* which, he said, referred to "the *coherence* and consequence of words. . . ." (*Humane Nature*, p. 32; *Works* I, 14). Reason is identified with discourse and is open to observation as discursion in what man says.

Descartes regarded the understanding (*intellectus*) as the power of knowing (*vis cognoscens*). There were grades of knowing, depending on the kinds of "simple things" or "simple natures" which were the proper objects of understanding. If the objects were those relating to self, self-consciousness, and awareness — such as were manifest when a man says he knows, or doubts, or wills — the understanding was operating in its purest grade. It was pure because states of consciousness were "mental" or "spiritual," uncontaminated by material things, as distinct from the body as the hand is from the eye. In working with pure states of consciousness, the understanding was acting alone, unaided by other powers and senses and needing no organ for its work. Its action was intuitive and it immediately knew truth and goodness. If the objects were "purely material simples [things]" having shape, extension, motion and the like, or if the objects were material or spiritual things that shared "common simples" such as existence, unity, and duration, the understanding called on imagination, memory, and sense. When objects having such simples were linked and combined, when they were said to exist or not, to be the same as, or different from, each other; when they were asserted to be true or false, good or bad, these operations were those of reason.[73] Hence to Descartes reason was "the power of forming a good judgment and of distinguishing the true from the false. . . ."[74] It appears that Descartes regarded reasoning as the understanding when it operated under special conditions. Yet it was not a principal faculty; Descartes did not place it among the four chief powers of what he called man's *ingenium*, or body-mind complex; understanding, imagination, memory, and sense.[75]

Having seen Bacon's distinction between understanding and reason, we have established a frame of reference within which we can appreciate other traits of the understanding. Bacon disclosed them when he treated of the "Idols of the Cave" and "Idols of the Tribe." The understanding is fond of darting around in all directions. It is unquiet; "it cannot stop or rest. . . ."[76] It "presses onward," looking for "final causes";[77] that is, it is looking for

---

[73] Descartes, *Rules, Philosophical Writings*, Rule XII.

[74] Descartes, *Discourse on Method, Philosophical Works*, I, 81.

[75] See the caption statement of Rule XII, Descartes, *Philosophical Writings*, p. 35.

[76] *Novum Organum* I, 45; *Works* IV, 57.   [77] *Ibid.*

purpose and design in nature that will satisfy its own cravings for order and form in everything. It desires regularity, perhaps because of "the homogeneity of the substance of the human spirit. . . ."[78] It seeks to give "a substance and reality to things that are fleeting. . . ."[79] The real business of the human understanding, Bacon repeats, is with "the figments of the human mind. . . ."[80] Except for a few natural forms — it will be recalled that quantity was one of them — the mind framed its own experience according to the categories and rubrics it found necessary and inevitable. By its own nature the mind was compelled to categorize and so by nature its own activity was channeled.

Such imperfections led Bacon to compare the condition of the understanding to a faulty mirror or to an uneven sheet of paper. At the beginning of life, the mind was a clean tablet as the ancients said, but it was not a smooth one. "The human understanding is like a false mirror, which, receiving rays irregularly, distorts and discolors the nature of things by mingling its own nature with it."[81] In support of the point, the widely known description — the joint creation of Bacon's reason and imagination — is so strikingly done that it is worth repeating: "the mind of man is far from the nature of a clear and equal glass, wherein the beams of things should reflect according to their true incidence; nay, it is rather like an enchanted glass, full of superstition and imposture, if it be not delivered and reduced."[82] The mind cannot be like "a fair sheet of paper with no writing on it."[83]

In speaking of idols, Bacon doubtless had in mind a Greek word *idola*, meaning phantoms, phantasms, spectres. He also suggested by *idol* (1) the firm hold that an idol or image may have on man, and (2) the misapprehension it carries. In *De Augmentis*,

---

[78] *Ibid.*, p. 59.   [79] *Ibid.*, p. 58.

[80] *Ibid.* Bacon goes on to say that all forms are figments unless one regards the "laws of action forms." When arrived at through the New Induction, a law of action was an axiom that immediately, not mediately, expressed the common feature of phenomena being observed. An axiom was a "Form," and a form was a law. Because of his desire to minimize abstraction at the first level of observation and statement, if not indeed to abolish it entirely, Bacon came close to viewing an axiom as a perceptual response.

[81] *Novum Organum* I, 41; *Works* IV, 54.

[82] *Advancement of Learning*, *Works* III, 394–395. Cf. *De Aug.* V, 4; *Works* IV, 431, where the mind is "dimned and clouded over as it were by the covering of the body."

[83] *Plan of the Work*, *Works* IV, 27.

V, 4, idols are called *images*, and in the *Advancement of Learning*, false appearances, that are imposed on man by the general nature of the mind.

Spedding says that Bacon used *idolon* in antithesis to *idea* (*Works* I, 89). But this cannot be. For in the passage in the *Novum Organum* I, 23, Bacon states that "there is a great difference between the Idols of the human mind and Ideas of the divine." An *idolon* involved images of sense; the term also meant images of other kinds of mental experience, such as ideas and feelings about ourselves, about things familiar and authoritative, etc. These might or might not be false, but when they were false Bacon always termed them *idol* rather than image. Hence, to him idols meant false appearances. There were four kinds of them, according to their sources or causes. As monitors to the understanding, the idols were to the interpretation of nature what the traditional doctrine of fallacies was to traditional logic.[84] They were errors of apprehension to be recognized, allowed for, and circumvented if possible.

From Bacon's description of his new method for the inductive investigation of nature, we also derive some insight into the processes of apprehending and abstracting.

In the rigorous study of nature, Bacon sought to control the process involved in moving from the sensory level of observation to the intellectual level of generalization. The journey was carefully laid out. ". . . all Interpretation of Nature commences with the senses, and leads from the perceptions of the senses by a straight, regular, and guarded path to the perceptions of the understanding, which are true notions and axioms. . . ."[85] Thus one may see what the senses can do, what the understanding can do, and one becomes aware of distinct levels of abstraction. The culmination of the method was to discover the nature of the nature being investigated, and this meant "to discover the form, or true specific difference, or nature-engendering nature, or source of emanation. . . ."[86] Obviously the object of search was at the top of an abstraction ladder, and a statement describing the nature discovered would reflect a high-level abstraction. When a change in concrete bodies was being investigated, one searched for "the

---

[84] *Novum Organum* I, 40; *Works* IV, 54.
[85] *Novum Organum* II, 38; *Works* IV, 192.
[86] *Novum Organum* II, 1; *Works* IV, 119.

latent process carried on from the manifest efficient and the manifest material to the form which is engendered; and in like manner the discovery of the *latent configuration* of bodies at rest and in motion." [87] True knowledge, after all, was the knowledge of causes, and this knowledge entailed statements that identified form, or "Forms."

The procedure started with "a muster of presentation before the understanding of all known instances which agree in the same nature [being investigated], though in substance the most unlike." [88] If the inquiry be, What is nature of heat?, instances of heat present and heat absent are to be mustered. The next step was to find and present instances of heat that manifested variations in degree. At this level of things there was a pause and a reckoning. Tables of observations were to be prepared. There were three: Heat Present, Heat Absent, and Heat Variable. During the stages described, the senses were being disciplined to observe similarities and dissimilarities, and the understanding was being disciplined against premature abstraction. But with the completion of the three tables, Bacon allowed the understanding to "indulge" itself, as he put it, and to engage in abstracting. The result was an axiom that stated the form, that is, the "absolute actuality" of heat. Such a statement Bacon also called a law. It is thus evident that an axiom is the outcome of abstracting and apprehending. It is an apprehension objectified in language.

As a rule, a first-level axiom is but tentatively true. The mind should withhold confidence. So Bacon devised subsequent stages of inquiry. These steered the mind through a series of twenty-seven "Prerogative Instances," all designed to test the truth of the axiom. For example, Striking Instances exhibited "the nature in question naked and standing by itself, and also in its exaltation or highest degree of power. . . ." [89] They invited attention to form. Clandestine Instances exhibited the nature in its "lowest degree of power," struggling to assert itself against contrary natures. They were "the best guides to *genera*, that is, to those common natures, whereof the natures proposed are nothing more than particular cases." [90] On the other hand, Constitutive Instances

---

[87] *Ibid.*   [88] *Novum Organum* II, 11; *Works* IV, 127.
[89] *Novum Organum* II, 24; *Works* IV, 158.   [90] *Ibid.*, p. 160.

showed "a single species of the proposed nature. . . ."[91] As compared with genera, these were "a sort of Lesser Form."[92] The search went on until the mind reached a level at which it was satisfied, that is, the mind recognized an axiom that was true of all the instances from which it came. "The eye of the understanding," said Bacon, "is like the eye of the sense; for as you may see great objects through small crannies or levels, so you may see great axioms of nature through small . . . instances."[93]

This same method of inquiry was to be applied to the investigation of other "natures," and other axioms were to be formulated. The understanding and reason then compared axioms, looking for forms of higher and higher generality. The outcome was a hierarchy of lesser forms and higher forms. Each art and each science produced its own hierarchy of axioms. Finally, metaphysics was to look for those forms that embraced "the unity of nature in substances the most unlike. . . ."[94]

The point to be emphasized here is that the entire scheme of inquiry into nature illustrates Bacon's belief that abstracting and forming are the proper activities of the understanding. Furthermore, one end of the spectrum of inquiry was closer to sense activity than the other. Among the Prerogative Instances, for example, Bacon described "*Instances Conformable*, or of *Analogy*; which I also call *Parallels* or *Physical Resemblances*. They are those which represent the resemblances and conjugations of things, not in Lesser Forms (as Constitutive Instances do) but merely in the concrete. Hence they may be called the first and lowest steps toward the union of nature. Nor do they constitute any axiom immediately from the beginning, but simply point out and mark a certain agreement in bodies."[95] Inquiry into concrete objects and behavior was at the level of the sense image; it was directed "to what may be called particular and special habits of nature, not to her fundamental and universal laws which constitute Forms."[96] On the other hand, inquiries into phenomena that revealed changes in structure were the primary concern of the understanding and reason. The search was for *schema*, the

[91] *Ibid.*, p. 161.   [92] *Ibid.*
[93] *Sylva Sylvarum*, 91; *Works* II, 377.
[94] *Novum Organum* II, 7; *Works* IV, 120.
[95] *Novum Organum* II, 27; *Works* IV, 164.
[96] *Novum Organum* II, 5; *Works* IV, 123.

configuration, of homogeneous parts. Since these were beyond observation, one had to resort to analysis; not by fire and violent physical methods, but by the "divine fire" of the mind, "by reasoning and true induction, with experiments to aid. . . ."[97] So the process of scientific observation and inference combined active and contemplative operations. Experience and practice supplied food for thought and theory. The senses were the reporters, and their sense images became the materials from which the understanding coined its concepts and the reason its judgments. We must, said Bacon, "begin and raise the sciences from those foundations which have relation to practice, and to let the active part itself be as the seal which prints and determines the contemplative part."[98] (The allusion here is to the active and passive intellects.)

Reason: Interpretation

Bacon seems to have dreamed of an understanding free of error. To designate concisely its operation, he reserved the word "interpretation." Of course the natural object of understanding was to know, and especially to know the causes of nature's operations. This the mind could manage to do if it were not misled by the idols into making "anticipations." These were a sort of foreknowledge or prediction that was built into language and was acquired through its processes. (Moderns should remember that *prediction* literally meant the moments preceding speech.) Language was the currency of everybody; it was everyman's reason. When the mind went on a search to find something among the accumulations of everyman's reason, it had some dim notion of what it would uncover. What it found was bound to be consistent with accepted language habits and thought. Thus it could be said to be anticipating. On this point Bacon cited Plato with approval: " 'whosoever seeks a thing knows that which he seeks for in a general notion; else how shall he know it when he has found it?' "[99]

Anticipatory behavior of this kind was fatal to the interpretation of nature. It was wrapped in the vocabulary of everyday life

---

[97] *Novum Organum* II, 16; *Works* IV, 145; *Novum Organum* II, 7; *Works* IV, 125.
[98] *Novum Organum* II, 4; *Works* IV, 121.
[99] *De Aug.* V, 3; *Works* IV, 423.

and this was not the vocabulary of nature. So Bacon could aver: "interpretation is the true and natural work of the mind when freed from impediments."[100] Again: "interpretation is the very natural and direct intention, action, and progression of the understanding, delivered from impediments. And . . . all anticipation is but a deflexion or declination by accident."[101]

Wit

Bacon appears to have been more ready to distinguish understanding from reason than he was to deal pointedly with wit and its relationship to the intellectual faculties. As a word *wit* appears often in his works. He thought of wit as a quality or accident of intellectual behavior, much as Hobbes did; and he used the word to refer to the intellectual faculties taken singly or in combination. In one place he associated it with works of art, apparently thinking of wit as a cause or condition of creativity.

In *The Great Instauration*, when speaking of "the strength and excellency of the wit," the reference is to the intellectual faculties generally.[102] Bacon may have had in mind what Hobbes did when he referred to wit as an intellectual virtue or "eminence." A natural wit Hobbes linked with "*celerity of imagining*, that is, swift succession of one thought to another; and *steady direction* to some approved end."[103] Quickness to find similitudes among images revealed a good wit or good fancy, and quickness to notice dissimilitudes and discern their fitness for the end in view showed a good wit or good judgment.

In a letter touching upon helps for the intellectual powers, Bacon referred to "the motions and faculties of the wit and memory. . . ."[104] Here *wit* is shorthand for two faculties, understanding and reason. The letter is built around a saying, *Faber quisque ingenii sui*, i.e., everyone is the maker of his own wit, or intellectual powers. Soon thereafter occurs the idea that man can help himself "not only in his appetite and affection, but in

---

[100] *Novum Organum* I, 130; *Works* IV, 115.
[101] *Of the Interpretation of Nature*, *Works* III, 251.
[102] *Works* IV, 19.
[103] Hobbes, *Leviathan*, *Works* III, 56 et seq. As an intellectual virtue, wit was both natural and acquired.   [104] *Works* VII, 97.

his power of wit and reason."[105] Here *wit* seems to refer to the
faculty of understanding only. Whenever the word appears in
the plural, *wits*, Bacon meant men of intellect and the products
of intellect. The "web of wit" was the web of the intellect or web
of the mind, a concept that embraced all four intellectual faculties: understanding, reason, imagination, and memory.[106]

In the *Novum Organum*, works of art as a class of things distinct from works of nature are called "*Instances of the Wit,
or Hands of Man.*"[107] Here is the understanding uniting with
imagination and memory in the role of inventor, when it finds
ideas for artistic ends, when it accepts and rejects ideas, and
when it shapes and elaborates them into a whole. The same
conception of wit appears plainly when Bacon declares that "particular phenomena of art and nature" are but few in number — a
"handful" as compared to "the inventions of the wit. . . ."[108]
Wit was not restricted to the humorous and the clever, and
Bacon would have not quarreled with Reynoldes, who viewed
wit as more than sudden flashes of conceit, "whether in Stile or
Conference"; it was also "a setled, constant, habituall sufficiency
of the Vnderstanding, whereby it is inabled in any kinde of Learning, Theory, or Practice, both to sharpnes in Search, subtilty in
Expression, and dispatch in Execution."[109] The "habitual sufficiency" is that general condition of the human being without
which there would be no mental life. All mental activity presumed
it. The tradition sometimes called it *intelligence*, sometimes *nous*.

It is evident that Bacon was not thinking of wit in unique ways.
It had no peculiar psychological function. He did not regard it,
as some had regarded it before him, as equivalent to the active
intellect, or *nous*, that "light" of man's mind. He did not locate
wit in the active and passive intellects as, for example, Thomas
Walkington did. This Elizabethan saw a quick, insightful wit,
fast in invention, whose seat was "in intellectu agente," in the
active understanding, and a "true wit" which kept decorum in
everything because it was "ever a consort with judgement." This

---

[105] *Ibid.*, p. 99.
[106] E.g., the furnishing and improving of "the wits of man"; the "succession
of wits" (*Works* III, 225, 226, 227, 231, 262); "the sharper wits," "the best
wits" (*Works* IV, 462).
[107] *Novum Organum* II, 31; *Works* IV, 170.
[108] *Novum Organum* I, 112; *Works* IV, 101. Bacon's Latin for wit is *ingenio*.
[109] Reynoldes, *A Treatise on the Passions of the Mind*, p. 514.

type of wit was in the passive intellect whose decorum consisted in judging the truth and falsity of "the species and *idea's* of objects" received from the active intellect.[110] Nor did Bacon limit wit to the particular power of invention, through which, said Elyot, the soul is "to espy, seek for, ensearch, and find out, which vertue is referred to wit, which is as it were the instrument of understanding."[111] Juan Huarte also saw wit as a "Generative Power."[112] Along with the understanding wit generated ideas or thoughts which issued in words and actions or lodged for a while in memory.

Bacon seems to have believed that wit was necessary to creative behavior of the intellect and imagination. Yet if it were true that some men were more apt or were quicker at invention than others, the difference was to be assigned not to wit, but to the understanding and imagination. If one man handled abstractions and reasoned formally more readily and surely than he produced images, the difference was due to his understanding, reason, and memory, which in his case, attributable perhaps to training and habit, were stronger than his imagination. Bacon would have approved Huarte's observation that the theorist is better at finding major premises, and that the practitioner – the physician, for example – is better at inventing particular, concrete premises. It is the special business of the understanding to grasp universals, and the theorist is known by this ability. In finding a minor premise, "the vnderstanding is of no value: for the same is particular and of another iurisdiction whose notice appertaineth to the imagination, borowing the proper and particular tokens of the disease, from the fiue outward senses."[113] In men of understanding, on the other hand, "the tokens before their eyes . . . worketh no manner of alteration in their senses, for that they want imagination."[114]

[110] Thomas Walkington, *The Optik Glasse of Hvmors* . . . (London, 1607), pp. 82, 94. In Chapter VII, Walkington recognizes nine "kindes" of wits.
[111] Elyot, *The Book Named the Governour*, p. 259.
[112] Huarte, *Examen de ingenios* (London, 1698), p. 3.
[113] Huarte, *Examen de ingenios* (London, 1594), p. 179.
[114] *Ibid.*, p. 180. When the physician enters a sickroom, his imagination goes to work. Because of its "certain vnutterable properties . . . it cleereth matters that cannot be expressed nor conceiued . . ." nor taught by art. ". . . by meanes of his sight, his hearing, his smelling, and his feeling, he knoweth things which seem impossible." He himself "cannot tell the reason:

An account of the higher faculties of man, presented faculty by faculty, can be misleading if it implies that Bacon believed that man's powers had definite boundaries, each power to be located in its own pigeonhole. A faculty, we must remember, was not an entity to Bacon; it was a mode of behavior, a distinctive movement of spirit. When it received a name, say the understanding, the label designated a certain modulation of spirit activity — the physical basis of all organic life — that seemed to be different from another modulation of spirit, say the reason. So two points must be kept in mind. First, the ranges of modulation overlap. Bacon intended them to. This can be seen when one compares the most general references to the faculties, first in the *Advancement of Learning* (1605) and its enlarged version, the *De Augmentis Scientiarum* (1623). In 1605 Bacon simply said that human learning was based on the three "parts" of man's understanding; in 1623 he preferred to say that the main divisions of human learning had reference to the three "faculties" of the understanding. A spatial term implying neat geographical areas has given way to a functional term difficult of precise definition.[115] Second, accompanying the change from *part* to *faculty* was a shift in the relationships among the powers. In 1605, the understanding seemed to embrace reason, memory, and imagination. This is the usage of La Primaudaye, who observed that "the *Vnderstanding*, if we consider it generally, it comprehendeth the whole minde: but beeing taken more specially, we meane a certain particular office thereof."[116] By 1623, one reads in Bacon of three faculties "Animae Rationalis," of the rational soul. The three specified were reason, memory, and imagination. They were powers of an encompassing soul. In the ensuing amplification and discussion, *intellectus* as understanding appears by name and by implication. But it was not dealt with pointedly until Bacon reached the logical arts. Then we find "Logic de Intellectu et Ratione . . .

---

for it is a grace which springeth from the fruitfulnesse of the imagination, which by another name is termed readinesse of capacitie, which by common signes and by vncertain coniectures, and of small importance, in the twinckling of an eie knoweth 1000 differences of things, wherein the force of curing and prognosticating with certainti consisteth." *Ibid.*

[115] Bacon made the shift in terminology as early as 1612, and once he had, let it stand. In *A Description of the Intellectual Globe* (1612) there are three "faculties." *Works* V, 503.

[116] La Primaudaye, *The French Academie*, p. 425.

disserit. . . ."[117] In short, although he always recognized six faculties, and only six,[118] and although his view of each remained consistent over the years, he never squeezed them into mutually exclusive compartments. Another sign of this fact is found when one ponders on the provinces of memory and imagination. They both partake of rationality; by nature and function they were more rational than sensory, no matter whether they were regarded as aspects of an understanding, of a rational soul, or of mind. The term faculty, accordingly, referred to a dominant feature or characteristic mode of human behavior. It referred to a *kind* of movement, to a species of movement of which motion itself was the genus. Bacon saw no reason for multiplying the number of man's powers and no cause for subdividing a power into subspecies. He did not, for example, chop up intellect into an active, a passive, and a possible intellect.

If Bacon could have carried out his proposals for study, he would have tried to explain the *movement* of the mind as it abstracted, apprehended, and reasoned. He would have proceeded along physical lines and looked for the efficient and material causes of mental action. His program for research called for the investigation of "simple motions," and for their measurement quantitatively. The study was to be conducted by a branch of knowledge called abstract physics.[119] It would consider his own theoretical analysis of simple motions "in which lies the root of all natural actions, subject to the configurations of matter." Among the motions is the "motion of *Signature* or *Impression*; that is, operation without the communication of substances." Here is the suggestion that the shape or form of motions and their amount (their "*how much* or *dose* in nature") are among the effective conditions to be looked for. One of the effective conditions to be measured is the influence "of the stimulus of surrounding things."[120]

But Bacon realized that "voluntary motion" in animal and human behavior could not be described entirely in terms of quantitative variations. Furthermore, the "actions of the senses, motion of imagination, appetite, and will; motion of the mind, determination, and intellectual faculties"— these were not entirely

---

[117] *Works* I, 615.   [118] *De Aug.* IV, 3; *Works* IV, 398.
[119] *De Aug.* III, 4; *Works* IV, 355–357.   [120] *Ibid.*, pp. 356, 357.

physical motions; and although their material and efficient causes should not be disregarded, their formal and final causes must receive prime attention.[121] Bacon never forgot that he was dealing with a whole man. Even when he concentrated on things intellectual, he was mindful of man's other parts and powers. Of all "living and breathing substances" man was the most susceptible of education, "and not only in his body, but in his mind and spirit, and there again not only in his appetite and affection, but in his power of wit and reason." [122]

---

[121] Bacon's suggestions were published in 1623. By 1963 research in psychology was reflecting the efforts of anatomy, physiology, neurology, physics, and statistics on the one hand, and logic, rhetoric, linguistics, and metaphysics on the other.

[122] *Helps for the Intellectual Powers, Works* VII, 99.

CHAPTER 7

Will and Appetite

The faculties, as we have seen, enabled man to know and to act. Man acquired knowledge because learning and knowing in themselves gave satisfaction and pleasure. Man also desired to know because he wanted to act better, that is, to conduct himself more effectively and acceptably among his fellows and before his God. Commonplace to Bacon and his contemporaries was Aristotle's distinction between knowledge for theory and knowledge for practice, between the philosopher and the man of action and affairs. Bacon seems to have been more interested in knowledge for use than in knowledge for its own sake. So in his observations on the nature of man, we expect him to describe how man acted. How were knowledge and experience, collected by the senses, stored by the memory, and worked over by the imagination, understanding, and reason, rendered effective for action?

Bacon thought that the faculties immediately setting off bodily movement were two, the will and the appetite. In Chapter 3 we encountered appetite as the efficient and effective cause of all involuntary movement. In this chapter we shall be concerned with voluntary movement. This sort of motion, Bacon would say, is the kind that man himself had control over; he decides whether to act or not to act, to believe or not to believe. As we shall see, appetite was held to be the efficient cause of actions that were affective or emotional, and nonreflective. The will, distinct from the appetite, was the efficient cause of reflective behavior. It was the power of saying yes or no prior to action. It was heralded in consciousness by moments of choice.

Bacon's conceptions of will and appetite are better understood if one first grasps Aristotle's account of the appetite. On this topic, as on scores of others, Bacon knew that his readers were acquainted with Aristotelian views.

All movement had to have causes, one of which was the efficient cause — that which made effective all other causal conditions of motion. In *De Anima* Aristotle asserted that there is "that which originates" any and all human movement. He called it appetite or desire. It was originative in the sense that it literally started or triggered off a motion. There were other less immediate causative conditions — material, formal, and final — but they were ineffective without the trigger. Furthermore, appetite was itself best thought of as a kind of conduct-oriented motion. It was the last of a series of events that prompted action, and hence could be said to have been moved or nudged by forces temporally prior to it. In turn it moved, and thus set things into motion, as, for example, the muscles involved in gesturing and speaking. The motion of appetite was like that of a ball and socket joint, having a convex and concave side. There was both a receiving aspect and an impelling aspect, a notion Bacon used when he postulated a receiving and giving force in the appetites of inanimate things, in their "consents" and "sympathies," and the like. The receiving aspect of the notion we still have in our idiom, as when we refer to the moving of the appetite, or to the moving of the will. The impelling aspect of the idea lingers in phrases such as "strength of will," "strength of appetite," and he "had the will to do" so-and-so.

The idea that appetite was itself moved prior to moving something else had an important consequence. It was easier to analyze the means of moving the appetite than to describe the "impelling" aspect of appetite; hence in most analyses of appetite as a force in voluntary movement one discovers much talk and description of the means of moving the appetite and will, and little about the mechanism involved when appetite and will are movers. Bacon is no exception.[1]

---

[1] The caption *"Appetites* and *Motions"* mentioned in Chapter 3, should be recalled here. Some of the "simple motions" listed and cited for study are probably also appetitive in nature. Through his caption, Bacon was calling attention to the reciprocal, though not convertible, relationship between motion on the one hand, and appetite as a kind of motion on the other. The same motions are discussed at some length in the *Novum Organum* and before the discussion is completed Bacon applies "appetite" to some of the motions, and "virtue" to their strength. The exposition ends in these words:

To return to Aristotle. There were two forms of appetite. One was the sensitive appetite, which was the efficient cause of all action and conduct that was habitually associated with the senses and emotions. The guides of appetite were pleasure and pain as features or outcomes of the immediate behavior in prospect. The vision of pleasure was enough to initiate a pleasurable act; the spectre of pain was sufficient to inhibit a painful act. The other form of appetite was rational in character, and is best verbalized in English as *will*. The will was the efficient cause of deliberative or calculative behavior. As a movement, it was preceded by activity of the rational faculties, notably reason and judgment, when they were directed to practical matters entailing choice and decision. In consciousness it was marked by feelings pleasant and unpleasant and by designations of "right" and "wrong," "good" and "bad."[2]

In Aristotle's theory of human action, the sensitive appetite beheld "apparent" good; the will always took into account the "real" good. In the one case, conduct looked good, because the image promised pleasure; in the other case, conduct was good, because it rested on the solid ground of valid and true judgment. Apparent good was that which passed the test of sense experience; real good was that which passed the test of reason.

To Bacon, though not to Aristotle, appetite and will were separate mechanisms. In his list of the faculties, they appear separately. Although the Englishman often linked them in the same phrase, he in no way interchanged them. The terms occur together most often when Bacon thought analytically about human action and conduct, about moral philosophy and ethics. In the *Advancement of Learning* the transition from rational knowledge to moral knowledge is signaled by the announcement, "We proceed now to that knowledge which considereth of the Appetite

---

"Thus then have I set forth the species or simple elements of motions, appetites, and active virtues, which are in nature most general." (*Works* IV, 230.) The complete exposition takes up *Aphorism* 48, Book II, pp. 214–232.

[2] In twentieth-century psychology, *will* seems to have been replaced by *desire*. This word entails connotations of both rationality and compulsion, and it avoids notions, often implied by *will*, of a distinct entity in mind and consciousness. To indicate Bacon's meaning, *desire* is better than other modern terms such as *motive* and *wish*. These can imply deliberation, but they do not invariably point to states of being that impel immediate action.

and Will of Man."[3] At the corresponding place in the Latin translation the will only is mentioned (*Voluntatem humanam*), doubtless because at issue was voluntary movement, i.e., all conduct
over which the human being can exercise control. "The will is
governed by right reason, seduced by apparent good, having for
its spurs the passions, for its ministers the organs and voluntary
motions. . . ."[4] Shortly after this declaration, in both the *Advancement* and the *De Augmentis*, we find that pictures of good,
virtue, duty, and felicity are the true objects for "the will and
desires" of man to aim at. The word *desire* here and elsewhere
seems to refer most often to the appetite of living things, although
it is applied metaphorically as in the "desire" of the magnet for
iron particles. In Bacon's writings *appetite* is a more general term
than *desire* and *will*; yet in any context bearing on the faculties
of man, appetite is kept distinct from will.

Function of Appetite and Will

Appetite and will were two different faculties, yet they had the
same function: they impelled man to action. Although not as
clear and explicit on the point as was Aristotle, Bacon seems to
have thought that the two faculties were essential to action. Appetite was the efficient and effective cause of processes not having
sense organs. It appeared, for example, in the movements of
nutrition and excretion. It seemed logical to postulate the same
kind of originative power for all kinds of movement. So Bacon
admonished the moral philosophers who "spend such an infinite
quantity of debate touching good and the highest good" to "cast
their eye abroad upon nature and behold the appetite that is in
all things to receive and to give. . . ."[5] With "receiving and giving" as the controlling idea, he suggested an analysis of appetitive
motions more precise than that of philosophers in their "long
and wandering discourses of pleasure, virtue, duty, and religion."[6]
Furthermore, if one looked deeply into the experience of human
desire he could detect movement, for "every obtaining [of] a de-

---

[3] *Works* III, 417–418.
[4] *De Aug.* VII, 1; *Works* V, 3.
[5] *Of the Interpretation of Nature, Works* III, 229.
[6] *Ibid.*, p. 230.

sire hath a shew of advancement, as motion though in a circle hath a shew of progression."[7] That is, a desire — say that of obtaining political office, or a mistress — directs one initially to a goal, and arriving at the goal is like returning to one's starting point. The will, too, seemed to be the immediate impetus to any action that was the outcome of reasoning and judgment. Reason might work well and true, judgment might be sound, but unless the will were moved the intellect would have cerebrated in vain. One function of the imagination, described previously, was that of making reason appealing to the will; and the art of rhetoric discharged its office by applying the dictates of reason to imagination for the "better" moving of the will.

As efficient causes, appetite and will allowed two different kinds of behavior, the sensuous and the rational. In sensuous actions, three features were always present. First, they were immediate and nonreflective; there was no thinking about consequences. Desire, for example, was often touched off by some "unlawful wish," and the wish "rashly granted before it has been understood and weighed. . . ."[8] Second, pleasure and pain attended sensuous actions, and hence were guides to desire. These qualities of experience were shown most clearly in the passions, some emotional experience giving pleasure, as with joy, other experience giving pain, as with anger. Pleasure and pain, declared Bacon, "are to the particular affections, as light is to particular colours." That is, pleasure or pain is always a feature of emotional experience, just as light is always present in color.[9] As a quality of experience, pleasure was most pure and satisfying when accompanying "knowledge and learning." Delight always attended upon learning; there was no satiety, for "satisfaction and appetite are perpetually interchangeable."[10] Many other kinds of behavior gave pleasure because of their novelty. Accordingly, some of life's pleasures could be graded, the pleasures of knowing exceeding those of the affections, the affections those of the senses, achieve-

---

[7] *Advancement of Learning, Works* III, 427.

[8] *De Aug.* II, 13; *Works* IV, 333. The most illuminating observations on the nature of desire occur in Bacon's interpretation of the stories told of Dionysius, or Bacchus. The god is held to personify desire.

[9] ". . . all colour is the broken image of light." *Topics of Inquiry Respecting Light and Luminous Matter, Works* V, 412.

[10] *Advancement of Learning, Works* III, 317.

ment and victory those of a song or a dinner.[11] If the pleasure of learning be not insatiable, why do "voluptuous men turn friars, and ambitious men turn melancholy"?[12]

The third feature of sensuous behavior in some manner involved the affections or passions; that is, sensuous actions were emotional to some degree, great or small. Bacon appears to have accepted the physician's belief that the center of emotional experience was in the heart or its region. Both affections and passions were linked to appetite rather than will. Their activity, strongly tinctured with pleasure and pain, powerfully "affected" the appetite. Their influence, however, need not be bad. In fact, in Bacon's scheme of things appetitive behavior was colored with good if it did not conflict with reason and will. The affections, indeed, could be properly enlisted by the imagination in efforts to move the will. The issues of appetite were evil only when the affections in their "perturbations" rose up to disturb judgment and overpower the will. As a general rule, behavior controlled by will was preferable to actions controlled by appetite.

Will as the Power of Choosing

The distinctive feature of will was the power of choice. Bacon was aware of this feature when he referred swiftly to the mind's faculty "of will and election."[13] Appetitive movement revealed no such feature: it was involuntary, habitual, unconscious of itself. In a completely literal sense, will could move or not move, act or not act. The power of will, as Hooker remarked, was always evident in the power to stay action.[14] If the will were to move it had to be moved; to act, it had first to be acted upon. Will was like an artist. As the efficient cause of his picture, the artist can elect to paint, or not; he can exercise his power of reviewing his intentions, inspecting his materials, and appraising his manner of treating and forming them so as to realize his intentions. So with the will. Furthermore, the will could call for the delay of action. It could put brakes on the appetite. It need not respond at once to the recommendations of reason. It could temporize

[11] *Ibid.*   [12] *Ibid.*
[13] *Helps for the Intellectual Powers, Works* VII, 101.
[14] Hooker, *The Works of . . . Mr. Richard Hooker . . .* , I, 221.

with reason, asking that noble faculty to review its processes; and it could expect imagination to do its proper work. Yet in checkmating ill-considered recommendations and impulses, the will could not expect either mind or body to do the impossible. It was restrained by a person's innate limitations. In talking of voluntary movement and its limits, Bacon observed, "It is in my power and will to run; but to run faster than according to my lightness or disposition of body, is not in my power nor will." [15] Knowledge of what was possible was derived from experience and reason; and many a contemporary of Bacon's shared Hooker's conviction that reason taught not only what was good but what was possible. [16]

Because a decision by the will was always necessary if rational thought were to result in action, classical and medieval tradition classified will as an intellectual faculty. Bacon, too, seemed to so class it when he spoke of the mind's faculty of will and election. In at least two instances will and intellect are put into the same family. "The doctrine concerning the Intellect . . . and the doctrine concerning the Will of man, are as it were twins by birth. For purity of illumination and freedom of will began and fell together; and nowhere in the universal nature of things is there so intimate a sympathy as between truth and goodness." [17] In thus alluding to Adam's fall from perfect wisdom and perfect goodness, Bacon recognized a sort of primordial intimacy between will and intellect. He asserted, too, that "the actions of life and the determinations of the will depend upon the intellect. . . ." [18] Yet in the discourse on helps for the intellectual powers, Bacon seems to exclude the will from their company. The discourse is a most carefully considered piece, addressed to a critical and knowledgeable reader, Sir Henry Savill. To emphasize the small number of ways of training and improving the understanding, reason, and memory, Bacon spent much time on the relatively large number of ways of molding will, appetite, and affections. The emphasis is suggestive. So also is Bacon's language. The will of man is "most maniable and obedient," and "admitteth most medicines to cure and alter it." But "the intellectual powers

[15] *Helps for the Intellectual Powers, Works* VII, 99.
[16] Hooker, *Works,* I, 222.
[17] *De Aug.* V, 1; *Works* IV, 405.
[18] *Wisdom of the Ancients, Works* VI, 720.

have fewer means to work upon them than the will or body of man. . . ."[19] Clearly, will is here not placed among things intellectual. Perhaps Bacon thought it unimportant, perhaps impossible, to characterize the will with any precision. It may have been important only that will be placed in the service of the rational angels and not at the command of the passionate devils. This Bacon did.

Movers of the Will

As is apparent, little could be said about will in its aspect as mover or impeller, though the power of choosing to act or not to act was sufficiently different from other features of human life to warrant a name. Much more could be said about the kinds of things, values, and forces that move the will and influenced men's conduct. Much was written — and has always been written — under the general heads of ethics, morals, moral philosophy, and politics. Bacon spoke more confidently and at greater length on these subjects than on the nature of the will. Best known are the essays: those aphorisms, counsels, and instructions that reflected educated opinion on motives, values, emotions, and sundry practical affairs in the late sixteenth and early seventeenth centuries. On the ways of influencing of the will we shall not linger long. We shall follow Bacon only so far as he appears to shed light on the nature of the will.

The main movers of the will had been traditionally regarded as the good (apparent good and real good), virtue, duty, and felicity.[20] These terms and things, Bacon said, were too vague to permit close analysis and study of conduct. Yet, having made the criticism, he subscribed to the classic generalization that apparent good was the mother of desire and real good the mother of virtue. Bacon's new classes of good were (1) the self-good, (2) the "Good of Communion" or duty, and (3) certain practical categories that related to the mind's culture.

The fresh approach to self-good and good of communion was to be based on the belief that "there is formed and imprinted in everything an appetite toward two natures of good: the one as ev-

---

[19] *Works* VII, 100.   [20] *De Aug.* VII, 3; *Works* V, 3.

erything is a total or substantive in itself, the other as it is a part or member of a greater body. . . ."[21] Self-good — sometimes called individual good — seemed to reveal a triple "appetite," that of preserving and protecting self, of perfecting self, and of multiplying self. Self-preservation was good because it brought pleasure in its "most pure and natural" form — though Bacon was prompt to add that this kind of pleasure was "the softest and lowest."[22] A higher and more active form of individual good was the appetite to perfect one's self. Even higher and still more dynamic in the scale of self-goods was the urge to extend and multiply the human species. In all manifestations of the good, the final end was the perfection of form; the mechanism or agent was that of instinct.

Bacon believed that man's desire to perfect himself and his own kind reflected a profound and eternal sensitivity to form. First, man seemed to have an "instinct of an advancement formal and essential. . . ."[23] Since his form and essence was his rationality, he would be most manlike when he showed "a mind well formed and composed in itself." The idea of *virtue* referred to just such a state in man. *Duty*, on the other hand, referred to "a mind well framed and disposed towards others."[24] Second, man's striving to perfect himself reflected the appetite in all things to approach the form next above them. ". . . there are some nobler natures to the dignity and excellence whereof inferior natures aspire as to their sources and origins."[25] In the case of man, "the perfection of his form" was his "assumption or approach . . . to the Divine or Angelical nature. . . ."[26] The affection of man for his higher nature may be what Bacon was referring to when he expressed belief in an "affection that is inseparable from human nature." He may be alluding, also, to the vestige of goodness that God vouchsafed Adam when he was banished from the Garden of Eden.

The will, then, was moved by considerations of self-good and of community good or duty. It was also influenced by those conditions that related to the "culture" or training of the mind. These conditions Bacon referred to in broad terms as the dispositions

---

[21] *De Aug.* VII, 1; *Works* V, 7.
[22] *De Aug.* VII, 2; *Works* V, 13.
[23] *De Aug.* VII, 2; *Works* V, 13.
[24] *Ibid.*, p. 15.   [25] *Ibid.*, p. 12.   [26] *Ibid.*

and characters of men. They were "inclinations . . . to virtue and vices" and to passions and perturbations.[27] The conditions were grouped under two principal divisions: those that the individual had no control over, and those that he could command. In the first division Bacon included "characters," that is, those "profound and radical" dispositions that seemed "to fit one man for business, another for art, one for the contemplative life, another for practical affairs, one for love, another for war, and the like." In the second division he placed a number of things that molded manners and affected both will and appetite. His language is clear and explicit:

I come now to those points which are within our own command, and have operation on the mind to affect and influence the will and appetite, and so have great power in altering manners; wherein philosophers ought carefully and actively to have inquired of the strength and energy of custom, exercise, habit, education, imitation, emulation, company, friendship, praise, reproof, exhortation, fame, laws, books, studies, and the like. For these are the things that rule in morals; these the agents by which the mind is affected and disposed; and the ingredients of which are compounded the medicines to preserve or recover the health of the mind, as far as it can be done by human remedies. . . .[28]

Since virtues were habits and could be learned, they too were among the moral conditions that influenced the will.[29] Yet virtue, in influencing the will, did not function quite like an agent; rather it was a guide, a goal, or an object; and in this respect it was in the family of good, duty, and felicity. These, said Bacon, were quite rightly "the true objects and scopes of man's will and desires." In fact, one function of ethical studies was "how to make the will of man conformable" to the pursuit of those objects. Bacon did not object to the concepts of virtue, good, duty, and felicity as general goals of conduct. He believed only that the classical analysis of the concepts did not yield practical and effective ways of moving the will; and for this reason he preferred his own method of analysis, namely, that through the con-

[27] De Aug. VII, 3; Works V, 21.

[28] Ibid., p. 24.

[29] ". . . virtues and vices consist in habit. . . ." (Advancement of Learning, Works III, 439.) By implication Bacon endorsed the statement that "the moral virtues are in the mind of man by habit, and not by nature. . . ." (De Aug. VII, 1; Works V, 4.)

cepts of self-good, the good of communion, and the culture of the mind.

The affections were movers of the will as well as of the appetite. Indeed, their influence was at times so direct and so great as to overpower the will. This happened whenever the appetite won imagination away from reason. Affective and emotional states furnished the materials for striking, irresistible images of desirable action. A man stirred up beyond reason was clearly "perturbed"; and "the perturbations and distempers of the affections" were regarded by Bacon and all rationalists as "the diseases and infirmities of the mind. . . ."[30] "It may be fitly said," Bacon remarked, "that the mind in its own nature would be temperate and staid; if the affections, as winds, did not put it into tumult and perturbation."[31] The affections, then, would seem to play a minor role — if any — in the life of the temperate, rational, and philosophic man. It is clear, however, that the affections played an essential role in the life of the man of action. They could be called upon to move the will quite properly and legitimately. For educated men in Elizabethan and Jacobean times, this point is well illustrated by Thomas Vicary: "acts of loving, fearing, etc., commonly called by the name of *affections* (I speake with submission to better Judgements) are only the motions [movers] of the will, by which it goeth forth to the embracing of its object which is good, which considered in the generall nature is loved, considered as in the fruition is delighted in; considered in the future as attainable, if with ease is desired; if with difficulty, is hoped for; if the will or these affections be fixed on their proper object, there is no danger in the excesse. . . ."[32] Whenever reason has had its chance to decide what is the right thing to do, when deliberation has taken place and the will must say yes or no, the affections may well unite with the imagination to urge the course of right reason, thus bringing to bear the full resources of the human being for the moving of the will. In fact, in the lives of practical men the dry light of reason alone did not usually secure action, contrary to what Stoic disciples believed. Nor for that matter did virtue secure good conduct when relied upon solely as an agent

---

[30] *Advancement of Learning, Works* III, 437.
[31] *De Aug.* VII, 3; *Works* V, 23.
[32] Thomas Vicary, To the Reader, *A Treatise of the Affections* (London, 1641).

of action. In reality, observed Bacon early in his career, "the virtues are moderators: they are laws of the mind; they restrain it, they limit it, they govern it, they amplify it not." They give "excellent form" to the mind, but they take away much of its natural vigor. But the affections "make the mind heroical . . . [give] it power to exceed itself, and fascinate and bind others." The affections are "the motions [movers] of the mind," and the virtues need them. A rational prudence takes its vigor from fear and wonder; it finds temperance in modesty, fortitude in indignation. In general, "all virtues take measure, power, and strength from the affections." [33]

It is probable that the affections, on their part, exerted their influence through the spirits. "The affections (no doubt) do make the spirits more powerful and active; and especially those affections which draw the spirits into the eyes: which are two, love and envy." [34] The general physiological principle is that "the spirits, in all passions, resort most to the parts that labour most, or are most affected." [35] In *Sylva Sylvarum*, 713, are described the physiological evidences of "the passions"; for example, "fear causeth paleness, trembling, the standing of the hair upright, starting, screeching. . . ." The nearest Bacon comes to an enumeration of the affections is at the point he deals with the effect *ad affectus et passiones animi* on the spirits and longevity. There he mentions joy, sorrow (grief and sadness), fear, anger, envy, compassion, shame, love, hope. [36] Fear and hope are the "predominant" affections. [37] Laughter is intellectual, not emotional; it is "scarce (properly) a passion, but hath his source from the intellect; for in laughing there ever precedeth a conceit of somewhat ridiculous; and therefore it is proper to man." [38]

Bacon seems to have believed that the impact of the affections upon the will — and upon man's conduct — produced more good than harm. If a man could recognize them, know their natures, and learn their proper uses, the affections would become the servant of reason, not the master of reason. Bacon recommended analy-

---

[33] *A Conference of Pleasure,* p. 9.
[34] *Sylva Sylvarum,* 944; *Works* II, 653.
[35] *Ibid.,* p. 722; *ibid.* II, 571.
[35] *Ibid.,* p. 722; *ibid.,* II, 571.
[37] *De Aug.* VII, 3; *Works* V, 24.
[38] *Sylva Sylvarum,* 721; *Works* II, 570.

sis of the affections, somewhat after the model of that appearing in the essays on emotions and character in Aristotle's *Rhetoric*. As for sources of "the best doctors of this knowledge," i.e., of the affections, he praised the poets and the writers of history.[39]

How close was the relationship between the will and the movers of the will? To Bacon the relationship appeared to be as intimate as the relationship of appetite to the causes of appetite was to Aristotle. Among the many ways of making a "new framed or formed human will" were measures that worked on the "affection and appetite," and these two, the affection and appetite, Bacon observed, were "but the inceptions and rudiments of will."[40] One cannot say that for Bacon the will and the forces that moved the will were one and the same; nevertheless, it may be that from time to time he thought so.

We may say in brief that the will was the immediate and effective cause of voluntary behavior. Appetite or desire was the immediate and effective cause of involuntary movement and action of the body. Appetite triggered physiological activity. Human desire revealed habits and patterns of conduct that had been learned under the guidance of the senses and affections. Will marked moments of deliberate choice. It was always associated with those forms of conduct that had both their origin and sanction in reason. An educated person in the days of Elizabeth and James never doubted that "the origin of action — its efficient, not its final cause — is choice. . . ."[41]

In reflecting on Bacon's view of the will, we can be certain that the will was regarded as a distinct power. Always accompanying it was a feature of deliberation marked by choice and decision. The decision either issued in action or in further deliberation; one could go down to the city to shop or decide to consider the matter at greater length. The difference between rationally doing something or not doing it was attributed to the power of will. Its presence was evident, if we may use Locke's terms, in the region of "liberty and necessity," wherever man enjoyed, in Bacon's terms, freedom "of will and election." Although in the letter to Savill

[39] See *De Aug.* VII, 3; *Works* V, 23–24.
[40] *Helps for the Intellectual Powers, Works* VII, 101.
[41] Aristotle, *Ethica Nicomachea*, 1139 a 31 (trans. W. D. Ross, in *The Works of Aristotle Translated into English Under the Editorship of W. D. Ross*).

Bacon appears to exclude the will from the company of the intellectual powers, at all other times it is associated with deliberative behavior. Probably Bacon would not have objected to Robert Burton's characterization of will as "the *rational* power *moving*,"[42] or as that power "*which covets or avoids such things as have been before judged, and apprehended by the understanding*."[43] But he might not have approved of Burton's calling the will a rational power and the rational appetite. Though Burton, with Aristotle, saw will as a species of appetite, Bacon did not.

Doubtless Bacon shared the opinions of his contemporaries, that the will was blind, that it required instruction, that it was moved by a variety of influences from a variety of sources. He would have found nothing essentially wrong with Edward Reynoldes' account of the relation of the will to the understanding. Reynoldes saw two "parts or principal powers" of the rational soul, understanding and will.[44] The understanding "contemplates" both objects and actions. Reynoldes makes the will a necessary feature of all action; so the will is encountered by the understanding when its contemplations are "accommodated unto any either Morall or Civill Actions." The will governs, moderates, and "overrules" all of man's behavior. It is the "imperium" of conduct. It rules except when the passions engulf it. In its proper function, the will is responsive to two sources of influence: the "seeds" of God's good "in the Nature of man" to which the will is sensitive directly; and information supplied by the understanding. This faculty, playing the role of minister or councillor, supplies the will with right ends in keeping with right desires, and with right means conducible to the ends desired.[45] The "liberty," or choice of means is "grounded on the Direction of the Judgement."[46] "So," concludes Reynoldes, "all the Acts of the Will necessarily presuppose some precedent guiding Acts in the Vnderstanding, whereby they are proportioned to the Rules of right Reason."[47]

Nor would Bacon have found much to criticize in John Locke's

---

[42] Burton, *The Anatomy of Melancholy*, p. 144.

[43] *Ibid.*, p. 146.

[44] Reynoldes, *A Treatise of the Passions*, p. 444.

[45] *Ibid.*, pp. 517–519.   [46] *Ibid.*, p. 537.

[47] *Ibid.*, p. 518. Reynoldes' vocabulary and full exposition is intriguing. The will is best seen in its three "peculiar Perfections": the Appetite and its role in selecting and shaping ends; Liberty and the choice of means to ends; and Dominion, or command over motor functions (p. 537).

view of the will. Though Locke lived later than Bacon, his conceptions of some of the faculties, particularly that of the will, are quite within the tradition of sixteenth- and early seventeenth-century thought. At times his descriptions are more explicit than those of writers preceding him.

This . . . I think evident, – That we find in ourselves a power to begin or forbear, continue or end several thoughts of our minds, and motions of our bodies, barely by the choice or preference of the mind. This power which the mind has to prefer the consideration of any idea, or the forbearing to consider it; or to prefer the motion of any part of the body to its rest is that which we call the Will. The actual preferring one to another is that which we call *volition* or *willing*.[48]

The use of *preferring* in 1690 emphasizes that the will's function consisted in choosing; in 1694 Locke found that the essence of choice resided in *forbearing*. "The forbearance of that action, consequent to . . . order or command of the mind, is called *voluntary*. And whatsoever action is performed without such a thought of the mind, is called *involuntary*." Locke has thus supplied an insight that in Bacon – if indeed it was implicit – was never verbalized.

Locke also called attention to the will's power to control and direct thought. The will could demand, as it were, that understanding supply all desired information prior to the act of choice. Confronted with a practical problem, the will could ask the understanding to think about, to reason, to judge the matter at hand, drawing upon the accumulated experience stored in memory.[49] The power of will over mind will seem less strange to us when we reflect upon the implications of such modern expressions as "I am trying to remember," "Try to think," and "You can at least *try* to work out the problem." The power of will over body movement is much more evident, thought Locke, than the effect of will on mental activity. "The idea of the *beginning* of motion we

---

[48] The language follows that of the first edition as indicated in this source: *An Essay Concerning Human Understanding* by John Locke, collated and annotated, with prolegomena by Alexander Campbell Fraser, I, 313–314.

[49] The influence of will on memory I have encountered most pointedly in Sir Kenelm Digby's enumeration of the forces that bring latent knowledge into play. In some part of the brain knowledge "resideth." There it remains until stirred up by natural appetite, by chance, or by "the will of the man in whom they [the ranks and files of stored experience] are, vpon the occasions he meeteth with of searching into them." The will, then, can stimulate memory to action. (Digby, *Two Treatises*, pp. 284–285.)

have . . . from reflection on what passes in ourselves; where we find by experience, that, barely by willing it, barely by a thought of the mind, we can move the parts of our bodies, which were before at rest." [50]

Bacon does not distinguish, as did Hobbes, between will as power and will as act. For the author of *Leviathan*, conduct is guided by man's appetites and desires and by his aversions. Entirely imperceptible, these are "small beginnings of motion," and may well be called "ENDEAVOUR." [51] If endeavor is toward something, it is "APPETITE, or DESIRE, the latter being the general name. . . ." [52] If endeavor is away from something, it is aversion. Conflict among desires, or between desire and aversion, sets the stage for deliberation, that is, for "a series of thoughts." The last step in the series just prior to movement is the will in act. Hobbes is referring, as he acknowledges, to the "rational appetite" of the Schoolmen, but he prefers his own terminology, "an appetite resulting from a precedent deliberation." [53] As an act, then, will is "the last appetite in deliberating"; and as a power, it is the final choice, whether to do or not to do, which "causes" action. [54]

How Bacon would have reacted to Descartes' account of the will is doubtful. In one respect the Frenchman's views do not differ substantially from those of Hobbes and Locke. So far as the will is an action or movement of the "soul" it is identified with volition or appetite. Volitions are of two kinds, movements terminating within the soul in which we direct our thoughts to our thoughts, and movements terminating in the body in which we tell ourselves, say, to walk, and we walk. In a second respect, Descartes differs radically. He held that the will could exert a direct effect on the pineal gland. "Now the action of the soul

---

[50] Locke, *An Essay Concerning Human Understanding*, I, 313.
[51] Hobbes, *Leviathan, Works* III, 39.
[52] *Ibid.*   [53] *Ibid.*, pp. 48–49.
[54] Hobbes also dealt with deliberation, appetite, and will in his treatise on the body (*De Corpore*), first translated in 1655 and incorporated in his *Elements of Philosophy*. If there is conflict between appetite and aversion "a series of thoughts" is set up, "which is called *deliberation*; which lasteth as long as they have it in their power to obtain that which pleaseth, or to avoid that which displeaseth them. Appetite and aversion, therefore, are simply so called as long as they follow not deliberation. But if deliberation have gone before, then the last act of it, if it be appetite [i.e., endeavor toward something] is called *will*; if aversion, *unwillingness*." (*The English Works of Thomas Hobbes*, I, 408–409.)

consists entirely in this, that simply by willing it makes the small
gland to which it is closely united move in the way requisite for
producing the effect aimed at in the volition." [55] Descartes believed that animal spirits flood the soul and body in all their parts
and that the parts communicate with one another only through
spirit channels that pass through the pineal gland. The will acted
to constrict or to dilate the gland subtly, thus causing movement
of the spirits in the desired part. In this manner the will not only
affected the muscles; it also stimulated the memory, imagination,
and understanding. Bacon of course knew of no gland that was
pivotal to the action of soul and body, although he was as committed to the omnipresence of spirits as was Descartes. He never
assayed to explain how the will moved man's parts; he was more
concerned with how the will itself was moved.

In other respects Bacon and Descartes appear to differ, but
perhaps not significantly. The Englishman never discussed free
will, doubtless because this concept, embedded in its long history of speculation and dogma, belonged to the theologians. The
Frenchman held convictions about the concept, of which the
most sweeping was that "the will is in its nature so free it can
never be constrained" by human powers.[56] Descartes believed,
furthermore, that man is most clearly aware of the will as a
power, or faculty, when he believes he is acting without being
influenced by any force external to him. ". . . the faculty of will
consists alone in our having the power of choosing to do a thing
or choosing not to do it (that is, to affirm or deny, to pursue or
shun it), or rather it consists alone in the fact that in order to
affirm or deny, pursue or shun those things placed before us by
the understanding, we act so that we are unconscious that any
outside force constrains us in doing so." [57]

On Bacon's behalf, finally, we can say that there was a faculty
or power of will sufficiently different in its manifestations — in
moving man to rational and motor activity, and in being moved —
to be dignified with a name. It was the efficient cause of voluntary,
deliberative behavior. Appetite was the efficient cause of invol-

---

[55] Descartes, *The Passions of the Soul, Philosophical Writings*, Arts. 39–41.
[56] *Ibid.*, Art. 41. Cf. *Meditations on First Philosophy*, in *The Philosophical
Works of Descartes*, trans. Elizabeth S. Haldane and G. R. T. Ross (2 vols.;
n.p.; Dover Publications, n.d.), I, 175.
[57] *Ibid.*

untary movements, of man's unreflective responses as well as of vital, vegetative processes that revealed no organs of control.

Bacon displays less information to us about the will than about any other faculty. Probably he saw no ways of submitting it to fruitful scrutiny in a manner comparable to the analysis and empirical study of physical and appetitive movement. I suspect that Bacon, along with any tight-thinking seventeenth-century scholar who could separate the study of nature from the assumptions of religion and theology, would have been in complete sympathy with Joseph Glanvill: "The sole difficulties about the *Will*, its nature, and sequency to the Understanding, etc. have almost quite baffled inquiry, and shewn us little else, but that our *Understandings* are as *blind* as it is." [58]

---

[58] Glanvill, *The Vanity of Dogmatizing*, p. 40.

Conclusion

The faculties were modes of spirit activity that marked behavior when man was observed to think, understand, reason, imagine, remember, act, and feel. Spirits were the material and substantial basis of inanimate and animate being. Two kinds of spirit movement were in animal and man: irrational and rational. In man the two kinds were called the irrational and rational souls, irrational spirit movement being the instrument of rational spirit activity. Rational behavior constituted a sort of dance of the spirits that Bacon called thinking. It was the stuff that appeared to reveal modes, or general forms, of activity: understanding, reasoning, imagining, and remembering. The modes were often spoken of as faculties or powers of the mind; they were distinctive kinds and types of rational behavior.

Man became aware of the physical world through his senses, those of vision, hearing, taste, touch, smell, and the Venus sense. He was aware of a suprasensory world, if at all, through his rational spirit, which was divine, and was infused into each man at birth. Man was aware of his faculties through his behavior. Memory stored the images of sense experience — the species of objects and events — and the products of the understanding, reason, and imagination. In the storehouse, these products, many in number and various in kind, were digested and altered in inexplicable ways. The imagination with the aid of memory revived sense images, and made them available to the reason and understanding, faculties whose operations gave form to imageless thought, and divided, combined, and organized mental experience in ways that were reflected in man's logical operations. The imagination also created images of its own, with unpredictable results.

Understanding and reason engaged in inventive, creative activity, and reason judged the products. Imagination came to their aid whenever mental activity had to be made available to the senses as symbolic experience in which thought was represented and transmitted to others. Thus in communication the imagination was said to illustrate the abstract operations of the mind. When man communicated with man, the imagination teamed up with reason to invent arguments and figures of speech appropriate and fitting to the persons addressed. When God communicated with man, his spirit spoke directly to the imagination and understanding, with the result that the imageless, ineffable experience of revelation was made accessible to reason.

The faculties of will and appetite were to feeling and action what the rational faculties were to knowledge. Bacon thought of them as the immediate causes of the changes man could recognize in his bodily processes and growth, and in his action and conduct. Appetite was that feature of spirit activity which Bacon called the power of giving and receiving. Its general forms were the consents and aversions, the sympathies and antipathies, among things. On the one hand, appetite controlled the vital processes of the body and, on the other, guided man's unreflective behavior through his feelings and emotions. The will was that mode of mental activity evident in arriving at, and in taking, decisions. It was moved by man's deliberations, and in turn moved him to act or to refrain from acting.

To Bacon man was the kind of creature who used his faculties as only a man could. Only a man could deliberate, make choices, and achieve ends. He might be a man of contemplation or a man of action, but as thinker and actor he was to be guided by notions of the true and the good. These could be known, Bacon believed, because man had within him the seeds of truth and goodness which God had vouchsafed Adam.

Bacon's view of man's faculties, as we have hinted from time to time, is a simpler one than the view held by most Englishmen in the late sixteenth and early seventeenth centuries. The classical account of the faculties Bacon understood, but he saw no place for a faculty labeled "common sense." The task given to this faculty, that of uniting and organizing the data supplied by separate senses through separate channels, was performed by nature herself. The senses were reporters and carried the species of things into the memory whole. The organization of man's inner experience into states, conditions, or habits of knowledge and feeling as well as the issue of such accumulated experience in specific thought and action Bacon assigned to the other faculties. The shapes of things were in objects and the senses responded to them. Bacon thus appears to have assumed that there were ultimate modes of being — whose signs were the categories — and that they organized man's object world quite apart from him. Man sees the tree in a quite literal sense. A common sense faculty, on the other hand, assumed a first level of organization immediately after sensory experience, where categories were brought to bear in producing sensible species, or percepts. Man does not see the tree; he perceives it. For Bacon a common sense faculty was unnecessary. Imagination and memory organized intermediate levels of experience, the object world becoming there less real and immediate, more ideal and remote. At the highest level of organization, the understanding, peculiarly attuned to forms and formal relationships, rendered experience conceptual.

In Bacon is encountered a quite different conception of the rational faculties and the internal senses from that rife in medieval thought. Illustrated in St. Thomas Aquinas, medieval practice recognized at least three internal senses — common sense, memory, and imagination — and three rational faculties — understanding, reason, and will. But Bacon saw little utility in this kind of division. It reflected the Schoolmen's habit of speculating abstractly in order to arrive at the essence of the faculties. The zenith of divison was reached when the Schoolmen named seven internal senses. Sometimes, as with Avicenna, imagination did the work of common sense.[1] They saw two kinds of memory and split the intellect into three: an active intellect, a passive intellect, and a possible intellect. Bacon's overriding purpose was different. He was more concerned with function than with essence. He wanted to advance man's ability to know and, knowing, to *use* knowledge. Accordingly, he so classified knowledge that man might see what had been learned and what was most needed to

---

[1] See Wolfson, "The Internal Senses," where the full account is admirably presented.

discover. His classification was based on the powers man required in acquiring knowledge, storing it, and using it. The powers were reason and understanding, imagination and memory. These he thought of as the rational faculties, and for him they comprised the mind of man. They were sufficient for contemplation and deliberation, but they needed the help of the appetite and the will in securing action. It is possible that Bacon's classification of knowledge and his conception of the faculties modified each other. It is probable, I think, that Bacon held a well-formed view of man prior to publication in 1605 of his scheme of knowledge. Ideas of the faculties were imbedded in the education of the times. The language Bacon used to announce his classification of learning implies an awareness of different ways of classification and deliberate choice of his own basis: "The *best* division of human learning is that derived from the three faculties of the rational soul, which is the seat of learning." (Italics mine.)

We observe, in epitome, that in making his account of man's nature simpler than the account he inherited, Bacon never lost sight of man's powers in their full context.

Bacon certainly saw man whole. Man could be divided into "parts" for the sake of study and analysis — as could also the world about him — but his parts were interrelated and constituted a functional whole. The faculties were parts, but they were related in two manifest ways. They shared, first, a common, material basis. The basis was spirit, a dynamic spirit always in motion, and in its vital and animal forms never at rest until death. Second, the faculties depended on each other and to some extent overlapped in their operations. The materials supplied through one kind of modulation of the spirit became the material of another. The senses, imagination, reason, and understanding fed memory and memory fed them. The rational faculties and affective powers as channels of knowing, feeling, action, and movement were not only inoperable but inconceivable without memory, the storehouse of experience. Some kinds of imagery, moreover, were the concrete obverse of abstract thought; thinking became "real" only through its image.

Embedded in Bacon's view of man's faculties are features of his intellectual system that seem to have escaped the notice of scholars.

His belief that the material basis of organic and inorganic life was to be found in ceaseless movements of spirits led Bacon to expect the discovery of ultimate elements or units of movement. He could not have imagined our submicroscopic world of sub-atomic particles and their universes. But he was convinced that there existed some kind of submicroscopic world of minute par-ticles in motion which once known would furnish a more exact basis of scientific knowledge than had ever been possible. To learn about the physical world beyond man's senses was to know about the forces behind magnetism and behind other evidences of what he called the consents and aversions, sympathies and antipathies of things.

Bacon was convinced, too, that to probe for natural forces more deeply than had been the habit was to break cleanly with time-encrusted methods of discovery. The old methods were tied to what man already knew. They were methods of invention devel-oped by dialectic, logic, grammar, and rhetoric. They were there-fore tied inevitably and permanently to men's language. Lan-guage symbolized or, to use Bacon's term, represented what man had thought and done and had stored in the files of memory. A system of invention, a scheme of topics, accordingly, could only be good for recalling past experience, for analyzing it, and for order-ing it anew. The old invention served for the finding of "speech and arguments," and worked well enough for the purposes of practical and poetical discourse only if one recognized the Idols of the Market Place and tried to discount their influence. If man were to uncover nature's secrets, if he were to acquire new knowl-edge of the physical world, he must abandon old ways of search and inquiry and must devise new ways of querying nature di-rectly. Man had to have a new organon, a new way of induction, and this is what Bacon thought he had provided.

To provide it he had to question the method and materials of finding knowledge that he and his contemporaries were taught. When Bacon referred to the ordinary and accepted division of knowledge he may have had in mind a system like that tradi-tionally presented by university professors. Stier's is one such system. It obtained at Cambridge in the time of James I and was probably not greatly different from the scheme of things Bacon learned at Cambridge in the 1580's.[2]

---

[2] Fletcher, *The Educational Development of John Milton*, II, 159–160 ff; M. Joanne Stierio, *Praecepta Doctrinae* . . . , 7th ed., 1671.

Stier's system is based on that of Aristotle and the Peripatetic commentaries. First comes logic, followed by ethics or moral philosophy. Then occurs physics (*physices*) or natural philosophy, followed by metaphysics. The last "division" was called Doctrine of the Spheres, or astronomy, and appended thereto, geography. The arrangement is not fully encyclopedic, that is, it does not depict the complete circle of learning, or philosophy. It seems to reflect a method-knowledge principle. The method of knowing is one that operates by logical principles and forms, and the things known are natural bodies and movements or their symbols. But though Bacon's classification of knowledge reflects his interest in producing knowledge he could not make the ordinary logic his method. He thought that the logic commonly used was a logic of disciplining language, not of disciplining nature, rather than a logic in which the understanding was linked with the senses to permit accurate observation and limited inference. He understood, of course, that the nature and reliability of knowledge could not be divorced from the method of acquiring it. He knew, too, that acquisition could be managed only through the powers of the human being; hence, any improvement in knowledge must mean better control over man's faculties of knowing.

The most novel feature of Bacon's thought, I believe, becomes evident when we pose this question: How did the "new" induction differ from the old way of invention? The new method was a way of controlling observation and abstraction by setting up two conditions. First, the understanding was to be tied directly to the senses and thus to increase the chances that a concept would emerge, or, as a gestaltist would say, a moment of insight would occur. Second, the understanding was to be governed by an order and procedure designed to delay and control abstraction.

In explaining these statements, it will help to start, as Bacon did in Book II of the *Novum Organum*, with the outcome of the inductive process. The explanation must again draw on materials from the *Novum Organum*, but the point of view now is different from that of Chapter 6. There Bacon's method of science helped to reveal the nature of the understanding as a faculty; here the attempt is to show that the view of man's faculties provided the basis of Bacon's inductive process.

The outcome of the process were axioms. These were of two kinds; one dealing with the "Form," or formal cause, of a number of related objects or movements under investigation, the other dealing with the efficient and material causes of processes and of objects. Axioms of the first kind Bacon assigned to what he called metaphysics; axioms of the second kind fell to physics. His method or "directions" for the discovery of such axioms embraced "two generic divisions; the one how to educe and form axioms from experience; the other how to deduce and derive new experiments from axioms."[3] The scientist's eduction of axioms from experience was to be improved by securing better control over the senses, the memory, and "the mind or reason."[4] Bacon did not live long enough to apply his method to the finding of axioms of the second kind. He chose to set forth in the *Novum Organum* his directions for the control of the mind when it was bent on discovering metaphysical axioms. These axioms were statements calling attention to the "Form" of the nature under observation. If the nature be that of heat, Bacon's directions for finding it produced this outcome: *Heat is a motion, expansive, restrained, and acting in its strife upon the smaller particles of bodies.* The statement points to the formal cause of heat, namely motion, whose form is that produced by small particles of bodies when their activity occurs under conditions of expansion and restraint. (Perhaps the statement also hints at the efficient cause.) Psychologically, the understanding has abstracted from occurrences and "instances" of heat phenomena reported through the senses and has formed a distinct apprehension.

In looking for the forms of nature and arriving at axioms, Bacon explains that one starts with "instances," and proceeds through two stages. The intellect is to be bound to real objects and experience; it is to be withdrawn no farther from the facts of nature "than may suffice to let the images and rays of natural objects meet in a point, as they do in the sense of vision. . . ."[5] Observation is disciplined and abstraction delayed until the understanding's innate tendency to abstract can no longer be held in check. At that point the understanding is "indulged," and a tentative axiom is framed. This stage Bacon calls the "First Vintage" of search and observation. The axiom produced corresponds to the modern scientist's hypothesis. Bacon outlines a definite

---

[3] *Novum Organum* II, 10; *Works* IV, 127.   [4] *Ibid.*
[5] Preface to *The Great Instauration, Works* IV, 19.

procedure designed to direct, perhaps to force, the understanding
and the senses to look for and consider special kinds of relevant
instances, as, for example, conditions in which heat is absent,
and instances where heat is unusual or striking. The procedure
for investigation and testing consists of twenty-seven "Prerogative
Instances." Only after the entire procedure has been completed
is the axiom entertained tentatively at first, then confirmed or
modified.

That the procedure was intended to keep the understanding
and the senses in direct communication may be seen from Bacon's
language. Merely a large collection of instances "confounds and
distracts the understanding"; they must be "ranged and presented to view in a suitable order," "a method and order" such
that "the understanding may be able to deal with them."[6] One
can arrive at a first vintage only by "a muster or presentation
before the understanding of all known instances which agree in
the same nature, though in substances the most unlike."[7] Lest
the understanding be dulled or become unduly channeled, as
further search goes on and testing is begun, there are five kinds
of instances that as a group serve "to digest the matters that enter
the understanding, and to correct the ill complexion of the understanding itself, which cannot but be tinged and infected, and at
length perverted and distorted, by daily and habitual impressions.
These instances therefore should be employed as a sort of pre-
parative for setting right and purging the understanding. For
whatever withdraws the understanding from the things to which
it is accustomed, smooths and levels its surface for the reception
of the dry and pure light of true ideas."[8] The instances of the Lamp
provide aid to the senses, which supply "first information" to the
understanding: "since all Interpretation of Nature commences
with the senses, and leads from the perceptions of the senses by
a straight, regular, and guarded path to the perceptions of the
understanding, which are true notions and axioms, it followed of
necessity that the more copious and exact the representations [and
presentations] of the senses, the more easily and prosperously

---

[6] *Novum Organum* II, 10; *Works* IV, 127.
[7] *Ibid.*
[8] *Ibid.*, 32; *ibid.*, p. 173. Bacon's Latin for the last phrase: *ad . . .
notionum verarum.*

everything will proceed."⁹ Some of the Lamps "strengthen, en-
large, and rectify the immediate action of the senses. . . ." Others
extend the senses to what they cannot get at directly — the tele-
scope, for example; others "excite the attention and notice" of
the senses.¹⁰ Some instances are intended to work "by narrow-
ing and indicating more nearly the Affirmative of the Form. . . ,"
others "by exalting the understanding and leading it to genera and
common natures; either immediately . . . or in the next degree. . . ."¹¹ In brief, wrote Bacon, as he closed the *Novum Organum*: "my logic aims to teach and instruct the understanding,
not that it may with the slender tendrils of the mind snatch at
and lay hold of abstract notions (as the common logic does), but
that it may in very truth dissect nature, and discover the virtues
and actions of bodies, with their laws as determined in matter,
so that his science flows not merely from the nature of the mind,
but also from the nature of things. . . ."¹²

Bacon thus recognized that in trying to discover knowledge of
natural things, man must virtually abandon his ordinary language.
Language reflected man's idols and warped his judgment. It was
imprecise. Above all, man's deductions from the concepts derived
through language produced conclusions saying much that was
familiar and little that was new. To acquire new knowledge of
natural phenomena by using an old system of invention that had
been developed through language and that had to be worked
through language was manifestly futile. Rather, man had to start
with natural objects, train his senses to search widely and report
accurately, and bend his understanding to dwell on relevant
instances. Man could learn to so discipline his senses and understanding, proceeding as described by the twenty-seven kinds of
instances, that he stood a good chance of finding an axiom or
Form that was truly new. In the language that Bacon used to
Lancelot Andrewes, we can say that the content of axioms are
not to be merely "a mixture of the new and old"; they will con-
tain, by comparison, "the new unmixed."

⁹ *Ibid.*, 38; *ibid.*, p. 192. ". . . necesse est ut quanto magis copiosae
et exactae fuerint repraesentationes sive praegitiones ipsius sensus, tanto
omnia cedant facilius et foelicius." (*Works* I, 306.) The meaning appears to
be: the better the sense works by supplying its images to the understanding
in large numbers rather than few, and by making its images precise rather
than inexact, the better are the forms apprehended.
¹⁰ *Ibid.*; *Works* IV, 192.   ¹¹ *Ibid.*, 52; *ibid.*, p. 247.   ¹² *Ibid.*, p. 246.

Bacon's interest in the faculties of man — an interest strong enough to produce a classification of knowledge based on the faculties — led him to see clearly that if man were to enhance his powers of creativity he had to try to control conditions of creative thought. Specifically, Bacon's view of the "exercise" of the understanding in its inventive role almost certainly led him to the fundamental requirement, namely, a specific procedure designed to encourage insight. His new induction was precisely of this nature. He may have had, moreover, some notion of insight itself, namely, its apparently accidental occurrence. A man might have spent his whole life, said Bacon, in contemplating the many kinds of "war engines," battering rams, and the like without hitting upon the idea of using gunpowder in a cannon. "Hence it is that all the discoveries which can take rank among the nobler of their kind, have (if you observe) been brought to light, not by small elaborations and extensions of arts, but entirely by accident."[13] If man were to reduce the intervals between accidents, to "anticipate" accidents as it were, he would set the stage for his wit to dart about among instances. Furthermore, if he were to strive for seminal discoveries — those of the nobler kind — he would look for instances that evoke his *wonder*. These would be found among things both of nature and of art that are "rare and extraordinary. . . ." Wonder is the "child of rarity," and men wonder at, and the understanding is excited by, the masterpieces of men and the mysteries of nature. The "singularities" of man's creativity are likely to be especially instructive in invention, because "the method of creating and constructing such miracles of art is in most cases plain, whereas in the miracles of nature it is generally obscure."[14] The method of man may suggest an analogue in nature, and vice versa.

In setting conditions for invention that brought the understanding in its most active state into direct contact with sense images of natural and artificial objects, Bacon makes no mention of the imagination. The omission is striking. Had the imagination no role in scientific discovery and in facilitating insight? It played no part. The reasons for its omission are evident. First, Bacon attributed to the understanding the exploratory activity — the

---

[13] *Ibid.*, 31; *ibid.*, p. 171.   [14] *Ibid.*, pp. 170, 171.

darting hither and yon, the to and fro movements — that other men, such as Reynoldes, attributed to the imagination. Such searching and probing activity Bacon sometimes thought of as wit. The imaginative faculty indeed had a creative role, but its inventive activity was limited to man's behavior when he appeared as rhetor, poet, communicator, and in general as a linguistic creature. In rhetoric, as we saw, imagination was evident as insinuative or imaginative reason and in poetry as images of remembered experience and as creations more or less credible. Second, the imagination's characteristic creations were tropes. These were regarded as ornaments of thought and language. Habits of thinking in terms of metaphor and synecdoche were useless and obstructive to scientific invention. In the moment of insight that brings forth a Form, in the moment of intellectual activity just prior to an axiom and revealed subsequently in the language of the axiom, thought was imageless. The role of imagination in science appeared only when it was necessary that thought be made accessible to sense. The necessary conditions were widely recognized by Bacon and his contemporaries and by the founders of the Royal Society: when thought had to be recorded for purposes of preservation and memory, when communication was desired, and when axioms as verbal entities became objects of discursive reason in acts of comparison and judgment. Under these conditions — as is well known to students of the rhetoric of science — the language produced by the imagination is literal; it must not be allowed to confound scientific invention and scientific communication by the intrusion of tropes and figures.

Another omission is striking. Bacon excludes mention of the reason from the *Novum Organum*. Had reason as a faculty no specific role in scientific invention? Seemingly not. The eduction of an axiom from particulars, no matter how long the procedure, is taken step by step and each step is nondiscursive. The movement of reason is typically discursive. The tables of presence and absence show that the understanding engages in comparing and contrasting, but it is not engaged in dividing or combining objects and qualities of experience. Analysis and synthesis is the work of reason. At any instant of comparison there is the simple question, Is the quality at issue present or absent? The understanding replies yes or no, for "the same action of the mind which

discovers the thing in question judges it. . . ."[15] Judgment there
is, but it is a sort of judgment different from that made by reason.
This faculty comes into play when one axiom is compared with
another, when one proposition is deduced from others, as goes
on typically in syllogistic inference. The movement of reason is
deliberative; the action of the understanding is nondeliberative.
Deliberation entails a criterion of judgment, and the criterion will
change according to the circumstances and contexts of judgment.
Scientific invention involves but one standard, the presence or absence of the quality under observation.

Bacon's attempt to make the understanding mind the senses,
as it were, becomes the more striking when one realizes that the
endeavor was contradictory to the best belief and dominant teaching of his day. For centuries men had firmly believed that the
understanding was working best and in keeping with its true
character when it was utterly divorced from sensory materials.
The senses cloyed and hindered the understanding. The highest
and best state of contemplation was at the highest level of abstraction, and the purest thought was that which was farthest from
the world of objects and events and closest to the world of angel
intelligences and the divine spirit. Confronted with a hoary tradition sanctioned by theology, Bacon had to show what the understanding could do when it was disciplined to sensory experience.
This would be possible only in a psychological system in which
the external senses unified their experience without the aid of a
common sense and the understanding could deal with incoming
sense images without the intervention of symbols. This Bacon's
system allowed. As a result, the second book of the *Novum Organum* becomes an example of what can be done when the understanding in its inventive behavior is disciplined to objects rather
than to symbols of objects. It may be remarked also that when
considered as an *example* in its rhetorical setting and the climate
of belief to which it was relevant, the second book is persuasive.

---

[15] *De Aug.* V, 4; *Works* IV, 428.

Bibliography

Bacon's Works

COLLECTED WORKS

Baconiana, or Certain Genuine Remains of Sir Francis Bacon Baron of Verulam and Viscount of St. Alban's; in Arguments Civil, Moral, Natural, Medical, Theological, and Bibliographical, Now for the First Time Faithfully Published. Edited by Archbishop Tenison. London, 1679.

Francis Bacon: A Bibliography of His Works and of Baconiana to the Year 1750. Compiled by R. W. Gibson. Oxford, 1950. *Supplement.* Privately issued under the auspices of the Francis Bacon Foundation, Inc., Pasadena, Calif., 1959.

The Letters and Life of Francis Bacon Including All His Occasional Works. . . . Collected by James Spedding. 7 vols. London: Longman, Green, Longman, and Roberts, 1861–74.

Mr. Bushell's Abridgement of the Lord Chancellor Bacon's Philosophical Theory in Mineral Prosecutions. 1659.

The Philosophical Works of Francis Bacon . . . Methodized, and Made English, from the Originals . . . by Peter Shaw. 3 vols. 2nd ed. London, 1737.

The Physical and Metaphysical Works of Lord Bacon, Including His Dignity and Advancement of Learning . . . and His Novum Organum, or Precepts for the Interpretation of Nature. Translated by Joseph Devey. London: Henry G. Bohn, 1853.

The Poems of Lord Bacon . . . with an Introduction by the Rev. A. B. Grosart. In *Miscellanies of the Fuller Worthies Library.* . . . By the Rev. Alexander B. Grosart. 4 vols. London: Blackburn, 1871–76.

The Works of Francis Bacon, Baron of Verulam, Viscount St. Alban, and Lord High Chancellor of England, collected and edited by James Spedding, Robert Leslie Ellis, and Douglas Denton Heath. 7 vols. London: Longmans & Co. . . . Virtue & Co., 1879.

SEPARATE WORKS

The Advancement of Learning. Edited by William Aldis Wright. 5th ed. Oxford: The Clarendon Press, 1900.

An Advertisement Touching the Controversies of the Church of England. London, 1640.

Apophthegmes New and Old. London, 1625.

Bacon's Advancement of Learning and the New Atlantis. With a Preface by Thomas Case. London: Oxford University Press, 1906.

Bacon's Essays and Colours of Good and Evil. With Notes and Glossarial Index by W. Aldis Wright. London, 1879.

Bacon's Novum Organum. Edited by Thomas Fowler. Oxford: The Clarendon Press, 1878.

A Briefe Discovrse, Touching the Happie Vnion of the Kingdomes of England, and Scotland. London, 1603.

Cogitata et visa: de interpretatione naturae, sine de scientia operativa; or Thoughts and Conclusions on the Interpretation of Nature or a Science of Productive Works. Translated by Benjamin Farrington, in *The Philosophy of Francis Bacon* (Liverpool: Liverpool University Press, 1964).

A Conference of Pleasure, Composed for Some Festive Occasion About the Year 1592 by Francis Bacon. Edited by James Spedding. London, 1870.

De dignitate et augmentis scientiarum libros ix. Edited by W. Rawley. London, 1623.

De sapientia veterum liber. London, 1609.

Descriptio globi intellectualis et thema coeli. First printed in *Scripta in naturali et universali philosophia.* Edited by I. Gruter. Amsterdam, 1653.

The Essaies of Sir Francis Bacon Knight the Kings Solliciter Generall. London, 1612.

The Essayes or Counsels, Civill and Morall, of Francis Lord Verulam, Viscount St. Alban, Newly Written. London, 1625.

Essayes. Religious Meditations. Places of Perswasion and Disswasion. London, 1597.

Essays, Moral, Economical, and Political. . . . By Francis Bacon. In *The Conduct of the Understanding* by John Locke. With an introductory essay by A. Potter. New York: Harper and Bros., 1844.

Filum labyrinthi. First printed in *Letters and Remains of the Lord Chancellor Bacon.* Collected by R. Stephens. London, 1734.

Francis Bacon's Promus of Formularies and Elegancies. Being a Literal Reprint of Part of the Harleian MS 7017. . . . London, 1898.

The Historie of Life and Death. With Observations Naturall and Experimentall for the Prolonging of Life. London, 1638.

Letter and Discourse to Sir Henry Savill, Touching Helps for the Intellectual Powers. First printed in *Resuscitatio, or Bringing into Publick Light Severall Pieces of the Works* . . . o*f Francis Ba-*

con. . . . With his Lordships Life. By W. Rawley. 2 pts. London, 1657.

The Novum Organon . . . a New Translation by Rev. G. W. Kitchin. Oxford: Oxford University Press, 1855.

Novum organum sive indica de interpretatione naturae. London, 1620.

Of the Advancement and Proficience of Learning, or the Partitions of Sciences, IX Bookes . . . Interpreted by Gilbert Wats. Oxford, 1640.

Of the Coulers of Good and Euill. London, 1597.

Redargutio philosophiarum, or the Refutation of Philosophies. Translated by Benjamin Farrington, in *The Philosophy of Francis Bacon* (Liverpool: Liverpool University Press, 1964).

The Remains of the Right Honourable Francis Lord Verulam . . . Being Essays and Severale Letters. . . . London, 1648.

Sylva sylvarum; or *A Natural Historie.* London, 1627.

Temporis partus masculus, or the Masculine Birth of Time. Translated by Benjamin Farrington, in *The Philosophy of Francis Bacon* (Liverpool: Liverpool University Press, 1964).

The Twoo Bookes of Francis Bacon, Of the Proficience and Advancement of Learning, Divine and Humane. London, 1605.

Valerius Terminus of the Interpretation of Nature. First printed in Stephens' *Letters.* London, 1734.

The Wisdom of the Ancients, and New Atlantis. . . . With an Introduction by Henry Morley. London: Cassell and Co., 1886.

The Wisedome of the Ancients . . . Done into English by Sir Arthur Georges Knight. London, 1619.

General

BOOKS

Abbott, E. A. *Francis Bacon*: An Account of His Life and Works. London, 1885.

Aiken, Lucy. *Memoirs of the Court of King James the First.* 2 vols. London, 1882.

Allen, Don Cameron. *The Legend of Noah*: Renaissance Rationalism in Art, Science, and Letters. ("Illinois Studies in Language and Literature," XXXIII.) Urbana: University of Illinois Press, 1949.

Allott, Robert (comp.?). *Wits Theater of the Little World.* London, 1599.

Alvarez, A. *The School of Donne.* London: Chatto & Windus, 1961.

Anderson, Fulton H. *The Philosophy of Francis Bacon.* Chicago: University of Chicago Press, 1948.

Anderson, Ruth L. *Elizabethan Psychology and Shakespeare's Plays.*

("University of Iowa. Humanistic Studies," III.) Iowa City: University of Iowa, 1927.

Ando, T. *Aristotle's Theory of Practical Cognition.* Kyoto, 1958.

Aristotle. *Aristotle on the Soul, Parva Naturalia, On Breath.* With an English translation by W. S. Hett. London: William Heineman, Ltd., and Cambridge, Mass.: Harvard University Press, 1957.

————. *Aristotle's DE ANIMA in the Version of William of Moerbeke and the Commentary of St. Thomas Aquinas.* Translated by Kenelm Foster and Silvester Humphries, with an introduction by Ivo Thomas. New Haven, Conn.: Yale University Press, 1951.

————. *Aristotle's Metaphysics.* Translated by Richard Hope. New York: Columbia University Press, 1952.

————. *Aristotle: The Nichomachean Ethics*; a Commentary by H. H. Joachim. Edited by D. A. Rees. Oxford: The Clarendon Press, 1951.

————. *Aristotle's Poetics*: The Argument. By Gerald F. Else. Cambridge, Mass.: Harvard University Press, 1957.

————. *Aristotle's Psychology.* By W. A. Hammond. New York: The Macmillan Co., 1902.

————. *The Politics of Aristotle.* Translated by E. Barker. Oxford: Oxford University Press, 1946.

————. *The Works of Aristotle Translated into English Under the Editorship of W. D. Ross.* 11 vols. Oxford: The Clarendon Press, 1912–31.

Ascham, Roger. *The Scholemaster*, or Plaine and Perfite Way of Teachyng Children the Latin Tong. London, 1589.

Atkins, J. W. H. *English Literary Criticism: The Medieval Phase.* London: Methuen and Co., 1952.

————. *English Literary Criticism: The Renascence.* 2nd ed. London: Methuen and Co., 1951.

————. *English Literary Criticism: 17th and 18th Centuries.* London: Methuen and Co., 1951.

————. *Literary Criticism in Antiquity*: A Sketch of Its Development. 2 vols. Cambridge: Cambridge University Press, 1934.

Augustine, Saint. *Concerning the Teacher (De magistro) and On the Immortality of the Soul (De immortalitate animae).* Translated by George G. Leckie. New York: Appleton-Century-Crofts, Inc., 1938.

————. *Of the Citie of God.* With the Learned Comments of Jo. Lrd. Vives. Englished by F. H. London, 1610.

————. *The Spirit and the Letter.* Translated with an introduction by W. J. Sparrow Simpson. Publications of the Church Historical Society. London, 1925.

Babb, Lawrence. *The Elizabethan Malady*: A Study of Melancholia in English Literature from 1580 to 1642. East Lansing: Michigan State University Press, 1951.

Bacon, Francis. *Francis Bacon, sa vie, son oeuvre, avec un exposé de sa philosophie par André Cresson.* Paris: Presses Universitaires de France, 1956.

Bacon, Roger. *The Mirror of Alchimy.* Into Which is Bound: An Excellent Discourse of the Admirable Force and Efficacie of Art and Nature, Written by the Famous Frier Roger Bacon. . . . [Translator not identified.] London, 1597.

———. *The Opus Majus of Roger Bacon.* Translated by B. B. Burke. 2 vols. Philadelphia and London: University of Pennsylvania Press, 1928.

Baldwin, William. *A Treatise of Morall Philosophy* . . . the Thirde Time Enlarged by Thomas Paulfreyman. London, 1567.

Bamborough, J. B. *The Little World of Man.* London, New York, and Toronto: Longmans, Green and Co., 1952.

Banister, John. *The Historie of Man,* Sucked from the Sappe of the Most Approued Anathomistes. London, 1578.

Bartholomaeus [Anglicus]. *Batman uppon Bartholome, His Booke De Proprietatibus Rerum.* [A translation by Stephen Bateman.] London, 1582.

Basse, William. *A Helpe to Discourse.* London, 1620.

Bevan, Bryan. *The Real Francis Bacon, a Biography.* London: Centaur Press, 1960.

Birch, Thomas. *The Court and Times of James the First.* 2 vols. London, 1849.

Blundeville, Thomas. *The Art of Logike* . . . According to the Doctrine of Aristotle, as of All Other Moderne and Best Accounted Authors thereof. . . . London, 1598.

Boaistuau, Peter. *Theatrum mundi,* or the theatre or rule of the world . . . to which is added a short discourse of the excellencie and dignitie of man. . . . London, 1581.

Boehner, Philotheus. *Medieval Logic:* An Outline of Its Development from 1250 to ca. 1400. Chicago: University of Chicago Press, 1952.

Boetius, A. M. T. S. *Five Bookes of Philosophicall Comfort.* . . . Translated by I. T. London, 1609.

Boring, Edwin G. *A History of Experimental Psychology.* New York: Appleton-Century-Crofts, Inc., 1950.

Bowen, Catherine Drinker. *Francis Bacon,* The Temper of a Man. Boston: Little, Brown and Co., 1963.

———. *The Lion and the Throne*: The Life and Times of Sir Edward Coke. New York: Little, Brown and Co., 1956.

Brathwait, Richard. *Essaies upon the Five Senses,* with a pithie one upon retraction. London, 1620.

Brett, George S. *Brett's History of Psychology.* Edited and abridged by R. S. Peters. New York: Humanities Press, Inc., 1953.

———. *A History of Psychology.* 3 vols. London: G. Allen and Co., 1912–21.

Bright, Timothy. *A Treatise of Melancholie by T. Bright,* Reproduced from the 1586 edition . . . with an Introduction by Hardin Craig. (Facsimile Text Society.) New York: Columbia University Press, 1940.

————. *A Treatise of Melancholy* . . . With divers Philosophicall discourses touching actions, and affections of the Soule, Spirit, and Body. . . . London, 1613.

Broad, C. D. *The Philosophy of Francis Bacon.* Cambridge: Cambridge University Press, 1926.

Browne, Sir Thomas. *Pseudoloxia Epidemica*: Or, Enquiries into Very Many Received Tenets and Commonly Presumed Truths. 7th ed. London, 1686.

————. *Religio Medici*, with Annotations. . . . London, 1685. [1642]

————. *The Works of Sir Thomas Browne.* Edited by Charles Sayle. 3 vols. Edinburgh: John Grant, 1927.

Bryskett, Lewis. *A Discourse of Civill Life*: Containing the Ethike part of Morall Philosophie. London, 1606.

Bullein, William. *A Newe Book Entituled the Government of Healthe.* London, 1558.

Bulwer, John. *Anthropometamorphosis*: Man Transformed: Or, the Artificiall Changling. . . . London, 1653.

Bundy, Murray W. *The Theory of Imagination in Classical and Medieval Thought.* ("Illinois Studies in Language and Literature," XII.) Urbana: University of Illinois Press, 1927.

Burley, Walter. *Burleus super octo libros physicorum* [of Aristotle. With the Text]. Venice, 1491.

Burton, Robert. *The Anatomy of Melancholy.* What It Is, with All the Kinds, Causes, Symptoms . . . by Democritus Junior. 5th ed. Oxford, 1638.

————. *The Anatomy of Melancholy.* Edited by Floyd Dell and Paul Jordan-Smith. New York: Farrar and Rinehart, Inc., 1938.

Campanella, Thomas. *De sensu rerum et magia.* Libros quatuor. . . . Paris, 1637.

Campbell, Lily B. *Shakespeare's Tragic Heroes*, Slaves of Passion. Cambridge: Cambridge University Press, 1930.

Cardano, Girolamo. *Cardanus Comforte.* Translated by T. Bedingfield. London, 1576.

Castiglioni, Arturo. *A History of Medicine.* Translated by E. B. Krumbhaar. New York: Alfred A. Knopf, Inc., 1941.

Charron, Pierre. *Of Wisdome Three Bookes.* Translated by Samson Leonard. London, 1658.

Church, R. W. *Bacon.* New York, 1884.

Cicero, M. T. *Those Fyue Questions Which Marke Tullye Cicero Disputed in His Manor of Tusculanum* . . . Englished by Iohn Dolman. London, 1561.

————. *Tusculanarum quaestionum.* Translated by J. E. King. (The Loeb Classical Library.) London: W. Heineman, and New York: G. P. Putnam's Sons, 1927.

Coffeteau, Nicolas. *A Table of Humane Passions.* With Their Causes and Effects. Translated by E. Grimeston. London, 1621.

Comenius [Komensky], J[ohn] A[mos]. *Porta linguarum aperta* . . . the Gate of Tongues Opened. . . . 2nd ed. London, 1633.

A Compendium of the Art of Logick and Rhetorick in the English Tongue, Containing All that Peter Ramus, Aristotle, and Others Have Writ Thereon. . . . London, 1651.

Copland, Robert. *The Art of Memory*, that otherwyse Is Called the "Phenix." A Boke Very Behouefull and Profytable to All Professours of Scyences. Grammaryens / Rethoryciens Dialectyke / . . . . ca. 1548.

Costello, William T. *The Scholastic Curriculum at Early Seventeenth-Century Cambridge*. Cambridge, Mass.: Harvard University Press, 1958.

Cotton, Sir Robert. *Cotton posthuma*. Edited by J. Howell. London, 1651.

Craig, Hardin. *The Enchanted Glass*: The Elizabethan Mind in Literature. New York: Oxford University Press, 1936.

Crakenthorp, Richard. *Introductio in Metaphysicam*. Oxford, 1619.

Crane, W. G. *Wit and Rhetoric in the Renaissance*. New York: Columbia University Press, 1937.

Crombie, A. C. *Robert Grosseteste and the Origins of Experimental Science*, 1100–1700. Oxford: Oxford University Press, 1953.

Crooke, Helkiah. *Microcosmographia*. A Description of the Body of Man . . . . London, 1615.

Crosse, Henry. *Virtues Commonwealth*. London, 1603.

Crowther, J. G. *Francis Bacon*. The First Statesman of Science. London: Cresset Press, 1960.

Culverwell, Nathaniel. *An Elegant and Learned Discourse of the Light of Nature*, with several other treatises. London, 1652.

———. *Of the Light of Nature*. Edited by John Brown, with a critical essay on the discourse by John Cairns. Edinburgh, 1857.

Curtis, Mark H. *Oxford and Cambridge in Transition, 1558–1642*. Oxford: Oxford University Press, 1959.

Cyril of Jerusalem and Nemesius of Emesa. Edited by William Telfer. ("Library of Christian Classics," IV.) Philadelphia: Westminster Press, 1955.

Davies, John [of Hereford]. *Microcosmos*. The Discovery of the Little World, with the Government Thereof. Oxford, 1603.

———. *Mirum in Modum*, a Glimpse of Gods Glorie and the Soules Shape. London, 1602.

Davies, Sir John. *Nosce teipsum*. London, 1619.

Dennis, Wayne. *Readings in the History of Psychology*. New York: Appleton-Century-Crofts, Inc., 1948.

Descartes, René. *Descartes' Philosophical Writings*. Selected and translated by Norman Kemp Smith. London: Macmillan, 1952.

———. *Discourse on the Method of Rightly Conducting the Reason and Seeking for Truth in the Sciences*. In *The Philosophical Works* of *Descartes*. Translated by Elizabeth S. Haldane and G. R. T. Ross. 2 vols. New York: Dover Publications, 1955.

―――. *The Passions of the Soul*. In *The Philosophical Works of Descartes*. Translated by Elizabeth S. Haldane and G. R. T. Ross. 2 vols. New York: Dover Publications, 1955.

―――. *Rules for the Direction of the Mind*. In *The Philosophical Works of Descartes*. Translated by Elizabeth S. Haldane and G. R. T. Ross. 2 vols. New York: Dover Publications, 1955.

Digby, Everard. *De duplici methodo libri duo*, unicam P. Rami methodum refutantes. . . . 1580.

―――. *Theoria analytica*, viam ad monarchiam scientiarum demonstrano. . . . London, 1579.

Digby, Sir Kenelm. *Observations on the 22. Stanza in the 9th Canto of the 2d Book of Spencers Faery Queen*. Full of Excellent Notions Concerning the Frame of Man, and His Rationall Soul. London, 1644.

―――. *Two Treatises*, in the One of Which the Natvre of Bodies, in the Other the Natvre of Mans Sovle; Is Looked into: in the Way of Discovery, of the Immortality of Reasonable Sovles. Paris, 1644.

Dixon, W. H. *Personal History of Lord Bacon, from Unpublished Papers*. Boston: John Murray, 1861.

Doni, Antonio F. *De natura hominis*. Lyon, 1581.

Dorchester, Dudley Carleton. *Letters from and to Sir Dudley Carleton . . . from January 1616 to December 1620*. London, 1757.

[Downame, John]. *Spiritual Physicke to Cure the Disease of the Soule, Arising from Superfluitie of Choller*. . . . London, 1600.

Du Vair, G. *The Morall Philosophy of the Stoicks*. Translated by Charles Cotton. London, 1664.

Elyot, Thomas. *The Book Named the Governour*. Edited by Arthur T. Eliot. London: Ridgeway and Sons, 1834.

―――. *The Castele of Health . . .* Newlie Perused, amended and corrected. . . . London, 1610.

Erasmus, Desiderius. *Enchiridion militis Christiana*. Translated by William Tyndale (?). 1518.

―――. *A Manual for a Christian Soldier*. Written by Erasmus and translated into English. London, 1687.

Evelyn, John. *Diary and Correspondence of John Evelyn*. Edited by William Bray. 4 vols. London, 1859–62.

Farrington, Benjamin. *Francis Bacon, Philosopher of Industrial Science*. London: Lawrence and Wishart, Ltd., 1951.

―――. *The Philosophy of Francis Bacon*. An Essay of Its Development from 1603 to 1609 with New Translations of Fundamental Texts. Liverpool: Liverpool University Press, 1964.

Fenner, Dudley. *The Artes of Logike and Rethorike*. Middleburg, 1584.

Fenner, William. *The Souls Looking-glasse*, Lively Representing Its Estate before God: With a Treatise of Conscience. . . . Cambridge, 1640.

————. *A Treatise of the Affections*, or the Soules Pulse. . . . London, 1641.

Fischer, Kuno. *Francis Bacon of Verulam*. Realistic Philosophy and Its Age. Translated by John Oxenford. London: Longman, Brown, Green, Longmans, and Roberts, 1857.

Fletcher, Harris Francis. *The Intellectual Development of John Milton*. 2 vols. Urbana: University of Illinois Press, 1956–61.

Fletcher, Phineas. *The Purple Island*, or *Isle of Man*. London, 1633.

Flud, Roberto [alias de Fluctibus]. *Tomi secundi Tractatus Primi, sectio secunda, De technica Microcosmi historia*. In Portiones VII. In *Utriusque Cosmi* . . . metaphysica, physica atque technica historia. . . . Oppenheim and Frankfort, 1617–24.

Fowler, Thomas. *Bacon*. New York: G. P. Putnam's Sons, 1881.

Fraunce, Abraham. *The Lawiers Logike*. London, 1588.

Galen. *Certaine Workes of Galens*, Called Methodus medendi . . . and an Epitome of the Third Booke of Galen, of Naturall Faculties. . . . Translated by Thomas Gale. London, 1586.

————. *An Epitome vpon Galens Three Bookes of Naturall Faculties*, verie necessarie for the Students both of Philosophie and Physicke: set forth by Maister Iames Siluius, Phisition. [Translated by Thomas Gale?] London, 1586. Bound into *Certain Workes of Galens*.

————. *Galen on Medical Experience*, First Edition of the Arabic Version. Translated by R. Walzer. London: Oxford University Press, 1944.

————. *Galen on the Natural Sciences*. Translated by Arthur John Brock. London: J. M. Dent and Sons, 1916.

Geminius, Thomas. *Compendiosa totius anatomie delineatio*. Translated by Nicholas Udall. London, 1553.

Gilbert, William. *De mundo nostro sublunari philosophia nova*. Amsterdam, 1651.

————. *William Gilbert of Colchester . . . on the Loadstone and Magnetic Bodies* . . . a New Physiology. . . . New York: J. Wiley and Sons, 1893.

Glanvill, Joseph. *An Essay concerning Preaching*. . . . London, 1678.

————. *Plus Ultra*: Or, the Progress and Advancement of Knowledge since the Days of Aristotle. . . . London, 1668.

————. *Saducismus triumphans*: or, Full and Plain Evidence concerning Witches and Apparitions. . . . London, 1681.

————. *The Vanity of Dogmatizing*: or Confidence in Opinions Manifested in a Discourse of the Shortness and Uncertainty of our Knowledge. . . . London, 1661.

————. *The Vanity of Dogmatizing*. . . . (Facsimile Text Society.) New York: Columbia University Press, 1931.

Gosse, Edmund. *Life and Letters of John Donne*. London: W. Heineman, 1899.

Granger, Thomas. *Syntagma Logicum: or the Divine Logike* (London, 1620).

Gratarolus, Gulielmus. *The Castel of Memorie*: Wherein Is Conteyned the Restoryng, Augmentyng, and Conservyng of the Memorie and Remembraunce. . . . Englished by William Fulwood. London, 1563.

Graves, F. P. *Peter Ramus and the Educational Reformation of the Sixteenth Century.* New York: The Macmillan Co., 1912.

Green, A. Wigfall. *Sir Francis Bacon, His Life and Works.* Denver: A. Swallow, 1952.

Grierson, H. J. C. *The First Half of the Seventeenth Century.* London: Charles Scribner's Sons, 1906.

Gruner, O. Cameron. *A Treatise on the Canon of Medicine of Avicenna,* Incorporating a Translation of the First Book. London: Luzac & Co., 1930.

Gunther, Edward T. *Early Science in Oxford.* 12 vols. Oxford: The Clarendon Press, 1939.

Hale-White, Sir William. *Bacon, Gilbert, and Harvey,* Being the Harveian Oration. . . . London: John Bales, Sons, & Danielsson, Ltd., 1927.

Hart, Charles A. *The Thomistic Concept of Mental Faculty.* Washington, D.C.: The Catholic University of America Press, 1930.

Harvey, Gabriel. *Gabriel Harvey's Ciceronianus.* Translated by C. A. Forbes, with introduction and notes by H. S. Wilson. ("University of Nebraska Studies in the Humanities," No. 4.) Lincoln: University of Nebraska Press, 1945.

Harvey, William. *The Works of William Harvey.* Translated by Robert Willis. Printed for the Sydenham Society. London, 1847.

Hawes, Stephen. *The Pastime of Pleasure.* Edited by William E. Mead. ("Early English Text Society," Original Series, No. 173.) London: Oxford University Press, 1928.

Heirdel, William A. *The Necessary and the Contingent in the Aristotelian System.* ("University of Chicago Contributions to Philosophy," No. 2.) Chicago: University of Chicago Press, 1896.

A Helpe to Memorie and Discourse . . . imprinted by B. A. London, 1621.

Herbert, George. *The English Works of George Herbert.* 3 vols. New York: Houghton, Mifflin and Co., 1905.

Herrick, M. T. *The Poetics of Aristotle in England.* ("Cornell Studies in English," XVII.) New Haven, Conn.: Yale University Press, 1930.

Hobbes, Thomas. *A Briefe of the Art of Rhetoriqve.* Containing in Substance All that Aristotle Hath Written in His Three Bookes of that Subject, except onely What Is Not Applicable to the English Tongue. . . . London, ca. 1637.

———. *Elements of Philosophy,* the First Section Concerning Body. London, 1656.

———. *The English Works of Thomas Hobbes.* Edited by Sir William Molesworth. 11 vols. London: J. Bohn, 1839–45.

———. *Humane Nature*: Or, the Fundamental Elements of Policie,

Being a Discoverie of the Faculties, Acts, and Passions of the Soul of Man, from Their Original Causes; According to Such Philosophical Principles as Are Commonly Known or Asserted. London, 1650.

——. *Leviathan.* Edited by M. Oakeshott. Oxford: B. Blackwell, [1946].

——. *Leviathan, or The Matter, Form and Power of a Commonwealth, Ecclesiastical and Civil.* London, 1651.

Holzknecht, Karl. *The Background of Shakespeare's Plays.* New York: American Book Co., 1950.

Hooker, Richard. *Of the Laws of Ecclesiastical Polity.* London, 1592–1662.

——. *The Works of . . . Mr. Richard Hooker. . . .* Arranged by Rev. John Keble. Revised by the Very Rev. R. W. Church and the Rev. F. Paget. 3 vols. 7th ed. Oxford: The Clarendon Press, 1888.

Huarte Navarro, Juan de Dios. *Examen de ingenios. The Examination of Men's Wits.* Englished by Richard Carew. London, 1594.

Hume, David. *Essays and Treatises on Several Subjects.* 2 vols. London, 1767.

——. *A Treatise of Human Nature.* Reprinted from the original edition in three volumes and edited by L. A. Selby-Bigge. Oxford: The Clarendon Press, 1888.

Hurault, Jacques. *Politicke, Moral, and Martial Discourses.* Translated by A. Golding. London, 1595.

James, D. G. *The Life of Reason: Hobbes, Locke, Bolingbroke.* New York: Longmans, Green, and Co., 1949.

Jewel, William. *The Golden Cabinet of True Treasure:* Containing the summe of Morall Philosophie. London, 1612.

Jones, John. *A Briefe . . . Discourse of the Naturall Beginning of All Growing and Living Things, Heate, Generation, Effects of the Spirits. . . .* London, 1574.

——. *Galens Booke of Elements.* London, 1574.

——. *The Arte and Science of Preserving Bodie and Soule in Health.* London, 1579.

——. *The Bathes of Bathes Ayde:* Wonderfull and most excellent, against very many Sicknesses. . . . London, 1572.

Jones, Richard Foster. *Ancients and Moderns:* A Study of the Background of the Battle of the Books. ("Washington University Studies in Language and Literature," New Series, No. 6.) St. Louis, 1936.

——. *Francis Bacon: Essays, Advancement of Learning, New Atlantis, and Other Pieces.* New York: Odyssey Press, 1937.

Keckerman, Bartholomew. *Gymnasium logicum.* London, 1606.

Klemm, Otto. *A History of Psychology.* New York: Charles Scribner's Sons, 1914.

Kocher, Paul H. *Science and Religion in Elizabethan England.* San Marino, Calif.: Huntington Library, 1953.

Kristeller, Paul O. *The Philosophy of Marsilio Ficino.* Translated by Virginia Conant. New York: Columbia University Press, 1943.

La Primaudaye, Pierre. *The French Academy*. [First Part.] Translated by T. Bowes. London, 1586.

――――. *The French Academie*: Fvlly Discovrsed in Fovre Bookes. 6th ed. London, 1618.

La Ramee, Pierre. *The Art of Logick* . . . Published by Anthony Wotton. London, 1626.

――――. *Dialecticae libri duo*. London, 1576.

――――. *The Logike of the Moste Excellent Philosopher P. Ramus Martyr*, Newly Translated. . . .by Roland MacIlmaine. London, 1574.

Lemnius, Levinus. *The Touchstone of Complexions* . . . for . . . Bodily Health. . . . Translated by Thomas Newton. London, 1581.

LeRoy, Loyc. *Of the Interchangeable Course, or Variety of Things in the Whole World* . . . whether It Be True or No, that there Can Be Nothing Sayd, Which Hath Not Bin Sayd heretofore: And that We Ought by Our Owne Inuentions to Augment the Doctrine of the Auncients; Not Contenting Ourselves with Translations, Expositions, Corrections, and Abridgements of Their Writings. Translated by Robert Ashley. London, 1594.

Lever, Ralph. *The Arte of Reason, Rightly Termed, Witcraft*. . . . London, 1573.

Levine, Israel. *Francis Bacon*. London: Small, Maynard, 1925.

Ling, Nicholas. *Politeuphuia*. Wits Common-wealth. 11th ed. London [1626?].

Locke, John. *An Essay Concerning Human Understanding*. Collated and annotated by Alexander Campbell Fraser. 2 vols. New York: Dover Publications, Inc., 1959.

――――. *An Essay Concerning the Understanding, Knowledge, Opinion, and Assent*. London, 1671.

M. S. *A Philosophical Discourse of the Nature of Rational and Irrational Souls*. London, 1695.

The Marriage of Wit and Wisdom, an Ancient Interlude. Edited by James Orchard Hallewill. Printed for the Shakespeare Society. London, 1846. [From a MS dated 1579.]

Mason, Robert. *Reason's Academie*. London, 1605.

――――. *Reason's Monarchie*. London, 1602.

Melanchthon, Philip. *Commentarius De Anima*. Strasbourg, 1540.

Merton, Egan S. *Science and Imagination in Sir Thomas Browne*. New York: Columbia University Press, 1949.

Mill, J. S. *Dissertations and Discussions*: Political, Philosophical, and Historical. 3 vols. Boston: W. V. Spencer, 1864.

――――. *A System of Logic*. 2 vols. London: J. W. Harper, 1843.

Milton, John. *Artis logicae plenior institutio*, as Petri Rami methodum concinnata. . . . [London, 1672.] Edited and translated by Allan H. Gilbert. In *The Works of John Milton*. Edited by Frank Allen Patterson, *et al.* 18 vols. New York, 1931–38. XI.

――――. *The Prose Works of John Milton*. Edited by J. A. St. John. 5 vols. (Bohn Standard Library.) London: Henry G. Bohn, 1848.

Montagu, Basil. *The Life of Francis Bacon.* London: Pickering, 1833.
Montaigne, Michel de. *The Essays, or Morall, Politike Discourses:* Done in English by J. Florio. London, 1603.
Montgomery, Robert L., Jr. *Symmetry and Sense:* The Poetry of Sir Philip Sidney. Austin: University of Texas Press, 1961.
A *Morality of Wisdom, Mind, Will, and Understanding. The Digby Plays.* ("Early English Text Society," Extra Series, No. 70.) Oxford: N. Trübner & Co., 1896.
Mulcaster, Richard. *The First Part of the Elementarie which Entreateth of Right Writing of our English Tung.* . . . London, 1582.
Mullally, Joseph Patrick. *The Summulae Logicales of Peter of Spain.* ("Notre Dame Publications in Mediaeval Studies," VIII.) South Bend, Ind.: University of Notre Dame Press, 1945.
Nani Mirabelli. *Polyanthea.* Cologne, 1552.
Nemesius [of Emesa]. *The Nature of Man.* London, 1636.
Nichol, John. *Francis Bacon:* His Life and Philosophy. 2 vols. Edinburgh: W. Blackwood and Sons, 1888–89.
Norris, John. *Essay Towards the Theory of the Ideal or Intelligible World.* 2 vols. 1704.
Palingenius, M. [P. A. Manzolli?] *The Zodiake of Life by Marcellus Palingenius.* Translated by Barnaby Googe. With an introduction by Rosemond Tuve. (New York: Scholars' Facsimiles & Reprints, 1947.)
Perkins, William. *The Art of Prophecying.* In *The Workes of* . . . *William Perkins.* 3 vols. Cambridge, 1609.
————. *A Treatise of Mans Imaginations.* Cambridge, 1607.
Petty, William. *The Advice of W. P. to Mr. Samuel Hartlib, for the Advancement of Some Particular Parts of Learning.* London, 1648. [Harlean Miscellany, VI.]
Pico della Mirandola, G. *On the Imagination.* The Latin text, with an introduction, an English translation, and notes by Harry Caplan. New Haven, Conn.: Yale University Press, 1930.
Plato. *The Dialogues of Plato.* Translated by B. Jowett. 2 vols. New York: Random House, 1937.
Porphyrius. *Isagoge.* Paris, 1538.
Porta, John Baptista. *Natural Magick* . . . wherein Are Set Forth All the Riches and Delights of the Natural Sciences. London, 1658.
Quarles, Francis. *Enchyridion Containing Institutions Divine and Morall.* London, 1640.
Rand, Benjamin. *The Classical Psychologists.* Boston: Houghton, Mifflin Co., 1912.
Randall, J. H., Jr. *Aristotle.* New York: Columbia University Press, 1960.
Redford, John. *Wit and Science.* Edited by Arthur Brown. (Malone Society Reprints.) Oxford, 1951.
Reisch, Gregorius. *Margarita Philosophica,* hoc est, habitvvm sev disciplinarvm omnivm, qvotqvot philosophiae syncerioris ambitu continentur. . . . Basileae, 1583.

Remusat, C. F. M. *Bacon, sa vie, son temps, sa philosophie et son influence jusquà nos jours.* Paris, 1877.

The Renaissance Philosophy of Man. Edited by E. Cassirer, P. O. Kristeller, J. H. Randall, Jr. Chicago: University of Chicago Press, 1948.

Reynoldes, Edward. *A Treatise of the Passions and Facvlties of the Sovle of Man.* London, 1640.

Rice, Eugene F., Jr. *The Renaissance Idea of Wisdom.* Cambridge, Mass.: Harvard University Press, 1958.

Richardson, Alexander. *The Logicians Schoolmaster.* London, 1629.

Ritchie, John. *Reports of Cases Decided by Francis Bacon . . . in the High Court of Chancery, 1617–1621.* London: Sweet and Maxwell, 1932.

Robin, P. Ansell. *The Old Physiology in English Literature.* New York: E. P. Dutton and Co., 1911.

Rogers, Thomas. *A Philosophicall Discourse Entituled, The Anatomie of the Minde.* London, 1576.

Ross, W. D. *Aristotle.* A Complete Exposition of His Works and Thought. New York: Meridian Books, 1959.

Saint Thomas Aquinas. *Philosophical Texts.* Selected and translated by Thomas Gilby. London and New York: Oxford University Press, 1951.

———. *Summa Theologia.* Translated by the English Dominican Fathers. In *Basic Writings of Saint Thomas Aquinas.* Edited and annotated, with an introduction by Anton C. Pegis. 2 vols. New York: Random House, 1945.

Sanderson, Robert. *Logicae artis compendium.* Oxford, 1615.

Sandys, J. E. *History of Classical Scholarship.* 3 vols. Cambridge: Cambridge University Press, 1921.

Sarton, George. *The Appreciation of Ancient and Mediaeval Science During the Renaissance (1450–1600).* Philadelphia: University of Pennsylvania Press, 1955.

———. *Galen of Pergamon.* Lawrence: University of Kansas Press, 1954.

———. *The History of Science and the New Humanism.* 3rd ed. New York: George Braziller, 1956.

———. *Introduction to the History of Science.* 3 vols. Baltimore: Williams and Wilkins Company, 1927–48.

Scheibler, Christopher. *Metaphysica.* Oxford, 1665.

———. *Opus logicum,* quatuor partibus universum huius artis systema comprehendens. . . . Geneva, 1651.

Science, Medicine, and History. Edited by E. A. Underwood. 2 vols. London and New York: Oxford University Press, 1953.

Senault, J. F. *The Use of Passions . . .* Put into English by Henry Earle of Monmouth. 1649.

Shute, Clarence. *The Psychology of Aristotle.* New York: Columbia University Press, 1941.

Singer, Charles, ed. *Studies in the History and Method of Science.* 2 vols. Oxford: The Clarendon Press, 1917.

Smith, G. Gregory, ed. *Elizabethan Critical Essays.* 2 vols. Oxford: Oxford University Press, 1904.

Smith, Preserved. *The Age of the Reformation.* New York: Henry Holt and Co., 1920.

————. *Erasmus: A Study of His Life.* New York: Harper and Bros., 1923.

Smith, Samuel. *Aditus ad logicam.* London, 1613.

Spedding, James. *An Account of the Life and Times of Francis Bacon.* 2 vols. Boston: Houghton, Osgood, and Co., 1878.

————. *The Collection of Books Used by James Spedding as His Working Library in Preparing His Edition of the Works of Sir Francis Bacon.* London, 1914.

————. *Evenings with Reviewer, or Macaulay and Bacon.* 2 vols. London: Kegan Paul & Co., 1881.

Spencer, Theodore. *Shakespeare and the Nature of Man.* 2nd ed. New York: The Macmillan Co., 1961.

Spencer, Thomas. *The Art of Logick,* Delivered in the Precepts of Aristotle and Ramus. London, 1628.

Steel, Byron. *Sir Francis Bacon, the First Modern Mind.* New York: Doubleday, Doran and Co., 1930.

Steeves, G. W. *Francis Bacon;* A Sketch of His Life, Works, and Literary Friends. . . . London: Methuen and Co., 1910.

Stierio, M. Joanne. *Praecepta doctrinae* logicae, ethicae, physicae, metaphysicae, sphoericaeq; brevitas tabellis compacta. . . . 8th ed. London, 1679.

Sturt, Mary. *Francis Bacon.* London: Kegan Paul & Co., 1932.

Svendsen, K. *Milton and Science.* Cambridge, Mass.: Harvard University Press, 1956.

Swan, John. *Speculum mundi,* or A Glasse Representing the Face of the World. Cambridge, 1635.

Taylor, Henry Osborn. *Thought and Expression in the Sixteenth Century.* 2 vols. 2nd rev. ed. New York: The Macmillan Co., 1930.

Telesius, Bernard. *Bernardini Telesii consentini de rerum natura.* . . . Libri IX. Naples, 1586.

Thesaurus Linguae Romanae and Britannicae. . . . London, 1584.

Thorndike, Lynn. *A History of Magic and Experimental Science.* 6 vols. New York: Columbia University Press, 1941.

Tillyard, E. M. W. *The Elizabethan World Picture.* London: Macmillan Company, 1943.

A Translation of Thirty-two Latin Poems in Honor of Francis Bacon, published by [William] Rawley in 1626. Translated by E. K. Rand. Privately printed. Boston, 1904.

Tropologia, or a Key to Open Scriptures. Metaphors Compleat in One Volume. London, 1682.

Tuve, Rosemond. *Elizabethan and Metaphysical Imagery.* Chicago: University of Chicago Press, 1947.
Tuvil, Daniel. *Essaies Politicke, and Morall.* London, 1608.
Valentinus, P. P. *Enchiridion medicum*: Containing an Epitome of the Whole Course of Physicke. . . . London, 1608.
Vaughan, William. *Directions for Health, Naturall and Artificiall.* . . . 7th ed. London, 1633.
Vergill, Polydore. *De inventoribus rerum prior editio.* . . . Paris, 1528.
Vesalius, Andreas. *De humani corporis fabrica.* Basileae, 1543.
Vicary, Thomas. *The Anatomie of the Bodie of Man,* by Thomas Vicary. . . . Edition of 1548. . . . Edited by F. J. Furnivall and P. Furnivall. ("Early English Text Society," Extra Series, No. 53.) London, 1888.
———. *A Treatise of the Affections.* London, 1641.
Vives, J. L. *Introduction to Wisedome.* Translated by R. Morysine. London, 1540.
———. *Vives on Education.* [A translation of the *De tradendis disciplinis* of Juan Luis Vives, by Foster Watson.] Cambridge: Cambridge University Press, 1913.
von Kunow, Amelie D. *Francis Bacon, Last of the Tudors.* Translated by Willard Parker. New York: Bacon Society of America, 1924.
Waddington, Charles. *Ramus: sa vie ses écrits et ses opinions.* Paris: C. Meyruels et Cᵉ, 1855.
Walker, D. P. *Spiritual and Demonic Magic from Ficino to Campanella.* London: Warburg Institute, University of London, 1958.
Walkington, Thomas. *The Optick Glasse of Hvmors,* or the Touchstone of a Golden Temperature. London, 1607.
Warren, Howard C. *Dictionary of Psychology.* Boston and New York: Houghton, Mifflin Co., 1934.
———. *A History of Association Psychology.* New York and Chicago: Charles Scribner and Sons, 1921.
Weld, C. R. *A History of the Royal Society.* . . . 2 vols. London: J. W. Parker, 1848.
Whitaker, Virgil K. *Shakespeare's Use of Learning*: An Inquiry into the Growth of His Mind and Art. San Marino, Calif.: Huntington Library, 1953.
Wightman, W. P. D. *Science and the Renaissance.* 2 vols. Edinburgh: Oliver and Boyd, 1962.
Williams, Charles. *Bacon.* London: A. Barker Ltd., 1933.
Willis, John. *Mnemonica, or, the Art of Memory* . . . also a Physical Treatise of Cherishing Natural Memory. . . . London, 1661.
Wilson, Thomas. *The Rule of Reason,* Conteinyng the Arte of Logique, Set Forth in Englishe. London, 1567.
Withals, John. *A Dictionarie in English and Latine for Children and Yong Beginners.* London, 1608.
Wolf, Abraham. *A History of Science, Technology, and Philosophy in*

the Sixteenth and Seventeenth Centuries. London: G. Allen and Unwin, Ltd., 1935.

Wolfson, Harry A. *Philosophy of the Church Fathers.* Vol. I: *Faith, Trinity, Incarnation.* Cambridge, Mass.: Harvard University Press, 1956.

Woolton, John. *A Newe Anatomie of the Whole Man as Well of His Body as of His Soul.* London, 1576.

———. *A Treatise on the Immortalitie of the Soule*: Wherein is declared the Origin, Nature, and Powers of the Same. . . . London, 1576.

Wotton, Sir Henry. *Reliquiae Wottonianae,* or a Collection of Lives, Letters, Poems, with Characters of Sundry Personages and Other Incomparable Pieces of Language and Art. . . . London, 1651.

Wright, L. B. *Middle-Class Culture in Elizabethan England.* Chapel Hill: University of North Carolina Press, 1935.

Wright, Thomas. *Queen Elizabeth and Her Times,* a Series of Original Letters, Selected from the Unedited Private Correspondence . . . of the Distinguished Persons of the Period. 2 vols. London: H. Colburn, 1838.

———. *The Passions of the Mind in General.* London, 1630.

Zilboorg, Gregory. *A History of Medical Psychology.* New York: W. W. Norton and Co., 1941.

Zwingerus, Theodorus. *Theatrum vitae humanae.* 1572.

ARTICLES AND DISSERTATIONS

American Baconiana. I (February, 1923), and II (November, 1927, and February, 1928). [Only numbers issued.]

Babb, Lawrence. "On the Nature of Elizabethan Psychological Literature," in *Joseph Quincy Adams Memorial Studies* (Washington, D.C.: Folger Shakespeare Memorial Library, 1948), 509–522.

Baconiana. London, 1886 – . [Vols. I and II titled *Journal of the Bacon Society.*]

Barnes, H. E. "The Historical Background and Setting of the Philosophy of Francis Bacon," *Scientific Monthly,* XVIII (May, 1924), 475–495.

Bensley, Edward. "Dr. Andrews and Bacon's Apophthegms," *Notes and Queries,* CXLVI (February 2, 1924), 85–86.

Boughner, Daniel C. "The Psychology of Memory in Spenser's *Faerie Queene,*" *PMLA,* XLVII (1932), 89–96.

Brennan, Joseph X. "The *Epitome troporum ac schematum* of Joannes Susenbrotus: Text, Translation, and Commentary." Unpublished Ph.D. dissertation, University of Illinois, Urbana, 1953.

Bundy, M. W. "Bacon's True Opinion of Poetry," *Studies in Philology,* XXVII (1930), 244–264.

———. "'Invention' and 'Imagination' in the Renaissance," *Journal of English and Germanic Philology,* XXIX (1930), 535–545.

———. "Shakespeare and Elizabethan Psychology," *Journal of English and Germanic Philology*, XXIII (1924), 516–549.

Camden, Carroll. "Memory, the Warder of the Brain," *Philological Quarterly*, XVIII (1939), 52–72.

Caplan, Harry. "Rhetorical Invention in Some Medieval Tractates on Preaching," *Speculum*, II (1927), 284–295.

Cochrane, Rexmond C. "Francis Bacon in Early Eighteenth-Century Literature," *Philological Quarterly*, XXXVII (1958), 57–79.

Crane, R. S. "The Relation of Bacon's Essays to His Program for the Advancement of Learning," in *Schelling Anniversary Papers* (New York: The Century Co., 1923), 87–105.

Crombie, A. C. "Early Concepts of the Senses and the Mind," *Scientific American*, CCX, No. 5 (May, 1964), 108–116.

Daly, Walter A. "The Educational Psychology of Juan Luis Vives." Unpublished Ph.D. dissertation, Catholic University of America, Washington, D.C., 1924.

Doran, Madeleine. "On Elizabethan Credulity," *Journal of the History of Ideas*, I (1940), 151–176.

Dowden, Edward. "Elizabethan Psychology," in *Essays Modern and Elizabethan* (London, 1910), 308–333.

Farrington, Benjamin. "On Misunderstanding the Philosophy of Francis Bacon," in *Science, Medicine, and History*, edited by E. A. Underwood (2 vols.; London and New York: Oxford University Press, 1953), I, 439–450.

Fookes, R. A. "The Player's Passion: Some Notes on Elizabethan Psychology and Acting," in *Essays and Studies, 1954: Being Volume Seven of the New Series of Essays and Studies Collected for the English Association by Guy Boas* (London: John Murray, 1954), 62–77.

Forest, Louise C. Turner. "A Caveat for Critics Against Invoking Elizabethan Psychology," *PMLA*, LXI (1946), 651–672.

Gilbert, Neal W. "The Concept of Will in Early Latin Philosophy," *Journal of the History of Philosophy*, I (1963), 17–35.

Halporn, James W. "*Magni Aurelii Cassiodori Senatoris Liber de Anima*: Introduction and Critical Text," *Traditio*, XVI (1960), 39–109.

Hendrickson, G. L. "Origin and Meaning of the Characters of Style," *American Journal of Philology*, XXVI (1905), 248–290.

———. "The Peripatetic Mean of Style and the Three Stylistic Characters," *American Journal of Philology*, XXV (1904), 125–146.

Herrick, M. T. "The Early History of Aristotle's Rhetoric in England," *Philological Quarterly*, V (1926), 242–257.

Hultzén, Lee S. "Aristotle's Rhetoric in England to 1660." Unpublished Ph.D. dissertation, Cornell University, Ithaca, N.Y., 1932.

———. "Charles Butler on Memory," *Speech Monographs*, VI (1939), 44–65.

Johnson, Francis R. "Elizabethan Drama and the Elizabethan Science of Psychology," in *English Studies Today*, edited by C. L. Wrenn and G. Bullough (Oxford: The Clarendon Press, 1951), 111–119.

Jones, Richard Foster. "Science and Language in England of the Mid-Seventeenth Century," *Journal of English and Germanic Philology*, XXXI (1932), 315–331.

————. "Science and Prose Style in the Third Quarter of the Seventeenth Century," *PMLA*, XLV (1930), 977–1009.

Kristeller, Paul O., and J. H. Randall, Jr. "The Study of the Philosophies of the Renaissance," *Journal of the History of Ideas*, II (1941), 449–496.

Larkey, Sanford V. "The Vesalian Compendium of Geminus and Nicholas Udall's Translation," *The Library*, 4th Series, XIII (1933), 367–394.

Larkin, James Francis. "Erasmus' *De ratione studii*: Its Relationship to Sixteenth Century English Literature." Unpublished Ph.D. dissertation, University of Illinois, Urbana, 1942.

Metz, Rudolph. "Bacon's Part in the Intellectual Movement of His Time," in *Seventeenth Century Studies, Presented to Sir Herbert Grierson* (Oxford: The Clarendon Press, 1938), 21–32.

Milhaud, G. "Descartes et Bacon," *Scientia*, XXI (1917), 185–198.

Montagu, M. F. Ashley. "Vesalius and the Galenists," in *Science, Medicine, and History*, edited by E. A. Underwood (2 vols.; London and New York: Oxford University Press, 1953), I, 376–385.

Ong, Walter J. "Hobbes and Talon's Ramist Rhetoric in English," *Transactions of the Cambridge Bibliographical Society*, I (1949–53), 260–262.

Peck, Arthur L. "The Connate *Pneuma*," in *Science, Medicine, and History*, edited by E. A. Underwood (2 vols.; London and New York: Oxford University Press, 1953), I, 111–121.

Pogson, Beryl C. "A Psychological Study of 'Measure for Measure,'" *Baconiana*, XXXIII (1949), 35–42.

Pratt, C. C. "Faculty Psychology," *Psychological Review*, XXXVI (1958), 228–236.

Rich, Audrey N. M. "Body and Soul in the Philosophy of Plotinus," *Journal of the History of Philosophy*, I (1963), 1–15.

Russel, H. K. "Elizabethan Dramatic Poetry in the Light of Natural and Moral Philosophy," *Philological Quarterly*, XII (1933), 187–195.

————. "Tudor and Stuart Dramatizations of the Doctrines of Natural and Moral Philosophy," *Studies in Philology*, XXXI (1934), 1–37.

Scott, William O. "Shelley's Admiration for Bacon," *PMLA*, LXXIII (1958), 228–236.

Soellner, R. H. "*Anima* and *Affectus*: Theories of the Emotions in Sixteenth Century Grammar Schools and Their Reflections in the Works of Shakspere." Unpublished Ph.D. dissertation, University of Illinois, Urbana, 1953.

Spurrell, Joan. "The Writings of Sir Francis Bacon Published Between 1750 and 1850." Unpublished thesis for Diploma in Librarianship, University of London, London, 1955.

Steele, Robert. "Roger Bacon and the State of Science in the Thirteenth Century," in *Studies in the History and Method of Science*, edited by Charles Singer (2 vols.; Oxford: The Clarendon Press, 1921), II, 121–150.

Thorndike, Lynn. "The Attitude of Francis Bacon and Descartes Towards Magic and Occult Science," in *Science, Medicine, and History*, edited by E. A. Underwood (2 vols.; London and New York: Oxford University Press, 1953), I, 451–454.

Trevor-Roper, Hugh. "Francis Bacon," *Encounter*, XVIII, No. 2 (February, 1962), 73–77.

Van Deusen, Neil C. "Telesio, the First of the Moderns." Unpublished Ph.D. dissertation, Columbia University, 1932.

Weisinger, Herbert. "The Study of the Revival of Learning from Bacon to Hallam," *Philological Quarterly*, XXV (1946), 221–247.

Wheatley, J. M. O. "Bacon's Redefinition of Metaphysics," *The Personalist*, XLII (1961), 487–499.

Whitaker, Virgil K. "Bacon and the Renaissance Encyclopedists." Unpublished Ph.D. dissertation, Stanford University, Palo Alto, Calif., 1933.

————. "Francis Bacon's Intellectual Milieu." A paper delivered . . . at the Clark Library, 18 November 1961, celebrating the 400th anniversary of Bacon's birth. William Andrewes Clark Memorial Library, Los Angeles, Calif., 1962.

Whitmore, C. E. "The Language of Science," *Scientific Monthly*, LXXX (March, 1955), 185–191.

Wilson, Harold S. "Some Meanings of 'Nature' in Renaissance Literary Theory," *Journal of the History of Ideas*, II (1941), 430–448.

Wolfson, Harry A. "The Internal Senses in Latin, Arabic, and Hebrew Philosophic Texts," *Harvard Theological Review*, XXVIII (1935), 69–133.

Index

Abstracting: the special work of the understanding, 101–112; reduction in materiality, 103; limits of, 104; revealed in speech, words, and discourse, 109; at work in discovering natural forms and axioms, 125; abstract notions, 161. *See also* Apprehending

Accident, in invention, 162

Acoustics, 43. *See also* Sound

Action, re goodness, 74

Active, re passive, 51

Active intellect: as the mind acting, 98; like light, 98; re *ingenium*, wit, intelligence, 98, 106–107; mentioned, 128

Adam, 85, 143

Advancement of Learning, The: and Bacon's system of knowledge, 2; mentioned, 11, 79, 97, 113, 132, 137

Aesthetics: hints for a psychology of, 46; sources of pleasure in seeing and hearing, 46

Affections, the: disturbers of reason, 80; the movers of the will and mind, 145, 146; a necessary aid to reason in securing action, 145; effective through the spirits, 146; those named by Bacon, 146; sources of knowledge about, 147; mentioned, 19–20, 80, 91, 134. — Vicary on the proper role of the affections, 145

Agent intellect, 98, 99. *See also* Active intellect

Alchemy, 51, 90

Analogue, in discovering method, 162

Anatomy, 3

Anderson, Fulton, 1, 4

Andrewes, Lancelot, 161

Animal spirit: function of, 30; as the efficient cause of sensation, 30; responsive to ideas of objects, 30; to pain and qualities of heat and cold, 46; properties of, 32; mentioned, 25. — Crooke on, 33–34; Descartes on its action and bodily channels, 151

Anticipation: of the object of search, 128. — Descartes on the mutual dependence of the new and old, 114–115

Antipathy. *See* Sympathy

Apparition. *See* Appearance

Appearance, Hobbes's meaning of, 45

Appetite: physics of "Appetites and Motions," 46; general power of giving and receiving, 48, 138; two categories of, natural, 48–52 (q.v.), and desire, 52–54 (q.v.); as applied to